the
BUSINESS PLAN
WORKBOOK

ROTHERHAM – SPACE AND SUCCESS FOR BUSINESS

Rotherham, at the heart of the UK, continues to prove to British and international investors that it offers what they seek – success for their companies, and payback on their investment.

Spearheading economic growth is Rotherham Investment & Development Office (RiDO), the regeneration arm of Rotherham Metropolitan Borough Council, which has an impressive track record in supporting companies ranging from start-ups to global players, attracting new businesses and working with expanding companies.

RiDO head Richard Poundford said: "Investors are impressed by what we offer – great sites, an energised workforce, excellent motorway links and the highest levels of business support in the EU. But it's the partnership approach, commitment and enthusiasm they find here that makes Rotherham different. The fact that more than 90 international companies have chosen to locate here, creating 7,500 jobs, and that we have 4,000 prospering UK and home-grown companies, is a clear sign that we're getting it right."

The scale of current developments confirms Rotherham's ability to bring massively ambitious projects to reality. Rotherham Renaissance, a 25-year-vision that will make the borough a better place in which to live, work and invest, is capitalising on the town's riverside location and is expected to attract £2bn of mostly private-sector funding.

The borough is also home to some of the largest investment projects in the North of England, including two £100m schemes. Both are in Manvers regeneration area, minutes from the M1 to the west and the A1(M) to the east. The first is transforming 84 brownfield acres into office and industrial space, while the second will regenerate about 280 acres, creating an 11-acre business park, lakeside homes, shops and extensive leisure facilities, with Manvers Lake as the centrepiece.

Interest in the Manvers Lake scheme is running high, with a number of leisure operators currently talking to the developers Express Park Group. For example, Britain's largest independent cinema group, Apollo Cinema Limited, which has 12 venues across the UK and 2.5 million visitors a year, has already signed up to develop a seven-screen multiplex.

To the south of the borough, regeneration of 200 brownfield acres is well under way at Dinnington. The emphasis will be on encouraging local business expansion as well as new inward investors. Among the latter is Johnston Press – successful publisher of the Yorkshire Post and a string of other newspapers – which is investing £60m in a printing plant there.

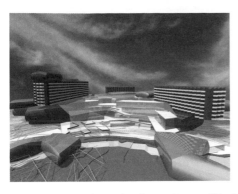

And that's not all. January saw a planning application submitted for the ambitious £300m YES! Project. Hailed as the largest indoor entertainment, leisure and tourism development in Europe, YES! will regenerate 320 acres and create 2,700 new jobs.

Another sign of success is the demand for office space, reflected in the fact that companies continue to build speculatively.

The success of Rotherham Council's drive to encourage entrepreneurs to start their own businesses has resulted in grow-on space being developed at one of the two business centres. Brampton and Century Business Centres provide 180 workspaces for a diverse range of businesses – and around 89% of these companies make it through the crucial first three years.

A third business centre opens this summer. Moorgate Crofts is a flagship project for Rotherham Council and partners, including the EU's Objective 1 office for South Yorkshire and Yorkshire Forward, and is creating a great deal of excitement.

The state-of-the-art development will be ideal for start-ups within high-growth sectors such as IT and digital, creative, professional and finance, and will provide entrepreneurs with a unique base from which to launch and grow their businesses. The high-quality building design also incorporates environmentally economic technologies such as geothermal heating and cooling, a literally green roof covered in rain-collecting plants and the use of recycled building materials.

The council's executive director of Economic & Development Services, Adam Wilkinson, summed up: "Every area chasing inward investment claims it's close to almost everywhere. Well – Rotherham is! We're right at the heart of the UK with excellent motorway and other links. But as well those, and a workforce that gives real commitment and financial incentives, we offer much more. We score top marks because we've got great quality products for investors and land and premises available now. And we back it all up with sound business support."

For further information, contact:
Paul Woodcock, Business Development Manager, RiDO, Reresby House, Bow Bridge Close, Templeborough, Rotheram S60 1YR
Tel: +44(0)1709-372099 email: info@rido.org.uk
www.rido.org.uk, www.dearnevalley.org, www.buy-local.co.uk, www.rotherham.gov.uk
EDS is part of Rotherham Metropolitan Borough Council, winner of the Government's Beacon Council award, 2002-2003, for Fostering Business Growth, and of the 2003-2004 Award for Removing Barriers to Work.

a **brighter**
business future...

SPACE & SUCCESS
Sites and premises readily available
More than four out of five businesses operating profitably

SUPERB TRANSPORT LINKS
At the heart of the UK, with comprehensive road, rail and air networks

COMMITMENT
Hard work and quality production

QUALITY OF LIFE
70% rural, with a quality of life that is hard to beat

space

prosperity

industry

...in

ROTHERHAM
UK

THE SUNDAY TIMES

the
BUSINESS PLAN
WORKBOOK

5TH EDITION

COLIN BARROW, PAUL BARROW & ROBERT BROWN

RECOMMENDED BY
INSTITUTE OF DIRECTORS

KOGAN
PAGE

London and Sterling, VA

First published in 1988, by Colin Barrow and Paul Barrow
Second edition by Colin Barrow, Paul Barrow and Robert Brown 1992
Reprinted in 1989, 1990, 1991, 1993 (twice), with revisions 1994, 1995 (twice), 1996, 1997 (twice)
Third edition 1998
Fourth edition 2001
Reprinted 2003
Fifth edition 2005

120 Pentonville Road
London N1 9JN
United Kingdom
www.kogan-page.co.uk

22883 Quicksilver Drive
Sterling VA 20166-2012
USA

British Library Cataloguing in Publication Data

A CIP record for this book is available from the British Library.

ISBN 0 7494 4346 4

Typeset by JS Typesetting Ltd, Porthcawl, Mid Glamorgan
Printed and bound in Great Britain by Cambrian Printers Ltd, Aberystwyth, Wales

Contents

natural   choice

North Lincolnshire: the natural
selection for evolving businesses.

We offer unrivalled transport
links, a multi-skilled workforce,
prime site locations and an
outstanding quality of life.
**All make a fertile growing
environment for businesses.**

Find out how we can nuture your
business call: **01724 297383** or
www.northlincs.gov.uk/business

**NORTH
LINCOLNSHIRE**
COUNCIL

NORTH LINCOLNSHIRE - THE NATURAL CHOICE

North Lincolnshire offers prime site locations plus the benefits of unparalleled access by road, air, rail and sea to over 370 million potential European customers. Investors take advantage of high quality serviced property, together with the skilled and adaptable employees that make North Lincolnshire the natural choice for business.

So what can North Lincolnshire offer your business?

North Lincolnshire is particularly attractive to the food, chemical, engineering, metals and manufacturing sectors due to the expertise and infrastructure existing in the area. For each cluster there are proactive networking opportunities, training, specialist support companies and experienced employees.

Natural Choice for a Skilled Workforce

The local workforce of 64,000 has an excellent track record for industrial relations, productivity and a reputation for flexible working. Training and education opportunities go hand in hand with the availability of a flexible workforce. North Lincolnshire boasts two colleges recognised nationally as centres of excellence with valuable links to the business community. Within a one-hour drive there are seven universities offering extensive research and development facilities and excellent graduate recruitment opportunities.

Unparalleled Access

Major investment has left the region with an excellent motorway network, allowing access to a potential market of 40 million UK customers and suppliers within a four-hour drive.

Proximity to the UK's largest and expanding ports complex – the Humber Ports – provides unrivalled access to Mid and Northern European markets. The complex handles in excess of 70 million tonnes of cargo a year, servicing 53 countries. Deep-sea facilities allow the landing of cargoes 24 hours a day. Fast overnight crossings mean hauliers can drive into the heart of mainland Europe within their time allowance.

The local rail freight terminal for the Channel Tunnel is only 20 miles away allowing excellent rail access to mainland Europe, Normanby Enterprise Park and Humber Bridge Industrial Estate offer potential for direct rail connections.

Humberside International Airport with a 30-minute check in time – has flights to Scotland and Amsterdam for transfers to the rest of the world. Close by Robin Hood Doncaster Sheffield Airport opens in 2005 offering new opportunities for business and pleasure.

Regional and Local Government Support

Within certain parts of the North Lincolnshire companies may be eligible for Selective Finance for Investment. A discretionary capital grant designed for businesses that are looking to invest but need financial help to go ahead.

A variety of 'top up' loan finance is available to enable businesses to facilitate projects as is equity finance through UK Steel Enterprise and other providers including 3i and Yorkshire Company Services.

The Learning and Skills Council provide formal but customised training packages and special recruitment packages are available through the local Employment Service. These packages save considerable costs for investors.

Winning Business Sites and Commercial Property

The right infrastructure for business is a priority; Normanby Enterprise Park is the area's most prestigious business location, offering fully serviced sites. A further 2000 acres are identified on the South Humber Bank for industrial development. The site is a natural base for the chemicals, ports/distribution and food manufacturing sectors. ConocoPhillips has already taken advantage of the strategic site to commission a combined heat and power plant.

Competitively priced greenfield and brownfield land is available with plot sizes ranging from less than 1 acre (0.405 hectares) up to 150 acres (60.71 hectares). The Economic Development Team can provide a free tailored search highlighting land and property in both public and private ownership.

Natural choice for Quality of Life

Few locations in the UK combine picturesque rolling countryside with ease of access to major cities. The area offers country parks, cultural events, quality restaurants and a choice of golf courses and sailing opportunities to rival some of the best in the country.

Added Value

The experienced and professional Economic Development Team can provide background information on the area, demographics, comparative technical data and information on other local companies. Saving significant expense and valuable management time.

North Lincolnshire offers unrivalled transport links, a multi-skilled workforce, prime site locations and an outstanding quality of life, which all make a fertile growing environment for business.

Find out how we can nurture your business, contact the Economic Development Team, Tel 01724 297383, or visit the web site **www.northlincs.gov.uk/business**

Neil Millar and Company Solicitors

Formed in 1998, we are a professional legal practice based in Manchester – the heart of the Northwest. We provide legal services to businesses and individuals at a national and international level. You may know our name from our successful personal injury department, or perhaps you may know us through Manchester's entrepreneurial community and other organisations supporting businesses. We have a varied business client base for whom we provide legal services and documentation at competitive prices.

Both small and medium sized businesses require contracts that provide a solid foundation for their business needs and future success. We understand that, particularly for businesses in their infancy, it can be tempting to put off implementing legal documentation. However, by not protecting your business and yourselves as owners, you leave yourself vulnerable to claims and disputes from customers, suppliers and employees. This can lead to an expensive court case or the employment tribunal. Legal costs are often greater than the amount in dispute – most notably in the case of employment tribunals where even if you win, you usually still have to pay your own legal fees.

The worst case scenario from our own experience involved a case whereby a company did not have any contracts of employment. The owner wished to sell his business to his senior employee who carried out most of the day to day company business. Negotiations broke down whereupon the senior employee left, set up independently in direct competition with his former employer and took most of the customers with him. Although not a large business, it was extremely profitable. On the company's own accountant's valuation, the failure of the company to protect its interests cost it over £ 1 million.

Some businesses try to address these issues by "borrowing" their contractual documentation from other businesses. Potentially, this can be as dangerous as having no documentation, as those businesses do not know whether their documentation is up to date or legally compliant and in addition they are almost certainly in breach of the copyright within that documentation.

As a result of dealing with issues arising from just these types of disputes, we felt that there was a need for businesses to have access to a standard range of fixed price documents to assist them in covering their basic legal needs.

With this in mind we have created a new web-site www.millarlaw.co.uk providing an easy to use service.

- You choose a document in which you are interested from our "document store".
- You can then read a brief description of the document and its contents.
- You simply log in, and pay the fixed price for the document; then immediately complete the document on-line with the aid of our unique wizard, or download it for completion later.

The document is on line to be used again and again. It takes about three minutes to complete our standard employment contract. Our wizard is completely user friendly and simple to follow.

We would like our document store to become your document store accessible twenty-four hours a day, seven days a week.

Of course, as a firm of solicitors we can also provide individual tailored legal documents to suit your specific needs. In addition we advise and assist over a range of other legal areas, including Business start-ups, Business Sales and Purchases, Disputes and Litigation, Employment and our dedicated Personal Injury Department deals with all injury claims. For more details of these services please visit our existing website www.neil-millar.co.uk

Telephone us on 0161 906 0789
Or Fax us on 0161 706 0799.

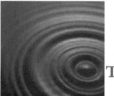

Business Manager Service have specialised in providing a full range of services to small and medium sized businesses over the past 10 years. The aim of the service is to provide business owners the freedom to focus on their business without the worry of the statutory requirements that their business is subjected to.

A full range of accountancy services are on offer to ensure everything a business may need can be provided. The services have been separately defined so they can be provided independently but are easily integrated if more than one service is required.

The range of services starts from the very basic through to a fully integrated and managed service, and every connotation in between. The services are provided depending on the specific requirement of the business to ensure no work is ever duplicated, nothing is missed and fees are only ever charged for what is needed and provided.

For each service that is provided a full range of facilities are available as an accompaniment. For example, the bookkeeping service also includes storage of the business documents that we and the business will have easy access to. The documents used to record bookkeeping transactions are stored as scanned images on a secure website that the business will be provided a unique link to. The online document storage is accepted by both H M Customs and Excise and the Inland Revenue and shows how our firm has achieved an innovative solution to the age old problem of storing paperwork.

Where the services provided include the completion of statutory paperwork and documents that require filing with different authorities we can offer the added service of filing these on behalf of you and your business. The business can be provided with a service that ensures it has no direct interaction with the Inland Revenue, H M Customs and Excise or Companies House. Our firm deal with these authorities on a regular basis and are happy to do so for our clients if they require. Where available the filing will be via the internet to help your business fit in with the recommendations to UK businesses from the government.

In addition to the services that are provided to help a business meet its requirements to the authorities a range of services can be also be provided focused more on the requirements of the business itself and its owners. Information a business needs to help it function is available and where required advice is available to ensure the business is efficient.

There is advice available to individuals thinking of setting up a business as well as advice to existing businesses covering its current position, future opportunities and if necessary eventual exit strategies. Where the business is owned by individuals there is also a range of advice available to these individuals to maximise their position within their business. Even a simple health check can be provided to ensure the business and its owners are efficient in their current position.

Our firm constantly reviews the rules and regulations that affect a business. Small businesses have seen some of the biggest changes in tax and status law over the last few years and our firm has been able to provide advice on the affects of these changes. This is an ongoing process and where a business is in any doubt over its particular exposure to rules and regulations a full review and advice can be provided.

Overall we aim to provide a conclusive range of services to a business and its owners covering everything that might be needed. Our firm is focused on providing a business with the optimum service without incurring fees for products and services that are not necessarily required. Our fee structure reflects this and shows our fees are competitive but also represent a fair value for the services provided.

Any business interested in discussing options available from Business Manager Service should contact the sales team to arrange an initial free no obligation consultation with the Business Advisor.

Tel: 01827 252291
email: sales@manager.co.uk
www.manager.co.uk

Preface

In this workbook we have attempted to distil the knowledge of the Enterprise Faculty within the Cranfield School of Management and, more importantly, the experiences of the many hundreds of 'student' entrepreneurs who have taken part in our enterprise programmes.

Business planning is at the core of everything we do with people who come to us at Cranfield, whether it is to start a new business or expand an existing one. Over the years we have developed and tested this method of helping people to research and validate their business ideas, and then to write up a business plan themselves.

Towards the end of each enterprise programme we invite a distinguished panel of senior bankers and venture capital providers to review and criticise each business plan presentation. Their valued comments not only have spurred our entrepreneurs to greater heights, but have given the faculty at Cranfield a privileged insight into the minds and thought processes of the principal providers of capital for new and growing enterprises.

This workbook brings together for the first time the processes and procedures required by the relative novice to write a business plan. Also included throughout are examples from the business plans of entrepreneurs who for the most part have gone on to start up successful enterprises.

In addition, we have included criticisms, warnings, and the experiences of investors and of recently successful entrepreneurs when they have a direct bearing on writing and presenting a business plan.

We don't pretend to have made writing up business plans an easy task – but we do think we have made it an understandable one that is within the grasp of everyone with the determination to succeed.

Thousands of students have passed through Cranfield's start-up and business growth programmes, raising millions in new capital and going on to run successful and thriving enterprises. Recently some of those earlier students have sold up to harvest their gains, in one case realising half a billion pounds!

How to use the workbook

The workbook contains 20 assignments that, once completed, should ensure that you have all the information you need to write and present a successful business plan. That is, one that helps to accomplish your objective, whether it is to gain a greater understanding of the venture you are proposing to start – its viability – or to raise outside money.

The workbook does not set out to be a comprehensive textbook on every business subject – finance, marketing, law, etc. Rather, it gives an appreciation as to how these subjects should be used to prepare your business plan. The topics covered under each assignment will often pull together ingredients from different 'academic' disciplines. For example, elements of law and marketing will be assembled in the assignment in which you are asked to describe your product and its proprietary position (patents, copyright, design registration, etc).

For some of the assignments you will almost certainly need to research outside the material contained in this workbook. However, 'technical' explanations of such subjects as cash flow, market research questionnaire design and break-even analysis are included.

The assignments are contained in seven phases that, as well as having a practical logic to their sequence, will provide you with manageable 'chunks' either to carry out yourself at different times, or to delegate to partners and professional advisers. While it is useful to make use of as much help as you can get in preparing the groundwork, you should orchestrate the information and write up the business plan yourself. After all, it is your future that is at stake – and every prospective financier will be backing you and your ability to put this plan into action, not your scriptwriter.

The seven phases are:

∎ *Phase 1: History and Position to Date*
Here you should describe your business or business idea so far as you have already developed it. In particular, explain your aims, objectives and eventual aspirations.

Introduce your management team, yourself included, and show how your skills and experiences relate to this venture.

Describe your product or service, its current state of development or readiness for the market, and whether or not you have any proprietary rights such as a patent, copyright or registered design.

∎ *Phase 2: Market Research*
This involves identifying the data needed both to validate your business idea and to decide upon the best start-up or growth strategy. In this phase you will be encouraged to gather market research data from as many sources as possible. Particular emphasis will be laid on researching customer needs, market segments and competitors' strengths and weaknesses. The appropriate research methodology and data sources are also described.

∎ *Phase 3: Competitive Business Strategy*
This involves planning how you will operate each element of your business, based upon the information collected and analysed in earlier phases. In relation to your chosen product or service, the market segment(s) you plan to serve and the competitive situation, you will decide on such factors as price, promotion, location, and channels of distribution.

∎ *Phase 4: Operations*
This involves detailing all the activities required to make your strategy happen. It will include such subjects as manufacturing, purchasing, selling, employing people, legal matters and insurance. Your business plan must demonstrate that you have taken account of all the principal matters that concern the operations of your venture.

∎ *Phase 5: Forecasting Results*
Based on the strategy evolved so far, in this phase you will carry out assignments enabling you to forecast the expected results of your venture. Projections will be made showing likely sales volume and value, pro forma profit and loss, cash-flow forecast and balance sheet, and a break-even analysis.

Although these first five phases are shown in sequence here and in the workbook, in practice you would expect to move backwards and forwards from phase to phase, as a result of new information or a modification of your earlier ideas.

∎ *Phase 6: Business Controls*
Here you must demonstrate how you will keep track of your business, both as a whole and for each individual element. As well as a bookkeeping system you will need sales and marketing planning records, customer record cards, personnel files and production control information.

■ *Phase 7: Writing Up and Presenting Your Business Plan*

The workbook assignments, when completed, are not your business plan. They are intended to help you to assemble the information needed to write up your business plan. The plan will require substantial editing and rewriting; the way in which it is written up will undoubtedly influence the chances of getting a hearing, if you are seeking outside support for your venture.

Finally, you must give some thought as to how you will handle the meeting with your bank, venture capital house or other backers. Presentation skills and good planning will all help to make for a good 'production', and showbiz counts for a surprising amount in the money world.

Here are some guidelines to help you and your colleagues complete the business plan assignments:

1. Each assignment will contain:
   (a) An introduction or brief description of the content and purpose of the assignment, usually broken down into two or more stages.
   (b) Examples as to how other entrepreneurs have answered or commented on parts of the assignment.
   (c) An explanation or amplification of any technical topics that need to be understood immediately.

   At the end there is an assignment worksheet with some specific questions for you to answer concerning your business. On this page you will also find suggestions for further reading on broader aspects of the subject of the assignment.

2. When tackling assignments this work pattern has proved successful:
   (a) Read up on the assignment and draft your own answer to the questions.
   (b) Discuss your answers, and any problems concerning the assignment with your prospective business partner(s), colleagues or some other knowledgeable individual such as an Enterprise Agency director, bank manager or accountant. If you are on, or plan to go on, a small business or new enterprise training programme, then your course tutor will also be able to help.
   (c) Revise your own answers in the light of these discussions – and then let your colleagues, and such other people as are involved, know your latest views on the assignment topic (you may need to go back and forth from steps (b) and (c) several times before you are entirely satisfied).

3. The contents of some assignments will suggest where and how to obtain the information needed to complete the assignment. However, don't expect to be told where to find all of the information about your business in these instructions. You will need to do some research yourself.

4. Example assignment completions taken from other business plans will also be presented to you in each assignment. These are presented only to give you a feel for the subject discussed. Your write-up of the assignment may need to be more or less elaborate, depending on your business.

5. The examples have been taken from actual business plans, but some have been changed in name and content, with some of the information purposely missing. Therefore do not copy a sample, however good it may sound; use it to help you to understand the purpose of the business plan assignment only.

6. Try to write up as much information as possible after reading each assignment. In this way you will know what remains to be researched (and do not wait until your information flows in perfect English before recording it).

7. Try to strike a balance between *qualitative* and *quantitative* statements in writing up your assignments. That is, try to back up as many of your statements as possible with numbers and documented sources of information. However, do not include numbers just because you have them; make sure that they really serve a purpose.

8. *Finally*, before attempting to write up your business plan, make sure the answers to all the assignments are internally consistent – and if you have business partners, make sure you are all in substantive agreement both at each stage and with the final outcome.

Believe it or not, the joint founders of one business fell out as they were making their presentation to a venture capital panel. They had divided up the workload of preparing the business plan, and one had not told the other of some fairly major modifications to the product range, provoked as a result of completing the workbook assignments. (There was a happy ending but for a moment it was a close-run thing.)

Why prepare a business plan?

Perhaps the most important step in launching any new venture or expanding an existing one is the construction of a business plan. Such a plan must include: your goals for the enterprise, both short and long term; a description of the products or services you will offer and the market opportunities you have anticipated for them; and finally, an explanation of the resources and means you will employ to achieve your goals in the face of likely competition. Time after time, research studies reveal that the absence of a written business plan leads to a higher incidence of failure for new and small businesses, as well as inhibiting growth and development.

Preparing a comprehensive business plan along these lines takes time and effort. In our experience at Cranfield on our new enterprise programmes, anything between 200 and 400 man-hours is needed, depending on the nature of your business and what data you have already gathered. Nevertheless, such an effort is essential if you are both to crystallise and to focus your ideas, and test your resolve about entering or expanding your business. Once completed, your business plan will serve as a blueprint to follow which, like any map, improves the user's chances of reaching his destination.

There are a number of other important benefits you can anticipate arising from preparing a business plan:

■ This systematic approach to planning enables you to make your mistakes on paper, rather than in the marketplace. One potential entrepreneur made the discovery while gathering data for his business plan that the local competitor he thought was a one-man band was in fact the pilot operation for a proposed national chain of franchised outlets. This had a profound effect on his market entry strategy!

Another entrepreneur found out that, at the price he proposed charging, he would never recover his overheads or break even. Indeed, 'overheads' and 'break even' were themselves alien terms before he embarked on preparing a business plan. This naive perspective on costs is by no means unusual.

∎ Once completed, a business plan will make you feel more confident about your ability to set up and operate the venture. It may even compensate for lack of capital and experience, provided of course that you have other factors in your favour, such as a sound idea and a sizeable market opportunity for your product or service.

∎ Your business plan will show how much money is needed, what it is needed for and when, and for how long it is required.

As under-capitalisation and early cash-flow problems are two important reasons why new business activities fail, it follows that those with a soundly prepared business plan can reduce these risks of failure. They can also experiment with a range of alternative viable strategies and so concentrate on options that make the most economic use of scarce financial resources.

It would be an exaggeration to say that your business plan is the passport to sources of finance. It will, however, help you to display your entrepreneurial flair and managerial talent to the full and to communicate your ideas to others in a way that will be easier for them to understand – and to appreciate the reasoning behind your ideas. These outside parties could be bankers, potential investors, partners or advisory agencies. Once they know what you are trying to do, they will be better able to help you.

∎ Preparing a business plan will give you an insight into the planning process. It is this process that is important to the long-term health of a business, and not simply the plan that comes out of it. Businesses are dynamic, as are the commercial and competitive environments in which they operate. No one expects every event as recorded on a business plan to occur as predicted, but the understanding and knowledge created by the process of business planning will prepare the business for any changes that it may face, and so enable it to adjust quickly.

Despite these many valuable benefits, thousands of would-be entrepreneurs still attempt to start without a business plan. The most common among these are businesses that appear to need little or no capital at the outset, or whose founders have funds of their own; in both cases it is believed unnecessary to expose the project to harsh financial appraisal.

The former hypothesis is usually based on the easily exploded myth that customers will all pay cash on the nail and suppliers will wait for months to be paid. In the meantime, the proprietor has the use of these funds to finance the business. Such model customers and suppliers are thinner on the ground than optimistic entrepreneurs think. In any event, two important market rules still apply: either the product or service on offer fails to sell like hot cakes and mountains of unpaid stocks build up, all of which eventually have to be financed; or it does sell like hot cakes and more financially robust entrepreneurs are attracted into the market. Without the staying power that adequate financing provides, these new competitors will rapidly kill off the fledgling business.

Those would-be entrepreneurs with funds of their own, or, worse still, borrowed from 'innocent' friends and relatives, tend to think that the time spent in preparing a business plan could be more usefully (and enjoyably) spent looking for premises, buying a new car or installing a computer. In short, anything that inhibits them from immediate action is viewed as time-wasting.

As most people's perception of their business venture is flawed in some important respect, it follows that jumping in at the deep end is risky – and unnecessarily so. Flaws can often be discovered cheaply and in advance when preparing a business plan; they are always discovered in the marketplace, invariably at a much higher and usually fatal cost.

There was a myth at the start of the Internet boom that the pace of development in the sector was too fast for business planning. The first generation of dot.com businesses and their backers seemed happy to pump money into what they called a 'business' or 'revenue' model. These 'models' were simply brief statements of intent supported by little more than wishful thinking. A few months into the new millennium, a sense of realism came to the Internet sector. In any business sector only ventures with well-prepared business plans have any chance of getting off the ground or being supported in later-stage financing rounds.

Live4now.com

Serena Doshi was working as an accountant at Schroders until a moment of serendipity changed her life: 'I called out an engineer to fix my printer,' said the 27-year-old from Fulham, London. 'This chap showed up and when we started talking, we just hit it off.' The young chap in question was 21-year-old Ewan MacLeod. Their business Live4now. com, a lifestyle site for 18- to 35-year-olds, raised £250,000 in seed capital and was valued at £20 million early in 2000.

But while the founders got on immediately, their business plan took a bit more work. In order to make their idea credible to prospective backers, Doshi spent six months working until 9 pm at Schroders then coming home and working until 3 am on the business plan. Doshi's four years at Arthur Andersen, the accountants, came in handy here.

What financiers look out for

Successful entrepreneurs with a proven track record can have as many problems raising finance for their ventures as can the relative novice, as Canadian-born but London-based Sherry Coutu was to find out:

Harvard MBA Sherry Coutu founded Internet Securities with venture-capital support with the goal of supplying supplied Western companies with timely and relevant East European market information. When Netscape offered free copies of its Internet software over the Web (and 3 million copies were downloaded in one weekend), Sherry decided the retail market could not be ignored – the Internet could be the vehicle to find and distribute vast quantities of financial information and research results not to companies this time, but to individuals.

Seeking funds to help set up a company devoted to the idea, Sherry sought the help of venture capitalists supporting Internet securities. Their reaction was, 'Make a choice – you can't run two companies'. Thwarted, she turned to Business Angels. They demanded a business plan. Sherry wrote it that night, including details of $250,000 worth of contracts from financial institutions wishing to advertise to her target audience. The next day Interactive Investor International (iii) was incorporated, backed with £1 million from Business Angels. Seeking partnerships with the UK unit-trust industry, Sherry was again rebuffed: 'Darling, nobody is going to buy investments over the Internet – go back to America.' Two weeks after her iii site went live, a leading fund manager sold a $10,000 unit trust to a customer via the site. Further venture capital funding was soon forthcoming and the company was floated in February 2000 (just before the City's, now over-exaggerated, love affair with the Internet cooled down!).

So, if you need finance, then as well as the operational benefits of preparing a business plan, it is important to examine what financiers expect from you, if you are to succeed in raising those funds.

It is often said that there is no shortage of money for new and growing businesses – the only scarce commodities are good ideas and people with the ability to exploit them. From the potential entrepreneur's position this is often hard to believe. One major venture capital firm alone receives several thousand business plans a year. Only 500 or so are examined in any detail, fewer than 25 are pursued to the negotiating stage, and only 6 of those are invested in.

To a great extent the decision whether to proceed beyond an initial reading of the plan will depend on the quality of the business plan used in supporting the investment proposal. The business plan is the ticket of admission giving the entrepreneur his first and often only chance to impress prospective sources of finance with the quality of his proposal.

It follows from this that to have any chance at all of getting financial support, your business plan must be the best that can be written and it must be professionally packaged.

In our experience at Cranfield the plans that succeed meet all of the following requirements:

EVIDENCE OF MARKET ORIENTATION AND FOCUS

Bookham Technologies

We saw the market opportunity and then went looking for the technology. That is the right way to do it.

Bookham Technologies, founded by Andrew Rickman in 1988, could well have been an example of a high-technology start-up in search of a market. With an honours degree in Mechanical Engineering from Imperial College, London and a PhD from the University of Surrey, Rickman certainly had the makings of a boffin. But an MBA from Cranfield changed his fervour for technology to an end in itself.

'Back in 1988 I came across the forerunners of the Internet and it struck me at the time that optical fibre was going to become a very important part of the Internet because it was the best way of transmitting lots and lots of information,' he says.

Rickman is part academic, part new-economy entrepreneur and part traditional businessman. He spurns the dressed-down uniform of the e-world for a sober suit, white shirt and tie, and is at his most animated explaining at a blackboard how data travel down optical cables.

Communication via *optical fibres* rather than copper wires uses light instead of electrical signals to carry and process information and is ideally suited to the heavy data traffic of the Internet age. Fibre-optic cables have been used for at least 10 years but the optical components at each end of the cables used to be expensive, involving the hand assembly of tiny lasers, filters and lenses.

This was the problem that Rickman set out to solve. He says: 'Our vision at the beginning of the business was to find a way of integrating all of the functions needed in optical components on to a chip in the same way that the electronics industry has done.' This simplification would allow automated volume manufacture, bringing down cost and encouraging growth in the use of the Internet. 'The only thing that is likely to prevent the continued exponential growth in the use of the Internet is that cost reduction in use does not come down fast enough,' he says.

The business started in a room above the garage of his home, with his wife as company secretary. But the idea did not stem from academic research work that Rickman, who holds a doctorate in integrated optics from the University of Surrey, had carried out. Rickman designed the business model to meet a market need rather than to exploit an existing technology. He says: 'I had briefly worked in the venture-capital community and, at the outset of Bookham Technologies, formulated a model for the ideal technology company. We saw the market opportunity and then went looking for the technology. That is the right way to do it.'

Once the initial scientific breakthroughs had been made, the company raised private equity finance totalling $110 million over several rounds and had backing from 3i, Cisco, Intel and others; 'It was a very long road to travel with substantial challenges, but now we are producing tens of thousands of components, scaling up in a way that has not been seen in the UK,' Rickman says.

Bookham Technologies, like Cisco, is a supplier of 'picks and shovels' to the Internet market. In May 2000 it employed 400 people and had annual sales of about £10 million. The company was listed on the London Stock Exchange and the NASDAQ in May 2000 and was valued at £5 billion. This made Rickman an addition to the growing list of European e-billionaires.

Entrepreneurs must demonstrate that they have recognised the needs of potential customers, rather than simply being infatuated with an innovative idea. Business plans that occupy more space with product descriptions and technical explanations than with explaining how products will be sold and to whom usually get cold-shouldered by financiers. They rightly suspect that these companies are more of an ego trip than an enterprise.

But market orientation is not in itself enough. Financiers want to sense that the entrepreneur knows the one or two things their business can do best – and that they are prepared to concentrate on exploiting these opportunities.

Two friends who eventually made it to an enterprise programme – and to founding a successful company – had great difficulty in getting backing at first. They were exceptionally talented designers and makers of clothes. They started out making ballgowns, wedding dresses, children's clothes – anything the market wanted. Only when they focused on designing and marketing clothes for the mother-to-be that allowed her still to feel fashionably dressed was it obvious they had a winning concept. That strategy built on their strength as designers and their experiences as former mothers-to-be, and exploited a clear market opportunity neglected at that time by the main player in the market-place – Mothercare.

From that point their company made a quantum leap forward from turning over a couple of hundred thousand pounds a year into the several million pound league in a few years.

EVIDENCE OF CUSTOMER ACCEPTANCE

Financiers like to know that your new product or service will sell and is being used, even if only on a trial or demonstration basis.

The founder of Solicitec, a company selling software to solicitors to enable them to process relatively standard documents such as wills, had little trouble getting support for his house conveyancing package once his product had been tried and approved by a leading building society for its panel of solicitors.

If you are only at the prototype stage, then as well as having to assess your chances of succeeding with technology, financiers have no immediate indication that, once made, your product will appeal to the market. Under these circumstances you have to show that the 'problem' your innovation seeks to solve is a substantial one that a large number of people will pay for.

One inventor from the Royal College of Art came up with a revolutionary toilet system design that, as well as being extremely thin, used 30 per cent less water per flush and had half the number of moving parts of a conventional product, all for no increase in price. Although he had only drawings to show, it was clear that with domestic metered water for all households a distinct possibility and a UK market for half a million new units per annum, a sizeable acceptance was reasonably certain.

As well as evidence of customer acceptance, entrepreneurs need to demonstrate that they know how and to whom their new product or service must be sold, and that they have a financially viable means of doing so.

PROPRIETARY POSITION

Exclusive rights to a product through patents, copyright, trademark protection or a licence helps to reduce the apparent riskiness of a venture in the financier's eyes, as these can limit competition – for a while at least.

One participant on a Cranfield enterprise programme held patents on a revolutionary folding bicycle he had designed at college. While no financial institution was prepared to back him in manufacturing the bicycle, funds were readily available to enable him to make production prototypes and then license manufacture to established bicycle makers throughout the world.

However well protected legally a product is, it is marketability and marketing know-how generally that outweigh 'patentability' in the success equation. A salutary observation made by an American professor of entrepreneurship revealed that fewer than 0.5 per cent of the best ideas contained in the US *Patent Gazette* in the last five years have returned a dime to the inventors.

FINANCIERS' NEEDS

Anyone lending money to or investing in a venture will expect the entrepreneur to have given some thought to his or her needs, and to have explained how they can be accommodated in the business plan.

Bankers, and indeed any other sources of debt capital, are looking for asset security to back their loan and the near certainty of getting their money back. They will also charge an interest rate that reflects current market conditions and their view of the risk level of the proposal. Depending on the nature of the business in question and the purpose for which the money is being used, bankers will take a 5- to 15-year view.

As with a mortgage repayment, bankers will usually expect a business to start repaying both the loan and the interest on a monthly or quarterly basis immediately the loan has been granted. In some cases a capital 'holiday' for up to two years can be negotiated, but in the early stage of any loan the interest charges make up the lion's share of payments.

Bankers hope the business will succeed so that they can lend more money in the future and provide more banking services such as insurance, tax advice, etc to a loyal customer.

It follows from this appreciation of a lender's needs that lenders are less interested in rapid growth and the consequent capital gain than they are in a steady stream of earnings almost from the outset.

As new or fast-growing businesses generally do not make immediate profits, money for such enterprises must come from elsewhere. Risk or equity capital, as other types of funds are called, comes from venture capital houses, as well as being put in by founders, their families and friends.

Because the inherent risks involved in investing in new and young ventures are greater than for investing in established companies, venture capital fund managers have to offer their investors the chance of larger overall returns. To do that, fund managers must not only keep failures to a minimum; they have to pick some big winners too – ventures with annual compound growth rates above 50 per cent – to offset the inevitable mediocre performers.

Typically, a fund manager would expect, from any 10 investments, one star, seven also-rans and two flops. It is important to remember that despite this outcome, venture capital fund managers are only looking for winners, so unless you are projecting high capital growth, the chances of getting venture capital are against you.

Not only are venture capitalists looking for winners, they are also looking for a substantial shareholding in your business. There are no simple rules for what constitutes a fair split, but *Venture Capital Report*, a UK monthly publication of investment opportunities, suggests the following starting point:

For the idea: 33%
For the management: 33%
For the money: 34%

It all comes down to how much you need the money, how risky the venture is, how much money could be made – and your skills as a negotiator. However, it is salutary to remember that 100 per cent of nothing is still nothing. So, all parties to the deal have to be satisfied if it is to succeed.

Venture capital firms may also want to put a non-executive director on the board of your company to look after their interests. You will have at your disposal a talented financial brain, so be prepared to make use of him or her, as his or her services won't be free – either you'll pay up front in the fee for raising the capital, or you'll pay an annual management charge.

As fast-growing companies typically have no cash available to pay dividends, investors can only profit by selling their holdings. With this in mind, the venture capitalist needs to have an exit route such as the Stock Exchange or a potential corporate buyer in view at the outset.

Unlike many entrepreneurs (and some lending bankers) who see their ventures as lifelong commitments to success and growth, venture capitalists have a relatively short time horizon. Typically, they are looking to liquidate small company investments within three to seven years, allowing them to pay out to individual investors and to have funds available for tomorrow's winners.

So, to be successful your business must be targeted at the needs of these two sources of finance, and in particular at the balance between the two. Lending bankers ideally look for a ratio of £1 of debt to £1 of equity capital, but have been known to go up to £4–£5. Venture capital providers will almost always encourage entrepreneurs to take on new debt capital to match the level of equity funding.

If you plan to raise money from friends and relatives their needs must also be taken into account in your business plan. Their funds can be in the form of debt equity, but they may also seek some management role for themselves. Unless they have an important contribution to make, by virtue of being an accountant or marketing expert or respected public figure, for example, it is always best to confine their role to that of a shareholder. In that capacity they can 'give' you advice or pass on their contacts and so enhance the worth of their (and your) shareholding, but they won't hold down a post that would be better filled by someone else. Alternatively, make them non-executive directors, which may flatter them and can't harm your business. Clearly, you must use common sense in this area.

One final point on the needs of financial institutions: they will expect your business plan to include a description of how performance will be monitored and controlled.

One budding entrepreneur blew an otherwise impeccable performance at a bankers' panel by replying when asked how he would control his venture: 'I'm only concerned with raising finance and getting my business started at the moment – once that's over I'll think about "bean counting".'

He had clearly forgotten who owned the beans!

BELIEVABLE FORECASTS

Entrepreneurs are naturally ebullient when explaining the future prospects for their business. They frequently believe that 'the sky's the limit' when it comes to growth, and money (or rather the lack of it) is the only thing that stands between them and their success.

It is true that if you are looking for venture capital, then the providers are also looking for rapid growth. However, it's as well to remember that financiers are dealing with thousands of investment proposals each year, and already have money tied up in hundreds of business sectors. It follows, therefore, that they already have a perception of what the accepted financial results and marketing approaches currently are for any sector. Any new company's business plan showing projections that are outside the ranges perceived as acceptable within an industry will raise questions in the investor's mind.

Make your growth forecasts believable; support them with hard facts where possible. If they are on the low side, then approach the more cautious lending banker, rather than venture capitalists. The former often see a modest forecast as a virtue, lending credibility to the business proposal as a whole.

JavaSoft/Hotmail

In September 1988, Sabeer Bhatia arrived at Los Angeles International Airport. He had won a transfer scholarship to Cal Tech by being the only applicant in the entire world to get a passing score on the notorious Cal Tech Transfer Exam in 1988 (there are usually about 150 who give it a try). Sabeer had scored a 62 out of 100 – the next highest score was 42.

Sabeer intended to get his degrees and then to go home to work – probably as an engineer for a very large Indian company. He was following a modest path of life like his parents. His mother was an accountant at the Central Bank of India for her entire career and his father spent 10 years as a captain in the Indian Army.

But as a graduate student at Stanford, Sabeer was drawn to the basement of Terman auditorium. There, the speakers were entrepreneurs like Scott McNealy, Steve Wozniak and Marc Andressen. Their fundamental message was always the same: 'You can do it too.' Sabeer knew that famous people always say such things – they want to be inspirational. But Sabeer's impression of these successful entrepreneurs was that they really were fairly ordinary smart guys – not much different from him and his classmates.

When he graduated, Sabeer did not want to go home. So, along with Jack Smith, he took a job at Apple Computer. Sabeer could have worked at Apple for 20 or 30 years, but he got swept up in the decade's fever: you haven't lived until you've gone solo.

Sabeer met a man named Farouk Arjani. Arjani had been a pioneer in the word-processing business in the 1970s and had since become a special limited partner of Sequoia Ventures. The two hit it off and Arjani became Sabeer's mentor. What really set Sabeer apart for Arjani from the hundreds of entrepreneurs was the size of his dream. Even before he had a product, before he had any money behind him, he was completely convinced that he was going to build a major company that would be worth hundreds of millions of dollars.

In mid-1995, Sabeer began taking around a two-page executive summary business plan for a net-based personal database called JavaSoft. When Jack Smith, by now a partner in the venture – albeit a reluctant one – and Sabeer came up with the Hotmail idea in December, JavaSoft effectively became the front for Hotmail. Sabeer knew that Hotmail was such an explosive concept, he didn't want a less-than-ethical venture capitalist to reject him, then turn around and copy his idea. He kept showing JavaSoft and showed Hotmail only to those venture capitalists for whom he had gained respect. 'It was fine that they were rejecting JavaSoft. But in so doing, I got to see how their mind worked. If they rejected JavaSoft for stupid reasons, then I said thank you and left. If they rejected it for the right reasons, then I showed them Hotmail.'

Sabeer presented his business plan to Steve Jurvetson of Draper Fisher Jurvetson. Jurvetson remembers 'Sabeer's revenue estimates as showing that he was going to grow the company faster than any in history. Most entrepreneurs have that trait, but they also are concerned with looking like a fool. Sabeer's projections were dismissed outright, but Sabeer's passionate belief was unchanged and he was right. He grew the subscriber base faster than any company in the history of the world.'

One might have presumed that, since Sabeer had been rejected by 20 venture capitalists previously and was virtually a nobody, he would be grateful to accept Draper Fisher Jurvetson's $300,000 on their terms. The venture capitalists made the perfectly reasonable offer of retaining 30 per cent ownership on a $1 million valuation. Sabeer held out for double that valuation, with their cut at 15 per cent. The negotiations got nowhere, so Sabeer shrugged, stood up and walked out of the door. His only other available option was a $100,000 'friends and family' round that had been arranged as back-up – not nearly enough money. If they had gone that route, Hotmail wouldn't exist today. What actually happened was that Draper and Jurvetson relented; they called back the next day to accept their 15 per cent.

It took enormous confidence to do what Sabeer did: first, to hide his real idea, and second, to hold out for the valuation that he thought the company deserved. Both of these actions are extremely rare. But Sabeer gives credit to the culture of Silicon Valley itself: 'Only in Silicon Valley could two 27-year-old guys get £300,000 dollars from men they had just met. Two 27-year-old guys who had no experience with consumer products, who had never started a company, who had never managed anybody, who had no experience even in software – Jack and I were hardware engineers. All we had was the idea. We didn't demo proof-of-concept software or a prototype or even a graphic printed on a piece of paper. I just sketched on Steve Jurvetson's whiteboard. Nowhere in the world could this happen but here.'

On New Year's Eve 1997, Sabeer sold Hotmail to Microsoft in exchange for 2,769,148 of their shares. At that time those shares were worth $400 million. It was barely nine years since Sabeer had stepped off his flight from Bangalore, India, with $250 in his pocket – the limit allowed by Indian customs officials.

SUGGESTED FURTHER READING

Barrow, Paul (2004) *Raising Finance: A practical guide to starting, expanding and selling your business*, Kogan Page, London

Cary, Lucius (1998) *Guide to Raising Capital for the Smaller Business*, Seed Capital (Publishing) Ltd and Venture Capital Report Ltd, Oxford Science Park

Vandermerwe, S and Taishoff, M (2000) *Interactive Investor International*, available from the European Case Clearing House, Cranfield, Beds MK43 0AL; tel: 01234 750903; fax: 01234 751125; Web site: www.ecch.cranfield.ac.uk; e-mail: ecch@cranfield.ac.uk

PLATINUM ENTERPRISE LIMITED

Commercial Finance

At Platinum Enterprise, we aim to search for sound but effective finance for your business.

Our business brokerage services include the following

Commercial Finance

We will be happy to consider most propositions of finance for your business. There are many products on the market ranging from:

★ Invoice discounting ★ Invoice factoring ★ Asset based finance ★ Leasing finance ★ Business loans Property Finance ★ Trade Finance ★ Stock Finance

Commercial Mortgages

Commercial mortgages and remortgages are available for most sites including:

★ Offices ★ Warehouses ★ Professional practices ★ Shops ★ Restaurants ★ Hotels ★ Post Offices ★ Leisure facilities ★ Care facilities ★ Commercial and Residential Investment

Property Finance

There are many sources for property finance and so the market is competitive. We aim to find a suitable product for most cases. The main areas of property finance are:

★ Land or Site finance ★ Development finance ★ Mezzanine finance

Buy-to-let Mortgages

We can arrange Buy to Let mortgages with a large number of lenders and so are able to find a product which meets your requirements from a wide selection.

Insurance

Please remember to consider the benefits of insurance regarding property, mortgages or other loans.

Please contact us for further information. Platinum Enterprise Limited 1 Berkeley Street London W1J 8DJ
Tel: 0845 850 0235 Fax: 0845 850 0245 Email: finance@platinumenterprise.co.uk www.platinumenterprise.co.uk

We subscribe to the NACFB code of practice. Insurance, security and a deposit may be required. Terms will be subject to circumstances. A Brokers fee of up to 1% of loan value may apply. Platinum Enterprises is an Appointed Representative of Network Data Limited which is authorised and regulated by the Financial Services Authority. Many of the services are not regulated by the Financial Services Authority.

Platinum Enterprise Limited

Commercial Mortgage

Many business will at some point own their own premises and at some point require a mortgage or remortgage. Most types of properties will be considered by lenders.

The first point to consider will be which mortgage will be available for the criteria allowed by the business. There are many lenders on the market and many will specialise within specific industry sectors and status.

The next point to consider is the flexibility of the product. Some lenders may be prepared to allow interest only periods and payment holidays. These may be points to consider where business is going through growth and changes.

The interest rates may also be flexible and where good status is available, there may be some room for negotiations for a better interest rate.

Factoring and Invoice Discounting

Companies which are growing may inevitably at some point find that due to timing of debtors receivable, cash flow issues occur and they have to be resoled.

Factoring services can be put in place and the sales ledger can be managed by a suitable lender. There is usually a quarterly charge in additional to interest payments.

In addition to costs, it is also important to consider the level of service provided to you and the flexibility offered to valued clients.

Invoice discounting is a more flexible and discreet way of debtor finance where your customers do not need to know that invoice has been factored. Insurance products are also available for bad debts.

Leasing Finance and Hire Purchase

Leasing finance offer flexibility to spread costs the life of the asset.

There are different types of leases which can allow the user to either purchase or return the asset at the end of the period. The benefits of return are clearly avoiding having to dispose of it at the end of the period.

Hire purchase options are also available with an option to purchase the product at the end of the period.

Items usually subject to finance include: Equipment, vehicles and information technology.

New business may be required to provide additional security.

Property Finance

Finance is available for investment property, land, development, and bridging.

Products are typically subject to the business status, exit strategy and loan to values.

Business Finance

A range of finances are available to support businesses.

These range from Stock finance, Trade finance and Business loans. Track record, management accounts, business plan and own contributions may be needed. Lenders will carry out thorough due diligence checks in many cases and lending is tightly controlled.

These products can allow businesses to trade effectively and most market needs.

Insurance

Please remember to consider insurance products in order to provide adequate cover against risk.

Platinum Enterprise Limited
1 Berkeley Street
London
W1J 8DJ
Tel: 0845 850 0235
Fax: 0845 850 0245
www.platinumenterprise.co.uk
Email: finance@platinumenterprise.co.uk

Choose
the **office** solution that's **right** for you

Team Office

Meeting Room

Choose from over 90 prime locations across UK, providing offices, meeting rooms and virtual offices tailored to your needs, on your terms and to suit your budget

Typical Reception Area

To receive a free cost comparison or for more information:

☏ **0870 880 8484**
🌐 **www.regus.co.uk**

Regus®

Why Regus makes good business sense

A small partnership sees expansion on the horizon. A sole trader working from home is finding it disruptive. A SME is seeking a more prestigious address for its corporate image.

Whatever the reason for moving into new premises, deciding on the right kind and where can be a nail-biting decision for any company – big or small.

What kind of property, in which location, and how much will it cost? These are just some of the questions that will need careful thought – particularly as most small businesses require flexible, cost-effective, low risk solutions in tune with their changing needs.

Why, therefore, do companies still lock themselves into conventional long-term property leases when a simple one-page agreement with Regus – the UK's top serviced office provider – is a good deal more cost effective and far more flexible? The myth that outsourcing office space is an expensive option, especially in rental hotspots such as London, is mostly to blame. Yet outsourcing to Regus is good value for money, and that's official!

High-cost myth dispelled

Recent independent research by Actium Consult and Cass Business School into total office costs – including capital expenditure on fitting out a new office, repairs, and maintenance and cleaning costs – concludes that Regus is up to 40 per cent cheaper than a conventional lease. 'The myth that serviced offices are an expensive option has once again been exploded by this research,' said David Ford, chief executive officer of Regus in the UK.

'Regus offers a cost-effective alternative to conventional property solutions at most levels and most locations. Our experience shows that once companies understand the value of the Regus product and experience the quality of the service, there's no going back. That's why almost two-thirds of our clients renew their agreements – the same people who, before coming to Regus, mistakenly assumed we were expensive.'

Savings on quality London offices

Despite London's high-rent reputation, 23 of Regus's 90 UK centres are in London, all offering excellent value offices with state-of-the-art IT and communications facilities. In the West End, for example, savings of 38 per cent could be made against a traditional office. The survey went on to show that savings could also be achieved in the hardest hit office markets in the City and Thames Valley.

And it's not just Regus' physical offices that offer excellent value. Its range of products is created with modern business in mind and can be tailored to fit the business and the budget. Regus Virtual Office, for example, offers 'everything but the office'. Companies have their own dedicated local telephone number, the use of a Regus address, and fax and post handling.

Regus also has 3,000 meeting rooms worldwide, offering a professional environment dedicated to business, with all the facilities and technology expected by modern business but with none of the distractions of a hotel.

Flexible, convenient and secure

But Regus doesn't only have the edge on costs. Conventional leases drain company resources as well as being inflexible to changing needs – businesses can't scale up or down or relocate easily if they're tied into an inflexible five, 10 or 15-year lease.

The real advantages of outsourcing to Regus are agility and mobility – particularly useful for growing businesses because it gives them the flexibility to manage their business effectively, without exposing it to too much risk. Regus offers immediate space for any length of occupation – that's everything from short-term rentals through to 12-month plus agreements. All companies have to do is walk into their Regus office, plug in and start work immediately.

It's a strategic benefit that more and more companies are recognising as they turn to Regus for outsourcing their property needs. So next time you're thinking of making an office move, call Regus for a no-obligation, cost comparison consultation.

Regus has more than 90 prime UK locations, in city centres, on motorway networks, and close to transport hubs such as airports and rail links. It has centres in many of London's most well known buildings plus strategically located centres throughout the country including Edinburgh, Newcastle, Manchester, Leeds, Birmingham and Bristol.

For more information, call Regus today on 0870 880 8484 or visit www.regus.co.uk.

Phase 1

History and position to date

1

Business purpose and aims

In this first assignment you should introduce your business idea to the future readers of your business plan. Explain something of how you arrived at your business idea, why you think people have a need for your product or service, and what your goals and aspirations for the business are. If your business needs financing, you could give some preliminary idea of how much you may need and what you intend to do with those funds. Remember, all these ideas are likely to be significantly modified later on – some more than others – but you need to have some idea at the outset of where you are going if you are to have any chance at all of getting there.

Edwin Trisk, manufacturer of paint-curing equipment, under the stewardship of managing director Robert Kilsby, has beaten off all international competition from Canada, Sweden and Italy to become the world leader in this niche market – and it is still growing at 20 per cent a year. Last year, Trisk, based in Sunderland, won the Queen's Award for Export Achievement.

The company has secured a presence in 58 countries by strong branding and a determined relationship with its importers. 'We set out on day one both in terms of products and customers to have a world market,' says Robert Kilsby, who bought out the company five years earlier. Since then Trisk has made its presence felt in every country in which it has a market. The strategy is to grant an importer exclusive rights to the company's range of drying equipment. The productivity advantages of Trisk's equipment means the time a body shop takes to dry a car can be cut from 4 hours to 10 minutes.

In return for Trisk's exclusivity, the importers have to adhere to stringent criteria. They have to agree to exhibit at local exhibitions, provide Trisk with market information, sales and stock reports, and use Trisk's own marketing strategy. The company is so hands-on that, should the importer wish to advertise in any local media, Trisk supplies the fonts and transparencies to be used. The policies might sound severe, but they work because Trisk has always been clear about where the company is going and how it is going to get there.

Trisk's success is helped by the fact that local competitors produce products of such poor quality. 'The Japanese are great with volume products, but in niche products it is a different world. There, they admire European technology.' Kilsby and his team place huge importance on what he calls 'worldwide brand-building'. As he says, 'we wanted to give the image of a bigger company'. The brochures are glossy, the products are glossy, all in a Day-Glo yellow much like the headquarters. And the philosophy has stood the company in good stead: turnover is up to £6m.

It may be useful to organise your information in this section using the pyramid of goals on page 23 as a framework.

Mission statements and objectives are important in two main ways:

█ to concentrate your own and your employees' efforts (rowing harder does not help if the boat is headed in the wrong direction);
█ to concentrate attention on problems to be solved (problem-solving is finding ways to get you from where you are to where you want to be).

Large companies may spend long weekends at country mansions wrestling with the fine print of their mission statements; in principle, given the narrower scope of the new business, the task facing the new business owner should be less daunting.

To take mission statements and objectives first, as they are inevitably inter-twined, these are direction statements intended to focus your attention on essentials, to encapsulate your specific competence(s) in relation to the markets/ customers you plan to serve.

First, the mission should be narrow enough to give direction and guidance to everyone in the business. This concentration is the key to business success because it is only by focusing on specific needs that a small business can differentiate itself from its larger competitors. Nothing kills off a new business faster than trying to do too many different things at the outset.

Second, the mission should open up a large enough market to allow the business to grow and realise its potential.

Interestingly enough, one of the highest incidences of failure in small busi-ness is in the building trade. The very nature of this field seems to mitigate against being able to concentrate on any specific type of work, or on customer need. One successful new small builder defined his mission in the following sentence. 'We will concentrate on domestic house repair and renovation work, and as well as doing a good job we will meet the customers' two key needs: a quotation that is accurate, and starting and completion dates that are met.' When told this mission, most small builders laugh. They say it cannot be done, but then most go broke.

Ultimately, there has to be something unique about your business idea or yourself that makes people want to buy from you. That uniqueness may be confined to the fact that you are the only photocopying shop in the area, but that is enough to make you stand out (provided, of course, that the area has potential customers).

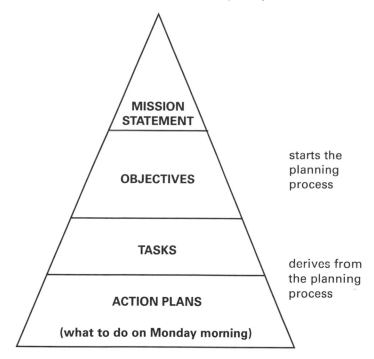

Note: Mission and objectives are 'what' statements; tasks and action plans are 'how to' statements.

Figure 1.1 The pyramid of goals

Also, within the objectives you need some idea of how big you want the business to be. Your share of the market, in other words. It certainly is not easy to forecast sales, especially before you have even started trading, but if you do not set a goal at the start and instead just wait to see how things develop, then one of two problems will occur. Either you will not sell enough to cover your fixed costs and so lose money and perhaps go out of business, or you will sell too much and run out of cash – in other words, overtrade.

Obviously, before you can set a market share and sales objective you need to know the size of your market. We shall consider how to find that out in later assignments.

The 'size' you want your business to be is more a matter of judgement than forecast – a judgement tempered by the resources you have available to achieve those objectives and, of course, some idea of what is reasonable and achievable and what is not. You will find the range of discretion over a size objective seriously constrained by the financial resources at your disposal – or realistically available from investors and lenders – and the scope of the market opportunity.

It will be useful to set near-term objectives covering the next 18 months or so, and a longer-term objective covering up to five or so years on.

In summary, the mission statement should explain:

- What business you are in and your purpose (eg Connect-Air, 'We are in the commuter/feeder airline business and we want to establish a profitable air-link between Cranfield and Heathrow as a forerunner for other links').
- What you want to achieve over the next one to three years, ie your strategic goal (eg Metropolitan Police, 'We aim to maintain a peaceful society, free of fear of crime and disorder'; NB this may take a little longer than one to three years).
- how, ie your values and standards (eg IBM, 'By dedication to customer service'; Sherry Coutu, 'By giving private investors an equal footing with investor services').

Above all, mission statements must be realistic, achievable – and brief. McKinsey's mission reads: 'As management consultants, to help our clients make distinctive, lasting, and substantial improvements in their performance and to build a great firm that attracts, develops, excites and retains exceptional people'.

Blooming Marvellous is a company formed by two young mothers who, while attending an enterprise programme, developed the following mission statement:

'Arising out of our experiences, we intend to design, make and market a range of clothes for mothers-to-be that will make them feel they can still be fashionably dressed. We aim to serve a niche missed out by Mothercare, Marks & Spencer, etc, and so become a significant force in the mail order fashion for the mothers-to-be market.

We are aiming for a 5 per cent share of this market in the South-East, and a 25 per cent return on assets employed within three years of starting up. We believe we will need about £25,000 start-up capital to finance stock, a mail order catalogue and an advertising campaign.'

Contrast the clarity of this mission with the blurred missions of some Internet company mission statements and it is not hard to see why so many of them have trouble raising additional financing.

iSKY

'iSKY provides a complete outsourced customer-loyalty management solution to both electronic businesses and traditional companies seeking to enhance their customers' online and offline experiences before, during and after a purchase. Our customer loyalty management services use interactive one-to-one communications, enhanced by real-time, personalised data collection and management, to find, win, keep and enhance profitable customer relationships. We offer our clients a customised, fully integrated, Web-enabled solution for interacting with their customers through a variety of media including real-time, text chat, e-mail, voice over Internet protocol, telephone and facsimile.'

iSKY was a company that had to pull its initial public offering (IPO) at lunchtime on that day in April 2000 when the NASDAQ plunged several hundred points. To be absolutely fair to its founders, the statement above was included in iSKY's IPO filing documentation under the heading 'Our Business', but we suspect many people would read it as a mission statement.

The Blooming Marvellous mission was evolved long before the Internet was even thought of, yet its founders had no difficulty absorbing it into the core of what they did by adding just the single word 'Internet' alongside 'mail order'. Even though they now derive much of their income from the Internet, they still have not used words commonly found in technology-based companies' mission statements.

Many companies separate out their specific objectives, which they wish to keep confidential, from the mission statement, which they realise they must communicate widely, via meetings and company literature, to promote greater company cohesion and concentration.

Thus the first paragraph alone of the Blooming Marvellous statement above could serve as the mission statement, for communication to all employees. Remember also that mission statements will change over time, as the environment and the company progresses. For example, Martin Sorrel at WPP set out in 1985 to establish 'a large multinational marketing services company and to be one of the best, by adding value and imagination to clients' products and services'. By the 1990s the mission had altered to being 'the largest multinational marketing company and THE best'. This will probably be modified again in the new millennium as Sorrel continues to add value from the centre.

Barrie Haigh revisited his mission statement with his top team for each of the six years after attending the Cranfield Business Growth Programme. Over that six-year period he took his business from £8 million a year turnover to a value of £550 million in a trade sale, netting himself some £350 million in the process.

Mission statements must not become too bland or too general. For example, can you tell what business this company is in, what it aims to achieve in the next three years and how?

Our key strategy is the aggressive pursuit of quality and performance in providing a wide and comprehensive range of business and consumer services.

Constantly developing these in line with our market driven approach to expanding into new areas of profitable growth, we are ready to meet the challenge of identifying and exploiting new opportunities where they exist.

No wonder that Sketchley plc, soon after the publication of the above in its 1998/9 Annual Report, was the subject of hostile takeover bids, ultimately failing and disappearing from the high street.

For the founders of Blooming Marvellous, the advantage of their clear mission statement lay in the fact that they could translate their principal objectives into specific key tasks and actions plans. This plan consists of 'how to' statements to achieve specific objectives and goals.

Objectives within three years:

▪ Achieve 5 per cent market share in south-east England.
▪ Obtain a 25 per cent return on assets employed.

Tasks:

▪ Identify mailing lists and promotion media within three months.
▪ Design 12 items of fashion clothes within six months.
▪ Produce mail-order catalogue within nine months.
▪ Locate packaging and distributor organisations within six months.

Action plan:

Monday morning:

▪ Start design on product.
▪ Write for mailing-list details.
▪ Look up trade directories for distributors.

It would also be useful at this stage to explain how you arrived at your business idea, what makes you believe it will succeed, and why you want to go ahead with it now.

McIntosh's business, Safariquip, equips safaris, or anyone else planning long, overland travel. The corporate and institutional market – involving expeditions and surveys for oil or minerals, or other projects in the Third World – is just beginning to open up too.

The idea was born out of the difficulties McIntosh experienced when he went exploring Africa by Land Rover and climbing mountains there. It took him two years to prepare for the trip. There was no single source of help, advice or supplies. This gave him the first inkling that there might be a market. Was it, he asked himself, the same for all similar overland travellers, whether going on safari, travelling for fun, mounting geographical expeditions or even prospecting for minerals?

Experience, he was to discover, showed that anyone travelling long distances over rough terrain and living in the bush for long periods while doing so needed much the same sort of equipment and advice. Much of the equipment, though basic, is special enough to be scattered among many different sources and difficult to obtain in total because of the problems involved in tracking down all the individual sources.

His other discoveries during his African safari included the disconcerting fact that roofracks on vehicles destroy the points at which they are anchored during the course of 21,000 miles of driving over rough ground. The solution as he saw it was to find better-designed and more easily stowable items in the first place, as well as redesigning stowage facilities inside the vehicle. He rebuilt his vehicle from the chassis up during two years in

South Africa, funding his work by taking a job as a middle manager in a mining company. He then, over a further two-year period, returned home, learning yet more about travelling and rough driving.

It was redundancy, after a variety of jobs, that pushed him finally into making his move. 'I decided to market my skills as a traveller. Many people need to know how to do it. I put an ad in *The Traveller* magazine, offering equipment and advice and started to pick up business very gradually.'

WORKSHEET FOR ASSIGNMENT 1: BUSINESS PURPOSE AND AIMS

1. Explain how you arrived at your business idea.
2. What makes you believe it will succeed?
3. Write a mission statement linking your product or service to the customer needs it is aimed at.
4. What are your principal objectives:
   (a) short term;
   (b) long term?
5. List your tasks and action plans as you see them at present.
6. How much money do you think will be needed to get your business started? Provide a short 'shopping list' of major expenses.

SUGGESTED FURTHER READING

Coulston-Thomas, J (2000) *Creating Excellence in Boardrooms*, McGraw-Hill, Maidenhead

Drucker, Peter (1994) *Managing for Results*, Butterworth-Heinemann, Oxford

Read, T with Chace, C and Rowe, S (2000) *The Internet Start-up Bible*, Random House, London

2

A description of your business

The two essential ingredients for success in any new venture are a good business idea and the right people to turn that idea into a business. Your business plan must therefore not only include a description of what your purpose or mission is, but give full details of your and your prospective partners' experience and 'suitability' for this venture.

You also need to explain the name of your business, why you chose it, and under what legal form you propose to trade. If your business has been trading for some time, you should give a brief description of achievements to date and a summary of financial results. Full accounts can be included in an appendix to your business plan. Let's look at each in turn.

YOU AND YOUR TEAM

The right stuff

To launch a new venture successfully, you have to be the right sort of person, your business idea must be right for the market, and your timing must be spot on. The world of business failures is full of products that are ahead of their time.

The entrepreneur is frequently seen as someone who is always bursting with new ideas, is highly enthusiastic, hyperactive and insatiably curious. But the more you try to create a picture of the typical entrepreneur, the more elusive he or she becomes. 'Is it genes or is it potty training, is it nature or nurture?', Cranfield's Professor Malcolm Harper liked to tease his entrepreneur class. Hermann Hauser (Amadeus Capital Partners), one of the founders of Cambridge's entrepreneurial renaissance, would reply: 'Britain has the right cultural genes, because we started the Industrial Revolution. We are not a lost cause, although we may have to rediscover, train and exercise these genes.'

Peter Drucker, the international business guru, captured the problem clearly with this description:

> Some are eccentrics, others painfully correct conformists; some are fat and some are lean; some are worriers, some relaxed; some drink quite heavily, others are total abstainers; some are men of great charm and warmth, some have no more personality than a frozen mackerel.

That said, there are certain characteristics that successful newcomers to business do have in common, and you should emphasise these in respect of yourself in the business plan.

Self-confident all-rounders

Entrepreneurs are rarely geniuses. There are nearly always people in their business who have more competence, in one field, than they could ever aspire to. But they have a wide range of ability and a willingness to turn their hands to anything that has to be done to make the venture succeed. They can usually make the product, market it and count the money, but above all they have self-confidence that lets them move comfortably through uncharted waters.

Paul Smith, who left school at 15, launched his clothing business and within a decade had opened three shops in London – one of which was in Covent Garden – and a further one in Tokyo, and turnover was above £2 million pa. Now 'Paul Smith' is an internationally recognised fashion brand.

Explaining his success, Smith states: 'It's not that I'm a particularly brilliant designer or businessman, but I can run a business and I can design. There are so many excellent designers or excellent people but so often the designers can't run the business and businessmen do not have the right product.'

Bob Payton, founder of the Chicago Pizza Pie Factory, explained how his first venture got started: 'I had no catering experience, but I've got a nose for what's going on. I flew to Chicago, located the best pizza chef and spent two weeks learning the business. I made dough, waited at tables and washed dishes – and then I set out to raise £25,000 to start up.'

The ability to bounce back

Rising from the ashes of former disasters is also a common feature of many successful entrepreneurs.

Henry Ford had been bankrupted twice before founding the Ford Motor Corporation with a loan of $28,000 in his fortieth year.

Timothy Waterstone, founder of one of the fastest-growing bookshop chains in the West, was fired from W H Smith's US operation in the most bloodcurdling circumstances. He took the first plane back to the UK and spent two months wondering what to do.

Until this time Waterstone's career path had been smooth and unmeteoric. After Cambridge he did a spell in the family tea-broking business in Cochin, followed by 10 years as a marketing manager for Allied Breweries. Books had always been his obsession, so he went to work for W H Smith. He was quickly sent to New York, where he remained for four years. His wife was in the UK for long periods, so he spent his spare time wandering around Manhattan bookshops. Brilliant places: lively and consumer-led with huge stock, accessible staff and long opening hours. He felt there was a gap for similar bookselling in Britain, but at the time did nothing about it.

A trip to the dole office acted as a catalyst. It was the most horrific experience of his life. Not waiting for his turn, he rushed out and sat in the car. Instead of trying to get a new job, he formulated the Waterstone's concept. High street banks turned him down. He then went to a finance house and struck lucky. He pledged his house, £6,000 savings, £10,000 borrowed from his father-in-law, and the rest was raised through the Government's loan guarantee scheme.

Three months later the first Waterstone's opened, based on a simple store plan an art student sketched out for £25. He filled the shops with the type of books that appeal to book lovers, not best-seller buyers. Midnight hours, Sunday trading (where possible) and bonus schemes for staff led to dazzling sales and the company employed 500 people in 40 branches, with a turnover of £35 million a year. The ultimate achievement was to sell back the company to W H Smith for the modest sum of £50 million. Don't get mad, start your own bookshop!

Innovative skills

Almost by definition, entrepreneurs are innovators who either tackle the unknown, or do old things in new ways. It is this inventive streak that allows them to carve out a new niche, often invisible to others.

Trees Unlimited, which passed the £1 million sales mark within three years of being started up, was launched by a nucleus of former managers of Porth Textiles, once Britain's largest manufacturer of decorations, garlands and plastic trees. Roger Freebody, Trees Unlimited's managing director, saw the writing on the wall before Porth collapsed with debts of £8 million, putting 364 people out of work in the Rhondda Valley.

Freebody and his colleagues saw the keys to survival as the ability to escape from old-fashioned manufacturing traditions and the ability to innovate and try new marketing approaches. Trees Unlimited introduced a whole range of coloured trees from brown to pink, thus bucking the tradition that said Christmas trees had to be green. It also introduced a new marketing concept of matching trees and their decorations with home decor. Even the Queen's florist in Berkeley Square has bought their products.

The Internet gave a boost to the business of a West Country village shop by drawing in customers from around the globe. Grocer Roger Biddle has been the boss of food shop Wessex Provender in South Petherton, near Yeovil in Somerset, for the past eight years. When he took on the village business the recession was at its worst, but selling his wares on the Internet has seen a dramatic upturn in his fortunes. Turnover has increased by 13 per cent in the few months since he opened Wessex Provender Mail Order Delicatessen on the World Wide Web; customers from all over the globe have placed orders for everything from smoked eels to cider brandy.

Mr Biddle, 57, who runs the shop with his wife, Sue, 49, said:

'The Internet gave this store a new lease of life. This technology could prove to be a lifeline for small rural businesses like ours. We always wanted to run a delicatessen and this seemed the perfect opportunity. Unfortunately, our launch coincided with one of the biggest recessions this country has ever known. It was really hard going at the beginning and we really struggled for the first few years. But over the last year things have started to come good and the Internet is a definite factor.'

Internet customers have come from as far afield as Japan, Australia and Poland. West Country folk abroad also use Mr Biddle's Internet site to keep apace of news and gossip in the Somerset village. Recent tittle-tattle on the Net has centred on a proposed one-way system and the risk of noise pollution from a new peal of bells at the parish church.

Results oriented

Successful people set themselves goals and get pleasure out of trying to achieve them. Once a goal has been reached, they have to get the next target in view as quickly as possible. This restlessness is very characteristic. Sir James Goldsmith was a classic example, moving the base of his business empire from the UK to France, then the United States – and finally into pure cash, ahead of a stock market crash.

Baltimore Technology

Baltimore Technology was typical of many companies that embarked on expensive acquisition programs during the dot.com era, seduced by forecasts about the future value of the security market. Its founder, Fran Rooney, bought a tiny Irish software company from an academic at Trinity College Dublin for less than £400,000 and built it into an FTSE 100 company in four years.

Rooney was strong on goals. At 29 he decided that by 40 he wanted to be heading a substantial company. By 45 he wanted his mortgage paid off, and by 50 he wanted to be in a position to retire.

By Rooney's 43rd birthday his business was worth £2.5 billion, but then reality caught up with it in July 2001, and with money running out, a restructuring programme was undertaken in a bid for survival. Since then it has sold its core PKI business to security and identity management provider Betrusted for £5 million, while Hewlett-Packard paid £8.3 million for its SelectAccess Web-based single sign-on software.

Baltimore has been reborn as a supplier of clean energy with a value of £22 million in August 2004, well down from its dizzy heights, but still a substantial business by any measure.

Professional risk-taker

The high failure rate shows that small businesses are faced with many dangers. An essential characteristic of someone starting a business is a willingness to make decisions and to take risks. This does not mean gambling on hunches. It means carefully calculating the odds and deciding which risks to take and when to take them.

Bob Payton's business plan for his first Chicago Pizza Pie Factory was modelled on the success he had seen the Hard Rock Cafe achieve on Hyde Park Corner. Uncertain, however, as to whether Londoners would take to his personally adored deep-pan Chicago pizzas, Bob, in order to minimise the risk, sought and found a six-month tail-end of a lease on small premises in Crown Alley passage, within walking distance of Hyde Park Corner. Within three months, queues in Crown Alley passage rivalled those at the Hard Rock Cafe and Bob could cheerfully negotiate a long and expensive lease on new premises in Hanover Square, knowing that he had sufficient customers from day one to cover all his outgoings.

Having total commitment

You will need complete faith in your idea. How else will you convince all the doubters you are bound to meet that it is a worthwhile venture? You will also need singlemindedness, energy and a lot of hard work to get things started; working 18-hour days is not uncommon. This can put a strain on other relationships, particularly within your family, so they too have to become involved and committed if you are to succeed.

At the age of 18, when his contemporaries were off to university, Darren Saunders chose the route of the inventor. In pursuit of his 'mad idea' of the Cyberquin – a highly realistic, moving mannequin for display in shop windows and exhibitions – he spent six months in a fruitless search for development cash. 'I must have spoken to 150 people,' he says. 'They all thought I was trying to achieve the impossible.' Finally, he clinched a DTI innovation grant; his father agreed to an overdraft with his bank to secure the remainder.

Darren got help with the patents from a local patent agent, and took a short course in exporting at the Cardiff Chamber of Commerce. After three long years of development, Saunders succeeded in creating a mannequin that would work 24 hours a day without a hitch, needed no maintenance, and could be easily shipped and effortlessly set up anywhere in the world. It took another 18 months of hard graft to get the product accepted, and it was all funded on a shoestring.

'Everyone advised me to stick to the UK,' says Saunders. 'But, I thought, the British never try anything new.'

He was right to follow his instincts. His budding company concentrated on visiting big shop-fittings exhibitions, including Euroshop in Düsseldorf, the biggest of them all. Here, the sight of a dynamic, lifelike mannequin attracted the crowds. The orders – despite a £5,000 price tag – came flooding in.

The Cyberquin has been exported by the dozen to 33 countries, including Japan, Korea, Chile, Australia and Kuwait. Cyberquins have been displayed at Disney World and on Fifth Avenue, New York.

All too often budding entrepreneurs believe themselves to be the right sort of person to set up a business. Unfortunately, the capacity for self-deception is enormous. When a random sample of male adults were asked recently to rank themselves on leadership ability, 70 per cent rated themselves in the top 25 per cent; only 2 per cent felt they were below average as leaders. In an area in which self-deception ought to be difficult, 60 per cent said they were well above average in athletic ability and only 6 per cent said they were below.

A common mistake made in assessing entrepreneurial talent is to assume that success in big business management will automatically guarantee success in a small business.

Lore Hap, who took her company Vector Graphics from a $6,000 investment to a £25-million company in five years, when asked if a grooming at IBM would have helped her on her way, replied:

'We are one of the pioneers of the micro-computer explosion. The buying as well as the selling process in this industry is different from what it had been before for computers. Buyers were much less sophisticated; they really didn't know what they wanted. So I think the principles that I might have learned at IBM, DEC, or any other computer company would probably not have served me well at all. We are dealing with a totally new element.'

BUILDING THE TEAM

Not surprisingly, an investor's ideal proposal includes an experienced and balanced management team, who have all worked together for a number of years. That will ensure management in depth, thus providing cover for every-thing from illness to expansion, and guaranteeing some stability during the turbulent early years. For this reason management buy-outs are a firm favourite.

At the other end of the scale is the lone inventor whose management skills may be in doubt, and who is anyway fully stretched getting his or her product from the drawing board to the production line. This type of proposal is un-likely to attract much investment capital. It has obvious risks beyond those every company expects to experience in the marketplace. In any case, without a management team in place the business is ill-prepared for the rapid growth required to service an investor's funds.

In practice, most business proposals lie somewhere between these extremes. Your business plan should explain clearly what the ideal composition of key managers should be for your business; who you have identified, or recruited so far; and last but certainly not least, how you will motivate them to remain with you and perform well for at least the first few all-important years.

F International, set up by a group of technologically skilled women whose family ties made it impossible for them to work standard office hours, nearly floundered when six full-time staff left to form their own business. They took with them many F International customers, as well as the business concept. F International's profits for the year up to this defection were £450,000. In the following year profits slumped to £124,000 and it wasn't until three years later that profits partially recovered to £340,000. Steve Shirley, the company's founder, subsequently went on to build a highly successful business and has been awarded an OBE.

Certainly investors will look for reassurance in this respect and will expect to see more reference to the steps you will take to encourage loyalty.

YOUR BUSINESS NAME

The main consideration in choosing a business name is its commercial usefulness. It is unlikely, for example, that Boris Karloff would have had such a successful career as a horror movie star using his own name, William Pratt.

Emma Bridgewater set up her business 18 months after completing an English degree at Bedford College, London. At first she wasn't sure what business to start but her boyfriend at the time, with whom she lived in Brixton, wanted to set up a craft studio to teach students how to slip-cast (an ancient method of making pottery with liquid clay poured into a mould). Emma visited factories in Stoke-on-Trent and discovered a number of people with this skill. 'Their mug shapes were revolting, though. So I drew my own. I found, doing so, that all my frustration evaporated just like that. Suddenly I knew what I wanted to do.'

The next few months were spent driving up and down the motorway in her Mini Metro, staying in travelling salesmen's hotels. She equipped herself with sponges and colours so that she could apply her designs to her mugs in the factories.

'At first the people in Stoke thought I was mad and were sceptical but helpful.' However, within a few months she won her first order, worth £600, from the General Trading Company, and in April she joined a lot of 'hysterical stall-holders with lavender bags' at a trade fair in Kensington: Brixton Spongeware was launched. She has since changed the name: 'I was fed up with jokes about reggae music and sweet potatoes. The name "Bridgewater" is far more appropriate. It sounds like an old, established industry. People often imagine it's a family business that has been going for years. That's exactly the mood I want to create.'

Just over two years later she had a file full of orders from top department stores in London and New York. Cheap imitators quickly started copying her designs. Now Bridgewater has an established name and a turnover in the millions.

When you choose a business name, you are also choosing an identity. Wally Olins, a corporate design expert, suggests that your business name should reflect:

- who you are;
- what you do;
- how you do it.

A good name, in effect, can become a one- or two-word summary of your marketing strategy; Body Shop, Toys R Us, Kwik-Fit Exhausts are good examples. Many companies add a slogan to explain to customers and employees alike 'how they do it'.

'Solaglas' was the name chosen by new owners to unify a group of some 40-plus previously independent and family owned glass and glazing merchants. The modest slogan 'Glass with the world's best service behind it' was added to all company literature to communicate to both customers and employees alike how the new group was to be run and would be different from competitors. The improved brand recognition achieved by the unifying name and slogan was reflected in the 10-fold increase in value of the company when the group was acquired six years later by St Gobain.

The John Lewis slogan, 'Never Knowingly Undersold', is almost better known than the company name itself. The name, slogan and logo combine to be the most visible tip of the iceberg in your corporate communications effort.

Spending time initially on trying to get your name and slogan right could pay off in the long term.

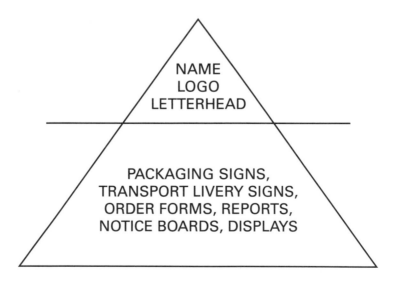

Figure 1.2 Hierarchy of branding

Perrier

The French sparkling water Perrier owes its name to Dr Perrier, a physician in south-west France at the turn of the 20th century who recommended the local spring water for his clients' good health. Nearly 80 years later, 80 per cent of the price that Nestlé paid to acquire the Perrier company was 'goodwill' – the brand value of the Perrier name.

Your company name can, in effect, be the starting and sustaining point in differentiating you from your competitors and, as such, should be carefully chosen, be protected by trademarks where possible (see page 58) and be written in a distinctive way.

If you have to use initials (and most companies in electronics do), try to make the initials into a name, to make recall easier.

Some people think that FIAT is an Italian family name; few, outside Italy, remember that it stands for Fabrica Italiana Automobile Turino. The name is always written in a distinctive way, making it a memorable company badge and logo. Given all the marketing investment you will make in your company name, you should check with a trademark agent (see *Yellow Pages*) whether you can protect your chosen name (descriptive words, surnames and place names are not normally registrable except after long use).

First, anyone wanting to use a 'controlled' name will have to get permission. There are some 80 or 90 controlled names, which include words such as 'International', 'Bank' and 'Royal'. This is simply to prevent a business implying that it is something that it is not.

Second, all businesses that intend to trade under names other than those of their owner(s) must state who does own the business and how the owner can be contacted. So, if you are a sole trader or partnership and you only use surnames with or without forenames or initials, you are not affected. Companies are also not affected if they simply use their full corporate name.

Guidance Notes entitled 'Choosing a Company Name' and 'Business Names and Business Ownership' are available from Companies House.

If any name other than the 'true' name is to be used, then you must disclose the name of the owner(s) and an address in the UK to which business documents can be sent. This information has to be shown on all business letters, orders for goods and services, invoices and receipts, and statements and demands for business debts. Also, a copy has to be displayed prominently on all business premises. The purpose of the Companies Act 1985 requirements is simply to make it easier to 'see' who you are doing business with.

If you are setting up as a limited company you will have to submit your choice of name to the Companies Registration Office along with the other documents required for registration. It will be accepted unless there is another company with that name on the register or the Registrar considers the name to be obscene, offensive or illegal.

REGISTER A DOMAIN NAME

If your company name is registered as a trademark (page 58), you *may* (as current case law develops) be able to prevent another business from using it as a domain name. A domain name identifies your business or organisation on the Internet, and it enables people to find you by directly entering your name into their browser address box.

Registering a domain name is simple (look at www.yourname.com, for example), although deciding on a domain name that is not already taken can sometimes be a process of elimination. Hundreds of domain names are registered every day and you must choose a name that has not already been registered. It is therefore important to have a selection of domain names before registering in case your first choice is unavailable.

Once you have decided on a selection of domain names, you can choose several different registration options:

- Use Nominet UK, which costs £80 plus VAT for each two-year period.
- Use Internet service providers (ISPs), which act as agents for their customers and will submit a domain name application for registration. Again, a successful application remains valid for two years, after which your ISP should make contact to notify you that your domain name is due for renewal.
- Register online. Hundreds of Web sites now offer domain-name registration online; it's a good idea to search the Internet for these sites, as they often sell domain names as loss leaders. Most of these providers also offer a search facility so you can see if your selected name has already been registered.
- Obtain free domain names along with free Web space by registering with an Internet community. These organisations offer you Web pages within their community space as well as a free domain name, but most communities only offer free domain names that have their own community domain tagged on the end – this can make your domain name rather long and hard to remember.

Legal ownership

Once your domain name has been registered and paid for, you will receive a registration certificate, either directly or through your ISP. This is an important document as it confirms you as the legal registrant of a domain name. If any amendments need to be made at any point during the registration period, the registry and your ISP must be informed.

Key points to remember are:

- Choose a domain name that is easy to remember – the shorter and snappier, the more likely it is to be remembered.
- If possible, choose a domain name that actually says what you do as a business, although this will depend on the availability of your chosen names.
- Make sure the company with which you register your domain name sends you a registration certificate as verification.
- Register all the core domain-name suffixes, including '.com', '.net', '.org', '.co.uk', '.uk', at the outset to avoid falling foul of 'copycat' sites.

Good domain names can be valuable, as in the case of Silicon.com.

Rob Lewis and Anna Russell, founders of the IT news site Silicon.com, were among the first to approach the original Californian owner of the domain name 'Silicon.com'. The original owner's computer services business had failed, so he was more than amenable to selling the name. His outstanding debts were $25,000, 'so we did a deal with him and he was a happy man and we were happy. A week later we had a phone call from the same man, who was now less happy, because he had just had an offer for £1 million for the domain name!'.

Here are some useful contact addresses:

Companies Registration Office
Crown Way
Maindy
Cardiff CF4 3UZ
Tel: 029 2038 0801
Fax: 029 2038 0329
Web site: www.companies-house.gov.uk

Department of Trade and Industry
1 Victoria Street
London SW1H 0ET
Tel: 020 7215 5000
Fax: 020 7215 6446
Web site: www.dti.gov.uk

Nominet UK
Tel: 01865 332 233
Web site: www.nominet.org.uk

DECIDING THE LEGAL FORM OF YOUR BUSINESS

Before you start trading you will need to consider what legal form your business will take. There are four main forms that a business can take and the one you choose will depend on a number of factors: commercial needs, financial risk and your tax position.

Each of these forms is explained briefly below, together with the procedure to follow on setting them up.

Sole trader

The vast majority of new businesses set up each year in the UK choose to do so as sole traders. It has the merit of being relatively formality free and, unless you intend to register for VAT, there are few rules about the records you have to keep. There is no requirement for your accounts to be audited, or for financial information on your business to be filed at Companies House.

As a sole trader there is no legal distinction between you and your business – your business is one of your assets, just as your house or car is. It follows from this that if your business should fail, your creditors have a right not only to the assets of the business, but also to your personal assets, subject only to the provisions of the Bankruptcy Acts (these allow you to keep only a few absolutely basic essentials for yourself and family).

It is possible to avoid the worst of these consequences by ensuring that your private assets are the legal property of your spouse, against whom your creditors have no claim. (You must be solvent when the transfer is made, and that transfer must have been made at least two years prior to your business running into trouble.) However, to be effective such a transfer must be absolute and you can have no say in how your spouse chooses to dispose of his or her new-found wealth!

The capital to get the business going must come from you – or from loans. There is no access to equity capital, which has the attraction of being risk-free. In return for these drawbacks you can have the pleasure of being your own boss immediately, subject only to declaring your profits on your tax return. (In practice you would be wise to take professional advice before doing so.)

Partnerships

Partnerships are effectively collections of sole traders and, as such, share the legal problems attached to personal liability. There are very few restrictions to setting up in business with another person (or persons) in partnership, and several definite advantages. By pooling resources you may have more capital; you will be bringing, hopefully, several sets of skills to the business; and if you are ill the business can still carry on.

There are two serious drawbacks that merit particular attention. First, if your partner makes a business mistake, perhaps by signing a disastrous contract, without your knowledge or consent, every member of the partnership must shoulder the consequences. Under these circumstances your personal assets could be taken to pay the creditors even though the mistake was no fault of your own.

Second, if your partner goes bankrupt in his or her personal capacity, for whatever reason, his or her share of the partnership can be seized by creditors. As a private individual you are not liable for your partner's private debts, but having to buy him or her out of the partnership at short notice could put you and the business in financial jeopardy. Even death may not release you from partnership obligations and in some circumstances your estate can remain liable. Unless you take 'public' leave of your partnership by notifying your business contacts and legally bringing your partnership to an end, you could remain liable.

The legal regulations governing this field are set out in the Partnership Act 1890, which in essence assumes that competent businesspeople should know what they are doing. The Act merely provides a framework of agreement that applies 'in the absence of agreement to the contrary'. It follows from this that many partnerships are entered into without legal formalities – and sometimes without the parties themselves being aware that they have entered a partnership!

The main provisions of the Partnership Act state:

- All partners contribute capital equally.
- All partners share profits and losses equally.
- No partner shall have interest paid on his capital.
- No partner shall be paid a salary.
- All partners have an equal say in the management of the business.

It is unlikely that all these provisions will suit you, so you would be well advised to get a 'partnership agreement' drawn up in writing by a solicitor at the outset of your venture.

One possibility that can reduce the more painful consequences of entering a partnership as a 'sleeping partner' is to have your involvement registered as a limited partnership. It means you (or your partner) can play no active part in running the business, but your risks are limited to the capital that you put in.

Unless you are a member of certain professions (eg law, accountancy, etc) you are restricted to a maximum of 20 partners in any partnership.

Cooperative

A cooperative is an enterprise owned and controlled by the people working in it. Once in danger of becoming extinct, the workers' cooperative is enjoying something of a comeback, and there are over 1,500 operating in the UK. They are growing at the rate of 20 per cent per annum.

Cooperatives are governed by the Industrial and Provident Societies Act 1965, whose main provisions state:

∎ Each member of the cooperative has equal control through the principle of 'one person one vote'.
∎ Membership must be open to anyone who satisfies the stipulated qualifications.
∎ Profits can be retained in the business or distributed in proportion to members' involvement, eg hours worked.
∎ Members must benefit primarily from their participation in the business.
∎ Interest on loan or share capital is limited in some specific way, even if the profits are high enough to allow a greater payment.

It is certainly not a legal structure designed to give entrepreneurs control of their own destiny and maximum profits. However, if this is to be your chosen legal form you can pay from £90 to register with the Chief Registrar of Friendly Societies, and must have at least seven members at the outset. They do not all have to be full-time workers at first. Like a limited company, a registered cooperative has limited liability (see under 'Limited liability companies') for its members and must file annual accounts, but there is no charge for this. Not all cooperatives bother to register, as it isn't mandatory, in which case they are treated in law as a partnership with unlimited liability.

Limited liability companies

In the UK, before the 1895 Companies Act it was necessary to have an Act of Parliament or a Royal Charter in order to set up a company. Now, out of the 3.5 million businesses trading in the UK, over 1.2 million are limited companies. As the name suggests, in this form of business your liability is limited to the amount you contribute by way of share capital.

A limited company has a legal identity of its own, separate from the people who own or run it. This means that, in the event of failure, creditors' claims are restricted to the assets of the company. The shareholders of the business are not liable as individuals for the business debts beyond the paid-up value of their shares. This applies even if the shareholders are working directors, unless of course the company has been trading fraudulently. (In practice, the ability to limit liability is severely restricted these days as most lenders, including the banks, often insist on personal guarantees from the directors.)

Other advantages include the freedom to raise capital by selling shares.

Disadvantages include the legal requirement for the company's accounts to be audited by a chartered or certified accountant. This is unlikely to cost much less than £500 per annum, and is more likely to run to four figures than three.

A limited company can be formed by two shareholders, one of whom must be a director. A company secretary must also be appointed, who can be a shareholder, director, or an outside person such as an accountant or lawyer.

The company can be bought 'off the shelf' from a registration agent, then adapted to suit your own purposes. This will involve changing the name, shareholders and articles of association, and will cost about £250 and take a couple of weeks to arrange. Alternatively, you can form your own company, using your solicitor or accountant. This will cost around £500 and take six to eight weeks.

The behaviour of companies and their directors is governed by the various Companies Acts that have come into effect since 1844.

Further information

Board of Inland Revenue
Press Office
Somerset House
Strand
London WC2R 1LB
Tel: 020 7438 6692
Fax: 020 7438 7541
Web site: www.inlandrevenue.gov.uk

Financial Services Authority
25 The Colonnade
Canary Wharf
London E14 5HS
Tel: 020 7676 1000
Web site: www.fsa.gov.uk

Institute of Chartered Accountants

In England and Wales:

PO Box 433
Chartered Accountants Hall
Moorgate Place
London EC2P 2BJ
Tel: 020 7920 8100
Fax: 020 7920 8600
Web site: www.icaew.co.uk

In Ireland:

Ulster Society
Belfast
Co Antrim
Belfast BT1 5JE
Tel: 028 9032 1600
Fax: 028 9023 0071
Web site: www.icai.ie

In Scotland:

21 Haymarket Yard
Edinburgh EH12 5BH
Tel: 0131 347 0100
Fax: 0131 347 0105
Web site: www.icas.org.uk

The Law Society
113 Chancery Lane
London WC2A 1PL
Tel: 020 7242 1222
Fax: 020 7831 0344
Web site: www.lawsociety.org.uk

The Registrar of Companies
Companies House
Crown Way
Maindy
Cardiff CF4 3UZ
Tel: 029 2038 0801
Fax: 029 2038 0329
Web site: www.companies-house.gov.uk

PAST ACHIEVEMENTS

If your business has already been trading for some time, your business plan should include a summary of past results and achievements. Annual reports, audited accounts, etc, if voluminous, can be included in an appendix, and referred to in this section of your business plan. Otherwise they can be shown in detail. You should emphasise what you have learnt so far that convinces you that your strategies are soundly based.

Windancer

Tim Langley Airwheels was set up as a limited company with an initial share capital of £20,000. The company's principal product is the Windancer, a unique land yacht using Langley's own invention, the air wheel.

The air wheel is a light, chunky, bouncy wheel whose tyre is treadless. It exhibits a number of useful properties that make it ideal for movement across both soft and rough ground.

The wheel was originally conceived with the idea of boat launching in mind. This has not proved a commercially viable proposition, so far at least. A number of reasons are involved: many launching sites are concreted because of known difficulties; launching trailers should ideally double as car trailers; air wheels have no tread, etc.

Commercial development has concentrated on using the air wheel, which now enjoys patent protection, as the unique element on the Windancer – a superior land/sand yacht.

This development took 18 months and the sales and profit history for Windancer are set out in Table 1.1.

Table 1.1 Sales and profit history of Windancer

Year	Sales (units)	£ Profit (loss)
1	10	(12,000)
2	30	(8,000)
3	70	350
4		
(1st quarter)	25	3,000 budget

The market, though difficult to quantify, grew from virtually zero to some 14,000 units per annum within a few years. It was much greater on the Continent, especially in France.

Distributor margins are around 50 per cent. So, Langley pitched his price and margins high. This allowed the company to make more profit for the distributors, thus making them keen to sell Windancer; it emphasised the company's 'uniqueness' and product superiority in the marketplace.

Its main competitor, the Landsailer, was lower in both quality and price, and Langley was confident that sales of 500 units could quickly be achieved with additional investment in manufacturing processes.

WORKSHEET FOR ASSIGNMENT 2:
A DESCRIPTION OF YOUR BUSINESS

1. What is your business name and why have you chosen it?
2. What experience and skills do you have that are particularly relevant to this venture?
3. Who else will be working with you and what relevant experience and skills do they have?
4. Draw an organisation chart showing who is responsible for which functions.
5. What people (or skill) gaps are there in the organisation you need to run your business? How do you plan to fill them?
6. How will you ensure that your key staff are motivated and loyal during the start-up period?
7. What professional advisers (accountant, lawyer, patent agent, etc) have you used, or do you plan to use?
8. Under what legal form will you trade and why?
9. If your business is already trading, give a brief summary of financial results and achievements to date.

SUGGESTED FURTHER READING

Clayton, Patricia (2004) *Forming a Limited Company*, 6th edn, Kogan Page/The Sunday Times, London

Clayton, Patricia (2004) *Law for the Small Business*, 9th edn, Kogan Page, London

Kirkland, Keith and Howard, Stuart (1998) *Simple and Practical Business Tax: A guide to PAYE, National Insurance, VAT and Schedule D Income Tax*, Kogan Page, London

3

A description of your products and/or services

Here you should describe what products or services you propose to market, what stage of development they are at and why they are competitive with existing sources of supply. Part of the information in this section is for the benefit of outside readers who may not be familiar with your business. It should also be useful to you since the research and analysis required will encourage you to examine your offering vis-à-vis your competitors'.

Explore these topics in this section of your business plan.

DESCRIPTION OF PRODUCTS AND/OR SERVICES

Explain what it is you are selling. Be specific and avoid unnecessary jargon. The reader should end up with more than just a vague idea about your products and/or services. Obviously, some products and services will require much more explanation than others. If you have invented a new process for analysing blood, you will need to provide the reader with many details. On the other hand, if you are selling your services as a bookkeeper, you may need to do little more than list the services you will provide. A danger of this section is in assuming that the reader can easily understand your products without your providing sufficient detail and description.

PNU-CLEEN, a new industrial cleaner aimed specifically at the metal-machining, wood-working and textile-manufacturing industries, included in its business plan this description of the product:

'The method of producing the suction in the cleaner is very simple. The technical term is a "jet-pump". In reality this is just a stream of high velocity air passed into a tube. It is a very similar device to the vacuum pumps found on the taps in chemistry laboratories but a "jet-pump" uses air as the prime mover instead of water (compressed air is readily available in most manufacturing units). The high speed air, when passing down the tube, will accelerate the surrounding air in the tube and draw air into the tube, similar to the draw of a chimney, causing a "vacuum" effect, an area of lower than atmospheric pressure.

'The air is accelerated by a small annular inlet supplied by a manifold surrounding the inlet. The air is controlled by a simple on/off valve. Incorporated into the valve is another position which allows for the provision of a supply of high speed air to be used to clean out difficult-to-get-at areas and to dislodge swarf from awkward places.

'Once the dirt/swarf/chippings have been picked up by the vacuum and passed the position of the inlet of accelerated air the dirt/swarf/chippings are blown down a flexible pipe. This blowing action is much stronger than the vacuum and means that the flexible pipe will never get blocked. It also means that the pipe can be of considerable length. In practice the length will be limited to between 2 and 3 metres to stop it getting in the way and allow for easy handling.

'The tube is clipped over the side of an existing dustbin where the air and dirt/swarf/chippings are separated out using a simple filter in order to stop the dirt/swarf/chippings being blown straight out of the dustbin again.'

In addition to listing and describing your products and/or services, you should note any applications or uses of your products that are not readily apparent to the reader. For instance, a photocopier can also produce overhead transparencies, as well as its more mundane output. When you make your list, show the proportion of turnover you expect each product or service to contribute to the whole, as illustrated in Table 1.2.

Table 1.2 Example showing products/services and their applications

Product/service	Description	% of sales
		100%

READINESS FOR MARKET

Are your products and/or services available for sale now? If not, what needs to be done to develop them? If you are selling a product, does it require more design work or research and development? Have you actually produced one or more completed products?

When Mark Saunders, Cranfield enterprise programme participant, put his proposal for the Strida, a revolutionary folding bicycle, before the venture capital panel, the only projections he could include with any degree of certainty were costs.

The business proposal for which he sought backing was to take his brainchild from the drawing board to a properly costed production prototype. For this he needed time, about two years, living expenses for that period, the use of a workshop and a modest amount of materials.

Saunders's business plan detailed how he would develop the product over this period and as a result the concept was backed by James Marshall, one-time manager of golfer Greg Norman. Marshall put together the manufacturing and marketing elements of the business plan, and within 18 months the Strida was in full-scale production and on sale through stores such as Harrods, Next Essentials, John Lewis, House of Fraser, Kelvin Hughes and many others.

If you are selling a service, do you presently have the skills and technical capability to provide it? If not, what needs to be done?

If additional inputs are required before your products or services are ready to be sold, state both the tasks to be done and time required, as shown in Table 1.3.

Table 1.3 Example showing products/services and additional inputs to be made

Product/service	State of development	Tasks to be done	Completion date

PROPRIETARY POSITION

Do your products or services have any special competitive advantage? If so, explain the advantages and state how long this proprietary position is likely to last. You should state any other factors that give you a competitive advantage, even though the advantage is not protected by contractual agreements of the law. Examples could include a special skill or talent not easily obtainable by others. (If you have none of these, and many businesses do not, do not just make something up!)

When Peter King (38) and Len Maxwell (28) had a good idea, they spent several months perfecting it and found themselves with a completely unique product. What was the next step?

'We had found a niche in the market and realised our product would satisfy it.' However, the ensuing product, Videoalert, a simple but ingenious video security system, was easy to copy. The size of two video cassettes, it is attached to the side of the video recorder. Once the recorder is lifted or moved even a fraction, the alarm lets off an ear-piercing shriek that will continue for eight hours.

The only way they could protect themselves from would-be imitators was to take out patents. As a further precaution they took out insurance against patent transgression, providing £250,000 for legal action. The patent for Videoalert was filed and then extended two years later to the whole of Europe, South Africa, the United States, Canada, Australia and Israel.

If, like King and Maxwell, you have a unique business idea, you should investigate the four categories of protection: *patenting*, which protects 'how something works'; *trademark registration*, which protects 'what something's called'; *design registration*, which protects 'how something looks'; and *copyright*, which protects 'work on paper, film and CD'.

Some products may be covered by two or more categories, eg the mechanism of a clock may be patented while its appearance may be design-registered.

Each category requires a different set of procedures, offers a different level of protection and extends for a different period of time. They all have one thing in common, though: in the event of any infringement your only redress is through the courts, and going to law can be wasteful of time and money, whether you win or lose.

PATENTS PROTECT 'HOW SOMETHING WORKS'

A patent can be regarded as a contract between an inventor and the state. The state agrees with the inventor that if he or she is prepared to publish details of the invention in a set form and if it appears that he or she has made a real advance, the state will then grant the inventor a 'monopoly' on the invention for 20 years: 'protection in return for disclosure'. The inventor uses the monopoly period to manufacture and sell his or her innovation; competitors can read the published specifications and glean ideas for their research, or they can approach the inventor and offer to help to develop the idea under licence.

However, the granting of a patent doesn't mean the proprietor is *automatically* free to make, use or sell the invention him- or herself, since to do so might involve infringing an earlier patent that has not yet expired.

A patent really only allows the inventor to stop another person using the particular device that forms the subject of the patent. The state does not guarantee validity of a patent either, so it is not uncommon for patents to be challenged through the courts.

What inventions can you patent? The basic rules are that an invention must be *new*, must involve an *inventive step* and must be capable of *industrial exploitation*.

You can't patent scientific/mathematical theories or mental processes, computer programs or ideas that might encourage offensive, immoral or anti-social behaviour. New medicines are patentable but not medical methods of treatment. Neither can you have just rediscovered a long-forgotten idea (knowingly or unknowingly).

If you want to apply for a patent, it is essential not to disclose your idea in non-confidential circumstances. If you do, your invention is already 'published' in the eyes of the law, and this could well invalidate your application.

There are two distinct stages in the patenting process:

- from filing an application up to publication of the patent;
- from publication to grant of the patent.

Two fees are payable for the first part of the process and a further fee for the second part. The whole process takes some two and a half years. Forms and details of how to patent are available free from the Patent Office.

It is possible – and cheaper – to make your own patent application, but this is not really recommended. Drafting a specification to give you as wide a monopoly as you think you can get away with is the essence of patenting and this is the skill of professional patent agents. They also know the tricks of the trade for each stage of the patenting procedure. A list of patent agents is available from the Chartered Institute of Patent Agents.

What can you do with your idea? If you have dreamt up an inspired invention but don't have the resources, skill, time or inclination to produce it yourself, you can take one of three courses once the idea is patented:

1. *Outright sale.* You can sell the rights and title of your patent to an individual or company. The payment you ask should be based on a sound evaluation of the market.
2. *Sale and royalty.* You can enter into an agreement whereby you assign the title and rights to produce to another party for cash but under which you get a royalty on each unit sold.

Anthony Robinson, the inventor of Holomedia, a novel hologram display system, decided while on a Cranfield enterprise programme not to make and market his product himself. Instead, he sold the patented product to a large, established company in a complementary field for a substantial six-figure sum, a £20,000 pa retainer and continuing royalties. His business subsequently concentrated exclusively on developing innovative products for other companies to make and sell.

3. *Licensing.* You keep the rights and title but sell a licence for manufacturing and marketing the product to someone else. The contract between you and the licensee should contain a performance clause requiring the licensee to sell a minimum number of units each year or the licence will be revoked.

Whichever option you select, you need a good patent agent/lawyer on your side.

TRADEMARKS PROTECT 'WHAT SOMETHING'S CALLED'

A trademark is the symbol by which the goods or services of a particular manufacturer or trader can be identified. It can be a word, a signature, a monogram, a picture, a logo or a combination of these.

To qualify for registration the trademark must be distinctive, must not be deceptive and must not be capable of confusion with marks already registered. Excluded are misleading marks, national flags, royal crests and insignia of the armed forces. A trademark can only apply to tangible goods, not services (although pressure is mounting for this to be changed).

The Trade Marks Act of 1938 and the Copyright, Designs and Patents Act of 1988 and subsequent amendments offer protection of great commercial value since, unlike other forms of protection, your sole rights to use the trademark continue indefinitely.

To register a trademark you or your agent should first conduct preliminary searches at the trade marks branch of the Patent Office to check there are no conflicting marks already in existence. You then apply for registration on the official trademark form and pay a fee (currently £200 for one class of goods or services, then £50 for each additional class).

Your application is then advertised in the weekly *Trade Marks Journal* to allow any objections to be raised.

Registration is initially for 10 years. After this, it can be renewed for periods of 10 years at a time, with no upper time limit.

It isn't mandatory to register a trademark. If an unregistered trademark has been used for some time and could be construed as closely associated with a product by customers, it will have acquired a 'reputation', which will give it some protection legally, but registration makes it much simpler for the owners to have recourse against any person who infringes the mark.

DESIGN REGISTRATION PROTECTS 'HOW SOMETHING LOOKS'

You can register the shape, design or decorative features of a commercial product if it is new, original, never published before or – if already known – never before applied to the product you have in mind. Protection is intended to apply to industrial articles to be produced in quantities of more than 50. Design registration applies only to features that appeal to the eye – not to the way the article functions.

To register a design, you should apply to the Design Registry and send a specimen or photograph of the design plus a registration fee (currently £90). The specimen or photograph is examined to see whether it is new or original and complies with other requirements of the Registered Designs Act 1949 and the Copyright, Designs and Patents Act 1988 and subsequent amendments to the Act. If it does, a certification of registration is issued which gives you, the proprietor, the sole right to manufacture, sell or use in business articles of that design.

Protection lasts for a maximum of 25 years. You can handle the design registration yourself, but, again, it might be preferable to let a specialist do it for you. There is no register of design agents but most patent agents are well versed in design law.

Wagamama, a small London-based restaurant chain, which has prospered by selling Japanese noodles to city trendies, sees the need to protect its idea as the main plank of its business strategy.

Alan Yau, who founded the business, came to the UK as an 11-year-old economic immigrant from Hong Kong. He joined his father running a Chinese takeaway in King's Lynn, Norfolk. Within 10 years he was running two Chinese restaurants of his own, one of which is close to the British Museum. From the outset he had plans to run a large international chain of restaurants.

Yau's food style is healthy, distinctive and contemporary. Wagamama conjures up someone who is a bit of a spoilt brat in Japanese, and the word lodged in Yau's mind. His informal communal dining room, opened under the Wagamama banner, received favourable reviews and the queues, which have become an essential part of the Wagamama experience, started forming. Realising he had an idea with global potential, Yau took the unusual step of registering his trademark worldwide. It cost £60,000. But within two years that investment began to pay off. A large listed company opened an Indian version of Wagamama. The concepts looked similar enough to have led ordinary people to think the two businesses were related. As Yau felt he could lose out, he decided to sue. The case was heard quickly and within three months Yau had won and his business idea was safe – at least for the five years his trademark protection runs for.

COPYRIGHT PROTECTS 'WORK ON PAPER, FILM AND CD'

Copyright is a complex field and since it is unlikely to be relevant to most business start-ups we only touch on it lightly here.

Basically, the Copyright, Designs and Patents Act 1988 gives protection against the unlicensed copying of original artistic and creative works – articles, books, paintings, films, plays, songs, music, engineering drawings. To claim copyright the item in question should carry this symbol: © (author's name) (date). At a diplomatic conference in Geneva in December 1996, new international copyright and performances and phonograms Treaties, which govern the protection of databases, were agreed on and came into force in January 1998.

You can take the further step of recording the date on which the work was completed for a moderate fee with the Registrar at Stationers' Hall. This, though, is an unusual precaution to take and probably only necessary if you anticipate an infringement.

Copyright protection in the UK lasts for 70 years after the death of the person who holds the copyright, or 50 years after publication if this is the later.

Copyright is infringed only if more than a 'substantial' part of your work is reproduced (ie issued for sale to the public) without your permission, but since there is no formal registration of copyright the question of whether or not your work is protected usually has to be decided in a court of law.

PROTECTING INTERNET ASSETS

Now that you have gone to so much trouble to develop a business model incorporating your mission, vision, objectives and culture so that you are all set for meteoric growth, it would be an awful pity if someone were to come along and steal it.

Even when times are hard, this is probably not an area to include in any cost-cutting exercise. In the Internet world, where all the value is placed in the anticipation of profits from day one, intellectual property may be all that's really worth saving.

Since the 1998 Supreme Court decision on the case of *State Street Bank* vs *Signature Financial Group*, a sort of business-method patent frenzy has swept over Internet companies (see Figure 1.3), resulting not only in a rise in the number of computer-related business-method patents issued, but also in a rise in lawsuits for patent infringement. By the end of 1999, DoubleClick was at the forefront of the lawsuit brigade, suing Internet ad network competitors such as Sabela (since acquired by 24/7 Media and LA-based L90).

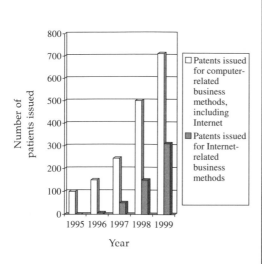

Companies	Subject
Amazon.com vs *Barnes & Noble.com*	'One-click' checkout
Broadvision vs *Art Technology Group*	Personalisation
Doubleclick vs *L90*	Ad monitoring and tracking
NetMoneyIN vs *Cybercourse, Elliance*	Third-party payment systems
Novadign vs *Marimba*	Updating applications
Priceline.com vs *Expedia.com* (Microsoft)	Reverse auctions for travel
Response Reward Systems vs *Planet U, e-centives, Coolsavings.com*	Coupons and promotions
Trilogy Software vs *CarsDirect.com*	Selecting options on cars

Figure 1.3   Internet business methods, patents and lawsuits

In a retaliatory move, 24/7 Media announced in May 2000 that it had filed a suit against DoubleClick for allegedly infringing its own patent (US Patent No 6,026,368: 'On-Line Interactive System and Method for Providing Content and Advertising Information to a Targeted Set of Viewers'). 24/7 Media was seeking monetary damages and requested an injunction barring DoubleClick from further infringement of the patent. The case is ongoing.

CoolSavings.com

CoolSavings, launched in 1995 by Steve Golden, provide a comprehensive suite of e-marketing services to both online and offline advertisers focused on building one-to-one customer relationships. In 1995, before launching their Web site, even before raising their first million dollars, the founders of CoolSavings.com Inc. sought a potentially more valuable asset for a young Internet company: a US patent. Shortly after receiving the patent in June 1998, CoolSavings put it to use. It sued nine other companies, which were also in the business of distributing coupons and promotions via the Internet, for infringement.

Those lawsuits quickly became the opening salvos in a multi-fronted war. Three rivals of CoolSavings acquired patents of their own and countersued. Henry Von Kohorn, an 86-year-old man from Florida, joined the fray, claiming he had invented electronic distribution of coupons in the 1980s. Mr Von Kohorn sued five market contenders, including CoolSavings.

CoolSavings.com had considerable foresight when it filed its patents. But suing is a long and painful process with unforeseeable outcomes. Three of the companies CoolSavings sued for patent infringement settled; one of them, emaildirect Inc, based in Aliso Viejo, California, claimed to have obtained a licence from CoolSavings that 'didn't cost us anything'.

Others have filed papers with the Patent Office challenging CoolSavings's patent, claiming they had developed some of the same ideas first.

In at least two cases, CoolSavings sued not just its rivals in the coupon business, but companies that did business with them. As part of a July 1999 settlement with Cool-Savings, the female-oriented Web site iVillage Inc, based in New York, agreed to stop doing business with a subsidiary of Catalina Marketing. A suit is being brought against Brodbeck Enterprises Inc, which operates the Dick's Supermarkets chain in Wisconsin and offers coupons through Planet U Inc, based in San Francisco – another Internet-promotions site.

CoolSavings.com is just the tip of what looks like a very large iceberg as rivals rush into patent and trademark offices to certify their latest innovations. Those smart – or lucky – enough to have obtained patents for which they applied four or five years ago increasingly wield them as weapons to prohibit others from employing the same technology.

FURTHER INFORMATION ON PROTECTING YOUR PRODUCTS

The Patent Office, Concept House, Cardiff Road, Newport, South Wales NP10 8QQ; tel: 01633 813930; fax: 01633 813600; Web site: www.patent.gov.uk. Publishes the following pamphlets: *Applying for a patent, Introducing patents – a guide for investors, How to prepare a UK patent application.*

Design Registry, address and telephone as for Patent Office (above). Publishes free of charge guides to registering designs.

Trade Marks Registry, address and telephone as for Patent Office (above). Publishes free of charge: *Applying for a trade mark; Trade Marks Journal* (every Wednesday).

The Patent Office material can also be viewed on the Internet: www.patent. gov.UK/snewcg/index/htme

Stationers' Hall, Ave Maria Lane, Ludgate Hill, London EC4M 7DD; tel: 020 7248 2934 (Mon–Fri 10 am–4 pm) for registration of copyright. Provides details and forms for registration.

The Chartered Institute of Patent Agents, Staple Inn Buildings, High Holborn, London WC1V 7PZ; tel: 020 7405 9450; fax: 020 7430 0471; Web site: www.cipa. org.uk. No advisory service but will put you in contact with a patent agent in your area. Publishes a Register of Patent Agents, which lists names and business addresses of all patent agents qualified to practise before the Patent Office.

COMPARISON WITH COMPETITIVE PRODUCTS AND SERVICES

Identify those products and/or services that you think will be competing with yours. They may be similar products/services or they may be quite different, but could be substituted for yours. An example of the latter would be a business that sells copying machines, which competes not only against other copying machines, but also against carbon paper and copy shops.

Once you have identified the major competing products, compare yours against them. List the advantages and disadvantages of yours vis-à-vis the competition. Later on, when you do your market research, you will probably want to address this question again and revise this section.

After making the comparison draw your conclusions. If your products/services will compete effectively, explain why. If not, explain what you plan to do to make them compete.

Returning to PNU-CLEEN Ltd, its business plan presented to the Cranfield enterprise panel included the following statement explaining its competitive advantage:

'As such there is no direct competition for the cleaner. This must be qualified by saying that there are some designs of vacuum cleaner that offer some but not all of the benefits that this design offers. The closest is a product made by Alpha Components Limited but it is based on a very small bore, almost unworkable.

'There is considerable indirect competition from electrically powered vacuum cleaners, pneumatic vacuum cleaners and the dustpan and brush. Overcoming this indirect competition should be achieved by making the customer aware that this cleaner is designed especially for use alongside a machine or workstation and offers the most convenient method at a low cost of keeping a high standard of cleanliness.'

Remember also that some products differentiate themselves from competitors by their service terms, while some services compete by the physical facilities offered, eg most makes of white goods are similar, but Philips Whirlpool seeks to differentiate its products by offering customers:

- replacement in its first year of any machine that cannot be repaired;
- guarantees on all parts for 10 years;
- payment of £12.50 if the repair engineer does not arrive within two days of call;
- a 24-hour call care line.

Additionally, all retailers in the distribution network are offered extended payment terms, finance for display stock and inventory as well as dealer support for advertising.

Similarly, most management consultants in the 'service' sector ensure that their 'products', their final reports, are faultless and immaculately presented, as are the premises and facilities of the best restaurants and fast food chains.

Guarantees and warranties

Will you be providing either of these with your product or service? Describe the scope of the warranty or guarantee, what it may cost, the benefits you expect from providing it, and how it will work in practice.

Possible future developments

If your product or service lends itself to other opportunities, with relatively minor alteration, which can be achieved quickly and will enhance your business, briefly describe these ideas.

SOME PRODUCT TURN-OFFS

Is one product enough?

One-product businesses are the natural output of the inventor, but they are extremely vulnerable to competition, changes in fashion and to technological obsolescence. Having only one product can also limit the growth potential of the enterprise. A question mark must inevitably hang over such ventures until they can broaden out their product base into, preferably, a 'family' of related products or services.

Cobra beer

Cambridge-educated and recently qualified accountant Karan Bilimoria started importing and distributing standard-size 660-millilitre bottles of Cobra beer, specifically brewed to complement Indian restaurant food in the UK. Soon it became 'the beer from Bangalore, brewed in Bedford'; it became available in 330-millilitre bottles and subsequently on draught. A low-alcohol version was then planned, followed by the addition of 'General Billy's Wine' as Karan widened the product range to meet Indian restaurant demand. Sales grew to over £60 million a year by August 2004.

Single-sale products

Medsoft was a business founded to sell a microcomputer and a tailor-made software package to hospital doctors. Unfortunately, the management had no idea of the cost and effort required to sell each unit. Worse still, there were no repeat sales. It was not that customers did not like the products: they did, but each user needed only one product. This meant that all the money and time spent on building up a 'loyal' customer were largely wasted.

In another type of venture, for example selling company cars, you could reasonably expect a satisfied customer to come back every two or three years. In the restaurant business the repeat purchase cycle might be every two to three months.

Non-essential products

Entrepreneurs tend to be attracted to fad, fashion and luxury items because of the short response time associated with their promotion and sale. Companies producing for these markets frequently run into financial difficulties arising out of sudden market shifts. Market security is more readily gained by having products that are viewed as 'essential'.

Worlds of Wonder was an immediate success, and immediately boomed. Sales in its second full year increased by 252 per cent to $327 million, and profits by 130 per cent, on the back of two blockbuster products – Teddy Ruxpin, a talking bear, and Lazer Tag, a game of catch using laser beams and sensors.

Worlds of Wonder's mistake was in failing to shield itself against the fickleness of blockbusters. Its choice for its second trading year was Julie, a hi-tech doll that responded to a child's voice, a genus known in the trade as 'interactive plush'. Technically imperfect and costing a high $100, Julie was an interactive flop with parents whose pockets proved less malleable than children's desires. WOW had nothing else to fall back on, and so – like other and earlier toy makers – it just fell.

The toy business has always been wickedly competitive. There is no shortage of entrepreneurs developing the greatest game since Scrabble and the best doll since Barbie (or, more recently, robot dogs). Margins are thin and entry costs low.

Diversification can be the best course for a firm with a blockbuster, rather than betting that its designers will have another winner next year. Coleco put $60 million of its earnings from Cabbage Patch Dolls into buying the American makers of Trivial Pursuit, Scrabble and Talking Wrinkles, an electronic puppy. That revived Coleco's sales. More diversified still, Fisher-Price, a wizard with pre-school toys, is owned by Quaker Oats. In such a group the toy maker becomes a high-risk fling with part of group profits. If children turn away, the company can survive.

Too simple a product

Simplicity, usually a desirable feature, can be a drawback. If a business idea is so basic that little management or marketing expertise is required for success, this is likely to make the cost of entry low and the value added minimal. This makes it easy for every Tom, Dick or Harry to duplicate the product idea, and impossible for the original company to defend its market, except by lowering the price.

The video rental business was a classic example of the 'too simple product' phenomenon. Too many people jumped on the bandwagon as virtually anyone with a couple of thousand pounds could set themselves up. Rental prices fell from pounds to pence in a year or so, and hundreds of businesses folded.

The founder of Character (Self-Assembly Furniture) Ltd included this product description in his business plan:

'The system at present allows the construction of chairs, tables, cupboards, chests of drawers, wardrobes, beds, a cot, climbing frame etc, in fact conceivably any item of furniture that a strong box-frame structure can be, or is required to be, an essential part of.

'The crux of the system is an easily screwed together (by hand, no tools required) joining method, that imparts rigidity and strength while being only hand tight. An aim of the design was to keep as many components as possible common to each item of furniture, so that certain ideas could evolve by additional follow-up purchases. An example of this idea would be the progression from cot through to playpen, then to climbing frame, some components of the latter being usable in other items such as shelves or chairs. Another aim was to enable the transformation from one item to another to be very simply and very rapidly achieved.

'The system will be available in a variety of solid woods or, where appropriate, veneered or laminated synthetic boards like medium density fibreboard (MDF). Metal fittings, where required, eg hinges, clips and holders, will be sturdy but discreet and, where possible, not visible externally.

'The appearance is modern, though not avant-garde, with a style expected to be favoured by the groups identified as being the most likely purchasers. The natural style, as a consequence of the method of construction, would not be out of place in a Habitat store.

'To summarise, the major features of this system which help to distinguish it are:

1. Speed of assembly.
2. Simplicity of assembly: no tools are required in the assembly of any piece – tools are only required for wall mounting of shelves or units and in these instances the design minimises the number of drilled holes required and maximises the simplicity of hanging.
3. Attractive 'up-market' appearance of the assembled item.
4. Consumer choice in the overall dimensions of the piece where possible, eg height of chairs, size and design of climbing frames, size and spacing of shelves in shelf system and room dividers.
5. Sturdiness – something missing from much self-assembly furniture (SAF).

6. The buy as you go along feature, especially of the shelf systems and climbing frames.
7. Ease and standardisation of manufacture. This should minimise manufacturing costs and offer the option of passing on the consequential benefit to the consumer.

'I am at present investigating the possibility of patenting certain aspects of the way in which the elements of this furniture system are put together. A preliminary search at the Patent Office produced an optimistic result and a subsequent discussion with a Patent Agent confirmed that this is a real possibility. To get satisfactory protection for the product in the major European markets will cost around £20,000.'

ONE PRODUCT MUST: QUALITY

One of the biggest problems for a new company is creating in the customer's mind an image of product quality. In the 1960s there was an almost faddish belief in 'dynamic obsolescence', implying that low quality would mean frequent and additional replacement sales. The inroads that the Japanese car makers have made on Western car manufacturers through improving quality, reliability and value for money have clearly demonstrated the fallacy of this proposition.

You cannot sell a product you do not believe in and as James Knock, founder president of a beer company, explained: 'in cold calling the only thing standing between you and the customers' scorn is the integrity of your product'.

The Cranfield entrepreneurs that we have seen prosper have all learned to fight the cost, quality and service trade-off: 'We are only interested in making the best quality and freshest pasta around,' explained Farshad Rouhani in describing how Pasta Masters had grown to become the leading supplier of fresh pasta to retailers and restaurants in London. Equally, David Sinclair and his team at Bagel Express were at work at 4 am each day to ensure that only freshly baked bagels were on sale each morning. To show the freshness of the product, the bagels were baked each day in open kitchens in front of the customers.

Quality is not just what you do, but also how you do it; each contact point between the customer and company is vital, be it on the telephone, at the counter, at the till. 'The customer who complains is our best friend,' explains Stu Leonard in the video *In Search of Excellence* – especially compared to the one you never see again! Getting your customers to help you maintain your quality and standards is perhaps one of the keys to business success. The quality obsession is clear; if you do not catch it, you will not survive.

WORKSHEET FOR ASSIGNMENT 3:
A DESCRIPTION OF YOUR PRODUCTS
AND/OR SERVICES

1. Describe your product or service, as if explaining it to a novice.
2. Is it currently available for sale? If not, what needs to be done, how much will that work cost and how long will it take?
3. Do you have, or plan to have, any legal protection such as patents? If so, explain what you have done so far to establish your rights.
4. How is your product or service different from those already on the market?
5. Will you be providing any warranties, guarantees or after-sales service?
6. Are there any possibilities of developing new products or services complementary to the one(s) described above?

SUGGESTED FURTHER READING

Bagel Express, Case History, Parts A, B & C, Start-Up and Growth, video and teaching note (Reference: 595-032-1) and Cobra Beer Ltd, A, B & C Start Up and Expansion, teaching note (Reference: 399-158-1), both available from the European Case Clearing House, Cranfield, Beds MK43 0AL; tel: 01234 750903; fax: 01234 751125; Web site: www.ecch.cranfield.ac.uk; e-mail: ecch@cranfield.ac.uk

Applegate, Jane (2002) *201 Great Ideas for Your Small Business*, Bloomberg Small Business, London

Cornish, William (1999) *Intellectual Property*, Sweet & Maxwell, London

Pressman, David and Elias, Stephen (1999) *Patent It Yourself*, 7th edn, Nolo, Berkeley, CA

Singleton, Susan (2003) *E-Commerce: A practical guide to the law*, Gower, London

Going for growth with MYOB

Your old classmates have tracked you down via Friends Reunited and invited you to a school disco reunion. Somewhere at the back of your wardrobe you've found your old school tie. But what about the blazer? Suitable trousers? A cap? Be honest, even if you'd kept them they wouldn't fit you now.

Sales to the Friends Reunited generation and School Disco phenomenon have helped fuel the recent growth of school wear and uniform retailer, SANCO. "Our business has really grown since 2000 - in fact we've seen double digit growth every year for the past five years," says Sandeep Sud of SANCO. The company now has four full-time employees and a turnover approaching £1 million.

SANCO was founded in 1973 by Sandeep's parents. Back in 2000 Sandeep was a solicitor, looking to take a year out to learn about business in the real world. Where better than the family firm? The business is now run by all three of them, although Sandeep does have plans to return to the legal profession, 'but only for fun and not for money'.

It was around this time that SANCO were starting to computerise their accounting function. "Our accounts were being done manually by a book-keeper. We were looking for a package that would change this and we found MYOB Accounting, which dramatically cut down our workload."

The MYOB software has helped the firm in a number of unexpected ways, too. "We can print reports detailing our total spend with a supplier during the year and use this to secure a discount on next year's orders," says Sandeep.

The Sud family are loyal Mac users, which was a significant factor in their decision to implement MYOB software. "We have always found Apple Macs to be incredibly reliable and, of course, good to look at. I wasn't prepared to sacrifice my Macs for the sake of a piece of accounting software but luckily that wasn't necessary. My sister, who is a Chartered Accountant, suggested MYOB because she

knew it was both Mac compatible and simple to use."

"Installation was extremely simple, and using the software has been equally straightforward. I use it, my 60 year old mother uses it, and we both feel completely comfortable with it because it has such a clear interface."

"The MYOB telephone helpline is fantastically useful," says Sandeep. "For example, I called the helpline to check I was inputting figures correctly and, because all the MYOB support technicians are accounting trained, they were able to tell me immediately."

As well as their retail outlet in Hounslow, SANCO sells wholesale to schools, who then sell the uniforms to pupils. SANCO's wholesale customers span the UK, West Africa and Europe.

The school uniform trade is inevitably seasonal and SANCO have responded to this challenge in a number of ways. As well as scouts and guides uniforms, they offer dancewear and a sportswear range, including karate, judo and cricket clothing. They will start selling school footwear in the next two months and Sandeep confidently predicts that this will increase business by ten percent. The company have closely guarded plans to introduce other lines which will extend their trading period.

"We are developing ideas that will capitalise on our existing relationship with schools, such as supplying them with specialist travel agency services for field trips," says Sandeep. As the company grows, their business accounting software will need to grow with them, but Sandeep does not foresee any problems. "In 1998/99 we installed Version 7 [of MYOB Accounting], and upgraded to Version 11 two years later. To be honest, the software has grown with us over that time, and it is not stretched in the slightest."

"The overall MYOB experience is outstanding," says Sandeep. "The MYOB system has helped us achieve the double digit growth we've seen since 2000. If it wasn't there, we'd be spending half our time doing basic accounting, rather than driving the business."

About MYOB
MYOB develops and delivers award-winning software, services and support for more than 500,000 businesses worldwide. Features range from basic to advanced and the software is quick to set up, easy to learn and makes accounting simple for everyone.

Mind Your Own Business. Smarter.

Phone: 020 8997 5500
Email: uk.info@myob.com
Web: www.myob.co.uk

Surveying Customer and Employee Opinions
Why Survey?
A thorough and objective survey provides you with in-depth insights into your people, customers, organisation, issues and challenges enabling you to take effective and relevant post survey action.

Surveying customers to:
- Identify customer expectations
- Measure level of customer satisfaction
- Identify areas for improvement
- Increase customer retention
- Increase profitability

Surveying employees to:
- Improve productivity & performance
- Improve communications
- Improve retention
- Improve morale
- Improve engagement and satisfaction
- Increase profitability

Achieving results from conducting opinion surveys
Objectives
Communicate to customers and employees why and what you are surveying. Commit to make results available to all.

Rate of return - Set a high target and work hard to achieve it.

Buy-In
Involvement – involve customers and employees in pre–survey research and let everyone know about it.

Motivation - ensure all connect completion of the survey with your commitment to disclose and act on the results.

Ownership – it's vital customers and employees feel the survey addresses issues that are important to them - Pilot test first, more involvement!

Qualitative Research
Conduct Focus Groups and interviews to establish issues and suggestions on survey topics.

Quantitative Research
Design a format to suit your circumstances – this could range from simple questions with yes/no answers to a 7-point response scale strongly agree to strongly disagree. Consider how to give respondents the opportunity for free-expression.

Data Collection & Processing
Consider the format-on-line, or paper, or both.

Confidentiality- demonstrate anomimity for all responses and inspire confidence to express opinions without being identified.

Diagnose & Interpret Results
Look for the underlying cause and effect behind the survey findings.

Read all free-expression - use a coding to analyse types of comments.

Feedback
Undertake to give feedback on the survey results.

Action
Take action on the priorities. Also select quick wins.

Communicate progress vs. Action Plan.

Re-survey to measure perception of progress.

Free Workshops & Support

In response to requests from organisations seeking to:

- Increase survey response rates and quality
- Conduct on-line surveys
- Benchmark survey results, including IiP, Balanced Scorecard, EFQM & Charter Mark
- Evaluate effectiveness of internal vs. external sourcing

We conduct free of charge workshops or evaluations:

One-day in-company workshop for all responsible for communications and surveys. Covers designing and conducting surveys, tailored to your needs and includes comprehensive workbooks and practical guidance.

Or

One-day in-depth evaluation of your current survey practices with recommendations on how to increase quality, depth and returns

Programmes tailored to suit your requirements, which has proved very valuable for organisations conducting surveys and those considering introducing surveys. Don't just take our word - read these references:

Anglia Co-op – *"A complimentary workshop. Too good to be true, I thought. Where's the catch? Well, after taking part in a one to one session with Enhancing, I had received a personal master class in conducting surveys, and guess what - no catch! I now have a head full of ideas that can only benefit our Society when we undertake our next survey."*

Comet – *"The excellent workshop enabled us to understand how we should be creating maximum survey buy-in."*

Moss Pharmacy – *"The workshop was very interesting and beneficial, with information provided in a clear concise way."*

About Enhancing

Enhancing specialise in opinion surveys, post-survey support and communications. Working with Board and Senior Executive clients, we develop close working relationships and are committed to making a real difference to their organisations and people.

Our team of highly experienced consultants, provides bespoke, high-quality support to enhance people and organisations internationally.

A selection of clients can be found on www.enhancingsurveys.com page together with client references. Our clients are from a wide range of sectors and include Finance, Legal, Services, Government, Construction, Manufacturing, Retail Distribution/Logistics, IT, Telecoms, Higher Education and the Voluntary Sector.

Enhancing people and organisations through bespoke, high quality, opinion surveys.

Enhancing Limited, 2nd Floor, Berkeley Square House, Berkeley Square, London, W1J 6BD
Tel 020 7396 5595 Fax 020 7396 5599
email enq@enhancingsurveys.com
web www.enhancingsurveys.com

Phase 2

Market research

Introduction

Assignments 4–6 are intended to help you to bring your customers, competitors and the marketplace more sharply into focus, and to identify areas you have yet to research.

The Duke of Wellington defined reconnaissance as 'the art of knowing what is on the other side of the hill'. Market research is the business equivalent of this military activity. It is the name given to the process of collecting, recording, classifying and analysing data on customers, competitors and any other influences in the chain that links buyers to sellers.

The research should be done *before* the business is started or a new strategy is pursued, so saving the time and cost incurred if expensive mistakes are made. Obviously, the amount of research undertaken has to be related to the sums at risk. If a venture calls for a start-up investment of £1,000, spending £5,000 on market research would be a bad investment. However, new and small businesses that do not want to join the catastrophically high first-year failure statistics would be prudent to carry out some elementary market research, whatever level their start-up capital is to be.

As the President of the Harvard Business School said: 'If you think knowledge is expensive, try ignorance.'

The data collected in this phase can be used to help you to decide on an appropriate strategy for your business.

The starting point in any market research has to be a definition of the scope of the market you are aiming for. A small general shop may only service the needs of a few dozen streets. A specialist restaurant may have to call on a much larger catchment area to be viable.

You may eventually decide to sell to different markets. For example, a retail business can serve a local area through the shop and a national area by mail order. A small manufacturing business could branch out into exporting.

People all too often flounder in their initial market research by describing their markets too broadly – for example, saying that they are in the motor industry when they really mean they sell second-hand cars in Perth; or saying they are in health foods, when they are selling wholemeal bread from a village shop,

While it is important to be aware of trends in the wider market, this must not obscure the need to focus on the precise area that you have to serve.

Shirt Point

Shirt Point was the brainchild of adman Robert Barclay and his friend since primary school, art dealer Jeremy Wayne. 'We were having lunch 18 months before we started the business, and complaining about the hassle we had trying to get shirts done,' says Barclay, aged 29. 'High performers in the City, earning perhaps £100,000 a year and working from 7 am until 7 pm, still had to get up at the crack of dawn to iron a shirt.' Their catchment area was initially restricted to the City and they were laundering up to 300 shirts a week within a few months. It means hard-pressed brokers and bankers could take their dirty laundry to the office, telephone Shirt Point, have it collected the same day and returned, hand-finished with buttons sewn on and collar bones renewed where necessary, within 48 hours.

Assignments 4 and 5 pose the main questions you need to answer concerning your customers and competitors, and Assignment 6 covers the principal ways in which basic market research can be conducted, and where such data can be found.

4

Customers

Without customers no business can get off the ground, let alone survive. Some people believe that customers arrive after the firm 'opens its doors'. This is nonsense. You need a clear idea in advance of who your customers will be, as they are a vital component of a successful business strategy, not simply the passive recipients of new products or services.

Knowing something about your customers and what you plan to sell to them seems so elementary it is hard to believe that any potential business-person could start a business without doing so. But it is all too common – and one of the reasons why many new businesses fail.

Here's a story that illustrates the pitfalls:

Tim Johnston took voluntary redundancy and decided to start his own business. His redundancy money combined with his savings gave him a total of £15,000, which he put into a vending machine business. He chose vending since he thought that with the demise of the tea lady it must be a growth market.

He surveyed the vending machine manufacturers and selected three machines that were easy to maintain and simple to fill and clean. He bought demonstration models at a discount, and installed them in his newly acquired office-cum-storeroom. He then looked for suppliers of ingredients, paying particular attention to the flavours, since he believed that vended drinks had a poor reputation.

Next he arranged with two leasing companies a deal by which they would finance the machines he sold to satisfactory customers.

All this took Tim four months and, by the autumn, he felt certain that he had a good product to offer.

He then started to sell. First he called on established medium-sized local companies. It quickly became clear that they already either had a vending machine or well-rehearsed reasons for not wanting one. So Tim moved downmarket and went to see small and new companies – and immediately hit a new problem. The leasing companies he had lined up would only take on clients with a good financial track record. Otherwise they required the directors or the company to provide personal guarantees in case the company defaulted. Now Tim had not only to persuade customers to buy a vending machine but to abandon the shelter of limited liability to do so!

By the end of the first month of his sales campaign, Tim had called on 250 people, seen 28 and given two quotes for machines.

His next task was to identify likely prospects via the telephone, but the closest he got to an order was from a firm that wanted a vending machine to provide refreshments for night-shift workers. The firm didn't care twopence about the quality of the ingredients; its only concern was that the machine could dispense all night on a single fill of drinks.

After six months 'in business' Tim closed down. Nearly half his cash was gone and he hadn't got a single order.

WHAT DO CUSTOMERS NEED?

The founder of a successful cosmetics firm, when asked what his business did, replied: 'In the factories we make perfume and in the shops we sell dreams.'

Businesspeople usually define their business in physical terms. Customers, on the other hand, see businesses as satisfying their needs. Compare a Bic with a Parker pen. Basically they are very similar: they both write well, are comfortable to hold, have clips that hold them in place and caps that protect your pockets from ink stains. One costs 50p, the other £5. Customers pay the extra £4.50 for largely intangible benefits such as status or the pleasure the pen will bring as a gift. Bic and Parker are both successful businesses, but the needs they satisfy are poles apart.

Until you have clearly defined the needs of your potential customers, you cannot begin to assemble a product to satisfy them.

In the mid-1980s, Andy Ingleston, a Business Studies graduate from Dover with a family transport background, noticed the increasing congestion at Britain's largest roll-on–roll-off port. Dover was the biggest port with the biggest problems: delays in clearing customs averaged 12 hours and could be 3 days! This was unproductive time for both the driver and the traction unit. Under the UK regulations, drivers were effectively counted as being 'on duty' while actually resting on board a ferry or awaiting clearance at a port. As a result, sailings could be missed during enforced rest periods, creating further expensive 'down time' while the vehicle was earning nothing. Andy identified five target customers – small northern hauliers with under 50 vehicles – who were suffering with this delay problem. By offering empty trailer units to these customers, clearing customs and trans-porting the original trailers across the Channel himself, he could turn idle time for the northern hauliers into work time for himself. One contract alone enabled him to break even in year 1. By 2004 Dockspeed Ltd, Andy's company, operated 43 vehicles, with a £9 million turnover and had won many transport industry 'small business of the year' awards.

Extra profitable growth had come from responding to new customer needs as port conditions at Dover improved; in particular, this involved importing refrigerated products for Gervais Danone and exporting cut bread and sandwiches for Marks & Spencer and German Railways. The bulk of Andy's fleet were state-of-the-art refrigerated vehicles.

Andy was able to sell the business to a major Danish transport conglomerate and take early retirement at 35! One of many Graduate Enterprise Programme millionaires!

The American psychologist Abraham Maslow says that 'all customers are goal seekers who gratify their needs by purchase and consumption'. He classifies consumer needs in a five-stage pyramid, called the hierarchy of needs:

1. self-realisation;
2. self-esteem;
3. social;
4. safety;
5. physiological (hunger and thirst).

Every product or service is bought to satisfy one or more of these needs. So, for example, as people's hunger and thirst needs are satisfied, they move up the hierarchy to satisfy other needs.

Try interesting someone who is starving and cold in 'higher' things; or see how much more food you buy if you shop when you are hungry than when you have just consumed a large meal.

Where are your customers on the needs hierarchy, and how can your product or service help them to achieve their goals?

It may also help to shape your business to distinguish between the needs of consumers of your product (eg children who eat sweets) and the needs of customers who make the buying decision (eg parents who pay for the sweets).

Autoglass, in setting up a skeleton network of depots to provide a quick windscreen replacement service to the motoring public, was concerned at the difficult task and cost of communicating the benefits of the service to millions of potential motoring consumers. Discussions with a major motor insurance company, which covered the cost of replacing windscreens for its insured motorists, indicated that the insurance company needed a reliable windscreen replacement company, with standard prices and credit payment terms, that would help the insurance company improve its service to motorists. In return for meeting this need, the insurance company 'customer' agreed to recommend Autoglass to all its insured motorists, at annual premium renewal time, solving the windscreen company's promotional problem and virtually guaranteeing customers for its new depots.

Segmenting the market

Market segmentation is the name given to the process whereby customers and potential customers are organised into clusters or groups of 'similar' types. For example, a shop or restaurant has regulars and passing trade. The balance between the two is a fundamental issue that affects everything the business does.

Also, each of these customer groups is motivated to buy for different reasons and your selling message has to be modified accordingly.

These are some of the ways by which markets can be segmented:

- *Psychographic segmentation* divides individual consumers into social groups such as 'Yuppies' (young, upwardly mobile professionals), 'Bumps' (borrowed-to-the-hilt, upwardly mobile, professional show-offs) and 'Jollies' (jet-setting oldies with lots of loot). These categories try to show how social behaviour influences buyer behaviour. Forrester Research, an Internet research house, has made rather a lot – perhaps even more than the subject deserves – of this type of segmentation. In a recent book by the company's vice-president of research, a 'secret' was shared with the readers: 'When it comes to determining whether consumers will or will not go on the Internet, how much they'll spend and what they'll buy, demographic factors such as age, race, and gender don't matter anywhere near as much as the consumers' *attitudes towards technology*.' Forrester uses this concept, together with its research, to produce Technographics® market segments as an aid to understanding people's behaviour as digital consumers.
- Forrester has used two categories: technology optimists and technology pessimists, and has used these alongside income and what it calls 'primary motivation' – career, family and entertainment – to divide up the whole market. Each segment is given a new name – 'Techno-strivers', 'Digital Hopefuls' and so forth – followed by a chapter explaining how to identify them, how to tell whether they are likely to be right for your product or service and providing some pointers as to what marketing strategies might get favourable responses from each group.
- *Benefit segmentation* recognises that different people can get different satisfaction from the same product or service. Lastminute.com claims two quite distinctive benefits for its users. First, it aims to offer people bargains that appeal because of price and value. Second, the company has recently been laying more emphasis on the benefit of immediacy. This idea is rather akin to the impulse-buy products placed at checkout tills, which you never thought of buying until you bumped into them on your way out. Whether 10 days on a beach in Goa or a trip to Istanbul are the types of things people 'pop in their baskets' before turning off their computers, time will tell.
- *Geographic segmentation* arises when different locations have different needs. For example, an inner-city location may be a heavy user of motorcycle dispatch services, but a light user of gardening products. However, locations can 'consume' both products if they are properly presented. An inner-city store might sell potatoes in 1-kilogram bags, recognising that its customers are likely to be on foot. An out-of-town shopping centre may sell the same product in 20-kilogram sacks, knowing its customers will have cars. Internet companies have been slow to extend their reach beyond

their own back yard, which is surprising considering the supposed global reach of the service. Microsoft exports only 20 per cent of its total sales beyond US borders, and fewer than 16 per cent of AOL's subscribers live outside the United States. However, the figure for AOL greatly overstates the company's true export performance. In reality, AOL does virtually no business with overseas subscribers, but instead serves them through affiliate relationships. Few of the recent batch of Internet IPOs have registered much overseas activity in their filing details. By way of contrast, the Japanese liquid crystal display industry exports more than 70 per cent of its entire output.

■ *Industrial segmentation* groups together commercial customers according to a combination of their geographic location, principal business activity, relative size, frequency of product use, buying policies and a range of other factors. Logical Holdings is an e-business solutions and service company that floated for over £1 billion on the London Stock Exchange and Tech-Mark index, making it one of the UK's biggest IT companies. It was formed from about 30 acquisitions, with sales of over £800 million, employing 2,000 people wordwide. The company was founded by Rikke Helms, formerly head of IBM's E-Commerce Solutions portfolio. Her company split the market into three: Small, Medium-Sized and Big, tailoring its services specifically for each.

■ *Multivariant segmentation* is where more than one variable is used. This can give a more precise picture of a market than using just one factor.

These are some useful rules to help decide if a market segment is worth trying to sell into:

■ *Measurability*. Can you estimate how many customers are in the segment? Are there enough to make it worth offering something 'different'?

■ *Accessibility*. Can you communicate with these customers, preferably in a way that reaches them on an individual basis? For example, you could reach the over-50s by advertising in a specialist 'older people's' magazine with reasonable confidence that young people will not read it. So if you were trying to promote Scrabble with tiles 50 per cent larger, you might prefer that young people did not hear about it. If they did, it might give the product an old-fashioned image.

■ *Open to profitable development*. The customers must have money to spend on the benefits that you propose to offer.

■ *Size*. A segment has to be large enough to be worth your exploiting it, but perhaps not so large as to attract larger competitors.

One example of a market segment that has not been open to development for hundreds of years is the sale of goods and services to retired people. Several factors made this a particularly unappealing segment. First, retired people were perceived as 'old' and less adventurous; second, they had a short life expectancy; and finally, the knockout blow was that they had no money. In the last decade or so that has all changed: people retire early, live longer and many have relatively large pensions. The result is that travel firms, house builders, magazine publishers and insurance companies have rushed out a stream of products and services aimed particularly at this market segment.

Segmentation is an important marketing process, as it helps to bring customers more sharply into focus, and it classifies them into manageable groups. It has wide-ranging implications for other marketing decisions. For example, the same product can be priced differently according to the intensity of customers' needs. The first- and second-class post is one example, off-peak rail travel another.

It is also a continuous process that needs to be carried out periodically, for example when strategies are being reviewed.

In just 15 years, Dawn Gibbons, co-founder of Flowcrete, took the company from a 400-square-foot industrial unit with £2,000 capital to a plc with a turnover of £9.5m in the field of floor screeding technology and clients including household names such as Cadbury, Sainsbury's, Unilever, Marks & Spencer, Barclays and Ford. Part of Flowcrete's success was down to a continuing focus on technical superiority. This attribute was engendered by Dawn's father, a well-respected industrial chemist with an interest in resin technology.

But arguably Dawn's skills contributed as much if not more to the firm's success. 'We want to be champions of change,' Gibbons claims. 'We have restructured a dozen times, focusing on new trends.' Markets and market segmentation are a vital part of any restructuring process – indeed, the best companies restructure around their customers' changing needs.

The first reappraisal came after seven years in business when Flowcrete realized that its market was no longer those firms that laid floors; it now had to become an installer itself. Changes in the market meant that to maintain growth Flowcrete had to appoint proven specialist contractors, train their staff, write specifications and carry out audits to ensure quality.

DEFINING THE PRODUCT IN THE CUSTOMERS' TERMS

Once you know what you are selling and to whom, you can match the features of the product (or service) to the benefits that customers will get when they purchase. *Features* are what a product has or is, and *benefits* are what the product does for the customer. For example, cameras, SLR or lens-shutters, even film are not the end product that customers want; they are looking for good pictures. Finally, as in Table 2.1, include 'proof' that these benefits can be delivered.

Table 2.1 Example showing product features, benefits and proof

Features	Benefits	Proof
We use a unique hardening process for our machine	Our tools last longer and that saves you money	– We have a patent on the process – Independent tests carried out by the Cambridge Institute of Technology show our product lasts longest
which means that	*you can see this is true because*	
Our shops stay open later than others in the area	You get more choice when to shop	– Come and see
Our computer system is fault tolerant using parallel processing	You have no down time for either defects or system expansion	– Our written specification guarantees this – Come and talk to satisfied customers operating in your field

Remember, the customer pays for the benefits and the seller for the features. So, the benefit will provide the 'copy' for most of your future advertising and promotional efforts.

WHO WILL BUY FIRST?

Customers do not sit and wait for a new business to open its doors. Word spreads slowly as the message is diffused throughout the various customer groups. Even then it is noticeable that generally it is the more adventurous types who first buy from a new business. Only after these people have given their seal of approval do the 'followers' come along.

This adoption process, from the 2.5 per cent of innovators who make up a new business's first customers, through to the laggards who won't buy from anyone until they have been in business for 20 years, is most noticeable with innovative products, such as computers, but the general trend is true for all businesses.

Until you have sold to the innovators, significant sales cannot be achieved. So, an important first task is to identify these customers. The moral is: the more you know about your potential customers at the outset, the better your chances of success.

Kentish hop farmer William Alexander first decided that there must be a market other than breweries for his flowering hop bines when he noticed that some of his bines were actually being stolen from the fields! Drying hop bines over his farmhouse Aga and trying to sell them for decoration purposes to local public houses drew no response. However, while standing in an early-morning flower-market queue at New Covent Garden, he was approached by buyers from the Sloane Street General Trading Company who offered to buy all the bines he was carrying and could produce.

Now equipped with his own drying kilns and a specialist dried-flower shop on his farm, he has daily contact with customers from all over the South-East. An article on the Hop Shop in the Saturday *Times* supplement produced orders from Hong Kong and Singapore. With an expanded dried-flower market range to meet customers' demands, production on 12 hectares of his farm now yields as much revenue as the traditional crops on the remaining 390 hectares.

The winning of a gold medal at the Chelsea Flower Show for dried flowers by his wife, Caroline, added to their growing customer network and reputation.

At the minimum, your business plan should include information on:

1. Who your principal customers are or, if you are launching into new areas, who they are likely to be. Determine in as much detail as you think appropriate the income, age, sex, education, interests, occupation and marital status of your potential customers, and name names if at all possible.

   Anthony Wreford was 35 when he started his PR company. He and partner Michael McAvoy invested £5,000 each, hired a secretary and rented three rooms in Mayfair. For the next two years they spent every waking moment getting McAvoy Wreford off the ground. 'We went through our complete list of contacts and invited anyone relevant over for lunch. To avoid wasting time, it became a standing joke to only deal with a MAN, which is shorthand for clients who have the Money, Authority and Need.'

   After four years they were approached with a brilliant buy-out offer. Two years and a performance-related contract later, Wreford and McAvoy knew that they were millionaires.

2. What factors are important in the customer's decision to buy or not to buy *your* product and/or service, how much they should buy and how frequently?

Tom Farmer, the son of a Leith shipping clerk who earned £5 a week, launched Kwik-Fit in 1971. Now the company has grown into a £418 million public company with almost 1,000 outlets. In his own words, the enduring philosophy behind his business, to which he ascribes its success, is '100 per cent customer satisfaction. Just giving service – phoning back in half an hour if you say you will, standing by promises – puts you miles ahead of anyone else in the field'. Knowing that service is as important as the exhaust pipes themselves is what has provided Kwik-Fit with a lasting competitive advantage.

Many factors probably have an influence and it is often not easy to identify all of them. These are some of the common ones that you should consider investigating:

(a) *Product considerations*
   (i)   Price
   (ii)   Quality
   (iii)   Appearance (colour, texture, shape, materials, etc)
   (iv)   Packaging
   (v)   Size
   (vi)   Fragility, ease of handling, transportability
   (vii)   Servicing, warranty, durability
   (viii) Operating characteristics (efficiency, economy, adaptability, etc).
(b) *Business considerations*
   (i)   Location and facilities
   (ii)   Reputation
   (iii)   Method(s) of selling
   (iv)   Opening hours, delivery times, etc
   (v)   Credit terms
   (vi)   Advertising and promotion
   (vii)   Variety of goods and/or services on offer
   (viii) Appearance and/or attitude of company's property and/or employees
   (ix)   Capability of employees.
(c) *Other considerations*
   (i)   Weather, seasonality, cyclicality
   (ii)   Changes in the economy – recession, depression, boom.

Since many of these factors relate to the attitudes and opinions of the potential customers, it is likely that answers to these questions will only be found through interviews with customers. It is also important to note that many factors that affect buying are not easily researched and are even less easy to act upon. For example, the amount of light in a shop or the position of a product on the shelves can influence buying decisions.

You could perhaps best use the above list to rate what potential customers see as your strengths and weaknesses. Then see if you can use that information to make your offering more appealing to them.

3. As well as knowing something of the characteristics of the likely buyers of your product or service, you also need to know how many of them there are, and whether their ranks are swelling or contracting. Overall market size, history and forecasts are important market research data that you need to assemble – particularly data that refer to your chosen market segments, rather than just to the market as a whole.

Character (Self-Assembly Furniture) Ltd

Philip Waddell researched published data on the self-assembly furniture market and conducted his own research via a questionnaire. Some of his conclusions as to the profile of customers for his products were:

1. Nearly 26 per cent of all men had assembled furniture from flat packs in the past 12 months – 53 per cent had done so at some time.
2. Thirty per cent of men had put up fitted shelves and cupboards in the past year – 60 per cent at some time in the recent past.
3. Over 75 per cent of these DIYers were in the 25–44 year age group.
4. Social groups A, B, C1 and C2 featured prominently, with the ABs significantly less interested than the Cs.
5. Owner-occupiers, especially those who had recently moved house, were most active in DIY, and in general people living in modern family housing on incomes 30 per cent or more higher than the national average.
6. Seventy-nine per cent said they would prefer DIY if the task was within their capabilities, in order to save money.
7. Women, in particular those who are married, in the AB social class and aged between 25 and 34, are generally favourably disposed to the concept of DIY.
8. There is a strong correlation between involvement in home decorating and a willingness to buy self-assembly furniture. This has important connotations for advertising and distribution.
9. The main reasons cited for not buying self-assembly furniture are lack of knowledge, lack of confidence and lack of time. This suggests that if the DIY task could be made evidently simpler and less time-consuming, then the numbers of people prepared to buy could be greatly increased.

The Oriental martial arts and fitness centre

The Oriental, a martial arts and fitness centre situated in the city of Cambridge, aimed to provide specialised facilities for martial arts clubs, not then available in Cambridge.

According to a publication at the time, *Sport in Cambridge*, sports and leisure generated £4.4 billion of consumer spending per annum and accounted for 376,000 jobs. Growth in indoor sports was linked with the growth in facilities. There were already 1,500 public sports centres and halls in the UK.

The Martial Arts Commission membership figures showed a growth in membership from 28,000 to 106,000 members in the five years prior to Oriental being started up. These figures do not include members of the British Judo Association, which had 41,700, an increase of 5 per cent over the previous year, or most self-defence classes, which have no governing body. Of martial arts instructors questioned, 77 per cent reported increasing interest in their martial art; none reported decreasing interest.

Fitness and exercise participation alongside sports in the past 20 years, with the popularity of jogging, fun-running, weight training and aerobics, have been the fastest growing area for women's activities. A Sports Council survey suggests that 2.4 million women take part regularly in movement and dance and that 10 per cent of women take part in aerobics and keep fit.

Customer benefits

The benefits offered by the centre were those of a well-equipped training area, large enough comfortably to hold courses and competitions for at least 200 people. The centre specialised in martial arts, but was also suitable for dance and keep fit.

For the primary customer, ie martial arts clubs, the centre offered the highest-quality training facilities for their needs in the area at affordable rates, and promoted their martial art, thus increasing participation levels.

For the secondary customer, ie the student of martial arts and participants in the other classes, the centre offered training in a pleasant atmosphere with good changing and showering facilities, a bar for relaxing in after training and a handy shop where equipment and books could be purchased.

Selected market segments

Two areas of the leisure market were selected for this venture: first, the martial arts sector, and second, the fitness (especially women's) sector.

The martial arts sector (including self-defence) covers the spectrum of income/occupation groups, drawing from all walks of life. Judo has the highest proportion of junior participants (three-quarters of the members of the BJA), whereas the other martial arts show participants mainly in the 25–35 age range.

Students mainly practise twice weekly (50 per cent), with 30 per cent training three or four times weekly and a further 16 per cent training in excess of four times per week; 47 per cent of students attend courses at least twice in a year, most travelling to those close to home, with a few (27 per cent) prepared to travel further than 300 miles, including going overseas.

The keep-fit market was fairly well served in the evenings in Cambridge by the community colleges and sports hall. There was a gap in women's weight training and in daytime classes for the unemployed or for mothers of younger children. This could be filled by offering crèche facilities during daytime classes.

Satisfying customers' needs or solving customers' problems must be the primary focus of any new or growing business. Customers change and companies must adapt to these changes; recent research by McKinsey & Co revealed that the major reason for companies losing customers was indifference to customer complaints; not price, not quality, but indifference! Stu Leonard views each of his customers as a potential £50,000 asset, as he intends that they will spend £100 a week for at least the next 10 years at his store.

WORKSHEET FOR ASSIGNMENT 4: CUSTOMERS

1. What is the geographic scope of the market you intend to serve and why have you so chosen?
2. What customer needs will your product or service satisfy?
3. List and describe the main difference types of customer for your product/service.
4. Which of these market segments will you concentrate on and why?
5. Match the features of your product/service to the benefits on offer to customers in each of your chosen market segments. Provide proof, where possible.
6. Who are the innovators in each of your market segments?
7. What factors are important in the customer's decision to buy or not to buy your product/service?
8. Is the market you are aiming at currently rising or falling? What is the trend over the past few years?
9. What share of this market are you aiming for, initially?

SUGGESTED FURTHER READING

Birn, Robin J (2004) *The Effective Use of Market Research*, Kogan Page, London

Dockspeed Ltd, Case History, Parts A, B & C, Start-Up and Growth, teaching note (Reference: 595-004-1) and the Hop Shop, Case History, Parts A, B & C, Start-Up and Growth, teaching note (Reference: 595-009-1), both available from the European Case Clearing House, Cranfield, Beds MK43 0AL; tel: 01234 750903; fax: 01234 751125; Web site: www.ecch.cranfield.ac.uk; e-mail: ecch@cranfield.ac.uk

Hague, Paul, Hague, Nick and Morgan, Carol Ann (2004) *Market Research in Practice: A guide to the basics*, Kogan Page, London

Mondahl, Mary (2001) *Now or Never: How companies must change today to win the battle for Internet consumers*, HarperCollins, London

5

Competitors

Researching the competition is often a time-consuming and frustrating job, but there are important lessons to be learnt from it. Some of the information that would be of most value to you will not be available. Particularly hard to find is information relating to the size and profitability of your competitors. Businesses, and particularly smaller businesses, are very secretive about their finances. Because of this, you may have to make estimates of the size and profitability of various firms.

RESEARCH ON COMPETITORS

When you begin your research, it is crucial that you make an accurate determination of your competitors. Remember, just because someone sells a similar product or service, that does not necessarily make him or her a competitor. Perhaps he or she makes the same product but sells it in an entirely different market. (By different market, we mean that it could be sold in a different geographical market, or to a different demographic market, etc). Conversely, just because someone sells a product or service that is different from yours does not mean that he or she is *not* a competitor. Completely dissimilar products are often substitutable for each other.

Once you have identified your competitors, you need to classify them further as to 'primary', 'secondary', 'potential', etc. There are two reasons for doing this. First, you need to limit the number of firms that you will do your research on to a workable number. If you try to research 25 firms in depth, you won't have time to do anything else. If you end up with more than 10 or 12 primary competitors, you should probably do your research on only a sample. Second, you may want to classify competitors into primary and secondary because your marketing strategy may be different for each group.

As mentioned previously, finding out the size and profitability of your competitors may be difficult. You may be able to get some valuable information from the annual accounts that each company has to file at Companies House. However, you should be aware that these are often not filed when required, or they may be incomplete, or contain information of no value.

A second source of information is local business directories, eg *Key British Enterprises*, *Kelly's*, etc. In addition to other types of information, these books list the category in which a particular company's sales volume falls. For instance, while it will not tell you the company's exact sales volume, it may tell you whether the company does less than £500,000–£1,000,000, etc.

Another way to find out size and profitability totals is to read the publications that cover the business scene. The financial section of your newspaper and trade magazine often contains stories that can be used for research.

If you have been unable to get the necessary information from published sources, try doing some primary research. Contact the company directly and ask them your questions. Usually, you will not get the information that you want, but occasionally this approach does work. Next, contact the firm's suppliers, or other individuals who are in a position to know or estimate the information. Sometimes you can get a ballpark figure, if not an exact one, from a wholesaler or other supplier.

Before starting his own bagel retail operation, David Sinclair studied a number of competitive bagel and croissant outlets. By counting the number of customers at peak hours and on different days, knowing what average purchase amounts were by his own personal visits (£2 per head), David was able to establish what the likely level of turnover would be for his competitors and hence his own future outlet. His first year's sales estimate of £216,000 was within 95 per cent of the actual figure.

Finally, you may be able to make a reasonable estimate from the bits and pieces of information that you were able to collect. This is commonly done with the use of operating ratios. To illustrate, let us assume that you are researching a large restaurant. You are unable to find out its annual sales volume but after striking up a conversation with one of the employees you find out that the restaurant employs 40 full-time people. Because of your knowledge of the restaurant industry, you feel confident in estimating the restaurant's payroll at £240,000 a year. From a book that lists operating ratios for the restaurant industry (published by the trade association) you find that payroll expenses, as a percentage of sales, average 40 per cent. With these facts you are able to estimate the annual sales volume of the restaurant at £600,000.

Several points should be noted here. First, operating ratios are published by a variety of trade associations and businesses. For most types of business they are not that difficult to obtain. Second, this approach is not limited to employment ratios. You can make estimates based upon inventory levels, rent or other expenses. Third, learning to use this technique is not difficult. Once you understand the use and logic of ratio analysis, you should be able to make estimates like the above. These estimates are derived by doing the ratio analysis in reverse. Instead of taking figures and working out the ratio, you start with the ratio and work out the figures. Fourth, the use of estimates resulting from this technique should be only a last resort, or used in conjunction with estimates derived in some other way. The reason for this is not that the ratio you found in the books may be 'average' but that the particular business may, for a variety of reasons, be far from average.

(See Assignment 13, 'Summary of performance ratios' (page 226) for a description of the key operating and financial ratios.)

USEFUL ADDRESSES

Company Registration Office. Keeps financial records of all limited companies. For England and Wales these records are kept at Companies House, 55–71 City Road, London EC1Y 1BB; tel: 020 7253 9393. For Scotland they are kept at the Registrar of Companies, 37 Castle Terrace, Edinburgh EH1 2EB; tel: 0131 535 5800. For Northern Ireland they are at the Department of Economic Development, 64 Chichester Street, Belfast BT1 4JX; tel: 01232 234488.

There are a number of commercial organisations that will obtain information from Companies House on your behalf for a modest fee. Extel can supply information on over 30,000 companies worldwide, and about 10,000 based in the UK. It provides a range of financial information for each company:

- accounts for five years: balance sheet, income statement, cash flow and so on;
- daily share prices back to 1988 for quoted companies;
- financial ratios such as gearing, liquidity and profit margins.

It is possible to search for an individual company, or to select a group of companies, say in a particular industry or using a specified criterion such as turnover or profit.

Extel services are provided by FT Interactive Data, 13 Epworth Street, London EC2A 4DL; tel: 020 7251 3333.

ICC Business Publications, Field House, 72 Oldfield Road, Hampton, Middlesex TW12 2HQ; tel: 020 8481 8720 produces 210 business sector reports analysing the performance of companies by providing 28 key business ratios, covering profitability, liquidity, gearing, asset utilisation, productivity, and growth rates.

Willings Press Guide is published by Hollis Directories, Harlequin House, 7 High Street, Teddington, Middlesex TW11 8EL; tel: 020 8977 7711. This directory lists and describes all the newspapers and periodicals of the world, by trade classification. So, for example, you could find the names of all the magazines published on the subjects of camping, caravanning and rambling – which would be a source of considerable information on companies, markets and products in that sphere of interest.

Directory of British Associations published by CBD Research Ltd, Chancery House, 15 Wickham Road, Beckenham, Kent BR3 2JS. Lists and describes all the trade and other associations in the UK by field of interest, each of which is an invaluable source of information in its respective field.

ANALYSING THE COMPETITION

The following are some of the areas that you should cover in this section of your business plan:

Description of competitors

Identify those businesses that are or will be competing with you. If the number is few, list them by name. If there are many, then describe the group without naming them individually ('47 charter fishing boat operators'). List any expected or potential competitors.

Jonathon Woodrow, a 25-year-old fine arts graduate who took part in a Cranfield enterprise programme, prepared the following preliminary analysis of the likely competitors to his company, Mainframe:

Framing outlets (franchised). A company called Fastframe, operates in the Newcastle area. They have adapted an American approach to the system, which incorporates the latest picture-framing machinery in workshops attached to the picture shops. They have now established nearly 50 outlets across the country, through a franchise operation which has a combined turnover of £4 million a year. None is based in the Greater London Area.

The Frame Factory operates in North London. Within five years of starting up they established 10 shops in Cambridge, Nottingham and secondary locations in Islington, Hampstead and London suburbs such as Streatham and Hornsey. Some of these were set up under a recent franchise operation.

Framing outlets (multi-location). Frame Express was set up in Wimbledon, London. This company closely followed the Fastframe approach (they were originally registered as Fastaframe). They have now established eight shops in central and south-east London.

A slightly different approach to fast framing has been introduced recently by a company called Fix-A-Frame. They operate two shops, in Old Brompton Road, Kensington and Swiss Cottage in north-west London. Here, customers are invited to do part of the work on their frames themselves, under supervision. This obviously cuts costs, and may appeal to certain customers, but for many people cost is acceptable if the service is good, and very often time is the important factor.

Independent shops. By far the majority of picture framing outlets in London are operated as independent shops providing a local service on a small scale. They offer diverse services which frequently take weeks to achieve, and are considerably more expensive than most fast-framing shops. This is because they incur greater labour charges and do not enjoy the benefits of bulk purchase, due to their comparatively low volume of trade.

Local competition. A survey of the area around Holborn confirms that there are no frame shops comparable to the Mainframe operation for at least a one-mile radius. There are three shops offering a framing service within a short walking distance of the site, of which only one treats framing as the primary activity. These are not seen as direct competition, as they appear to be aiming at a local domestic market, which is not the principal Mainframe target.

Size of competitors

Determine the assets and sales volume of the major competitors. Will you be competing against firms whose size is similar to yours or will you be competing against giant corporations? If assets and sales volume cannot be determined, try to find other indications of size, such as number of employees, number of branches, etc.

The proprietor of 'Scoops', a proposed pick'n'mix sweet shop, got something of a shock researching his market while on an enterprise programme at Cranfield. He found out from Companies House that the small shop in Bath he proposed to emulate was owned by a multinational food company, and was not a one-man band as he thought. Further research revealed that this multinational planned a chain of franchised outlets if the Bath shop was a success.

His original strategy was to open a similar shop in another town and then perhaps grow slowly over five more years. This new information on his competitive environment confirmed that the market was very attractive, but forced him to adopt a different strategy on premises. He couldn't hope to match a franchisee-resourced chain head on, so he went for a shop-in-shop approach. This meant he could open new outlets at least as fast as his competitor, but use even less capital. His first concession in Hamley's in Birmingham was successful, leading to three more outlets in his first year of operations – a rate of growth he could not have sustained adopting his original strategy. Subsequently, however, when all 'out of London' Hamley's stores were sold, he found himself in difficulties with the new store owners.

Profitability of competitors

Try to determine how profitable the business is for those companies already in the field. Which firms are making money? Losing money? How much?

Operating methods

For each of the major competitors, try to determine the relevant operating methods. For example, what pricing strategy does each firm use? Others, besides price, that you may consider are:

- quality of product and/or service;
- hours of operation;
- ability of personnel;
- servicing, warranties and packaging;
- methods of selling: distribution channels;
- credit terms: volume discounts;
- location: advertising and promotion;
- reputation of company and/or principals;
- inventory levels.

Many of the above items will not be relevant to all businesses. Location will not be relevant, perhaps, to a telephone-answering service. On the other hand, there are many items that are not listed above that may be very relevant to your business. In the motor trade, trade-in value and styling may be as relevant as the price. So, it is very important for you to determine the relevant characteristics on which you will do your research.

Summary of analysis of competitors

After you have completed your research it is useful to summarise your findings in tabular form, such as shown in Table 2.3 (page 101). Keep in mind that the characteristics listed are for illustration only. You must decide the relevant characteristics that will go into your own table.

When the table is complete, analyse the information contained in it to reach your conclusions. Is there a correlation between the methods of operation and other characteristics, and the size and/or profitability of the competitors? A thoughtful analysis is essential because there may be many patterns shown. For instance, you may find that all the profitable companies are large, and all the unprofitable companies are small. That would be an easy pattern to spot (and an important one, as well) because it involves only two factors, profitability and size. However, it is more common that success and failure correlate with a number of factors that are not always so easy to discern, even when your findings are summarised on one page.

Looking for patterns is not the only type of analysis that is needed. You may find that a company is very successful, even though its characteristics are completely different from those of the other profitable firms. What factors apparently contribute to its success? Or you may find that a company is failing despite the fact that its operational characteristics are similar to those of the profitable firms. Can you identify the reason?

Once you have reached conclusions about the competition, relate them to your business. What is the competitive situation in the market? Is everyone making money and expanding, or is it a dog-eat-dog situation? Are your competitors likely to be much larger than you? If so, what effect will this have? Are there some operating methods that appear critical to success in this market? If so, will you be able to operate in the necessary fashion? Are there operating methods or characteristics not being widely used in the market which you think have merit? If so, why are they not found at present? Is it because they have been overlooked, or because they have problems that you have not foreseen?

The above are some of the questions that you will want to address. You will probably have many others. The important thing, though, is for you to decide the general outlook for your business. At this point in your research, does it appear that you will be able to compete successfully in this market? Do you now feel that you know what it will take in order to compete successfully? If you can answer these two questions to your satisfaction, you have probably done an adequate job of research.

Brighton Furniture Co Ltd

Despite the fact that there are over 100 furniture dealers in Brighton, the bulk of the new flats and town house developments get their furniture packages from only six firms. In my market research I found that from 80 to 99 per cent (depending on who you talk to) of the 'packages' were sold by those six firms. The firms are identified by name in Table 2.2 (page 99).

Product characteristics

To get information on the products sold by each of the firms, I talked to eight developers who had selected one or more of the six firms to provide a furniture package for their units; I also talked to 23 individuals who had purchased a package for their premises from one of the six firms. In general, the purchasers felt that their furniture was performing about as they had expected. The one exception was that buyers of the Apartment Furniture Co products all felt that the quality was not as good as they had been led to believe.

A summary of other characteristics for each company is presented in Table 2.2. Based upon these findings, I have divided the six into three groups, and labelled them as follows:

High quality, high price. The only firm in this category is Rattan Imports, which sells only rattan furniture. As one would expect, its sales are to the more expensive developments.

Moderate price, high quality. Again, only one firm, Georgian Furniture, is in this category. The bulk of its sales were made in developments where one-bedroom units cost from £75,000 to £100,000, although it did get the contract for one more expensive building.

Low price, varying quality. Four of the six firms appear to be competing in the lower end of the package-deal market. Three of the four sell 'casual' furniture, and the fourth sells bamboo furniture. Overall, there is not much difference in warranty and delivery service, but there is some variation in price (from a low of £4,200 to a high of £5,100) and upkeep (Apartment Furniture Co and Bamboo Things Ltd products appear to require less maintenance than the other two). There is, however, a wide disparity between the firms in trade-in value.

Bamboo Things furniture holds its value much better than the other firms' products, being almost 2.5 times better than the products of AAA and Apartment Furniture.

Company characteristics

By talking to four of the six firms (the other two refused) and by researching various published sources, I was able to prepare Table 2.2. Some characteristics that bear mentioning are:

▓ All six firms use in-house salespeople rather than manufacturers' representatives.
▓ There does not seem to be any particular correlation between performance and the number of years in business.
▓ Although the sales of the two firms that concentrate on the higher-price furniture are relatively small, their profits as a percentage of sales are very high.
▓ The two firms that manufacture their own furniture have the lowest profits as a percentage of sales.

Analysis of competition

Based upon the data gathered, the following analysis of the competition seems reasonable:

▓ The high-price, high-quality segment of market seems the most profitable. There is only one competitor; the firm has been in existence only a few years and sales are already over £500,000 a year; profit/sales is running at 25 per cent; and the firm is not quite as aggressive as it could be since it requires full payment on delivery.
▓ The moderate-price, high-quality segment of the market also seems to have good potential since there is only one firm presently in the market. On the negative side, this firm has been operating a year longer than Rattan Imports and seems to be more aggressive than Rattan (as shown by its lower profit/sales ratio and its more liberal credit policy), yet its total sales ratio may be low because of some inefficiencies on the company's part.
▓ The lower-price segment of the market seems to be very competitive. Of particular concern is the fact that two of the firms manufacture their own furniture. AAA Furniture

Table 2.2 Example showing company characteristics

Competitors' names	Sales (£)	Profits (£)	Year started	Credit terms	Salespeople/ Reps	Manufacturer
Condo Supplies Co	750,000	125,000	1993	50% deposit	Salespeople	No
Georgian Furniture	300,000	60,000	1997	50% deposit	Salespeople	No
AAA Furniture Inc	1,250,000	75,000	2000	COD	Salespeople	Yes
Rattan Imports Inc	500,000	125,000	1999	COD	Salespeople	No
Bamboo Things Ltd	600,000	150,000	1998	50% deposit	Salespeople	No
Apartment Furniture Co	400,000	10,000	1999	COD	Salespeople	Yes

is the leader in terms of both price and sales, and yet its profits and those of the other manufacturer, Apartment Furniture, seem very low.

It seems likely that both these companies are willing to accept low profits because they are making the bulk of their money from manufacturing. This fact is important because it means that they could even afford to sell at a cheaper price and make money, whereas I have to make a profit on the retail sales.

The fact that Condo Supplies is able to remain profitable in the face of this competition is due to the company's years in business, and the reputation for quality and service that it has cultivated with the big developers. A new firm, such as mine, would be at the mercy of the manufacturers since I do not have the reputation of Condo Supplies, nor a unique product such as Bamboo Things Ltd.

Based on this, I conclude that I have neither the unique line nor the reputation to compete successfully in the lower-priced end of the market. However, I feel that I can upgrade sufficiently to enter the moderate-price, high-quality or the high-price, high-quality segment. Of the two, the high-price segment seems most likely since Rattan Imports is not as aggressive as Georgian Furniture; also, the high-price segment seems to be larger and faster growing than the moderate-price segment.

The purpose of your competitive analysis is, therefore, as Harvard's Professor Michael Porter has researched, twofold:

▮ to determine where your competitor is weak and how he or she might retaliate to your activity.
▮ to help you define what should be your product's point of difference, based on your understanding of the key factors for success in your industry sector. (See outline example, Table 2.3.)

Canon, for example, in developing its personal copier, set production benchmarks based on competitors' products: copy quality had to be as good as for IBM office copiers, price slightly below major competitors' and weight below 20 kilograms compared with 35 kilograms for the leading competitor. This analysis forced managers to find novel ways to meet objectives in manufacturing and marketing areas.

So, you must buy and analyse competitors' products, study competitive advertisements and visit trade exhibitions to learn all you can about competitors' offerings at first hand, and continue to do so, as competitors, like customers, change all the time. And never, ever underestimate the opposition!

Table 2.3 Example showing an analysis of the competition

Name	Assets	Profits	Sales	Quality	Credit terms	Location	Price	Customer service	Inventory levels	Direct sale or wholesale

Conclusions – Key factors for success in your industry are:

WORKSHEET FOR ASSIGNMENT 5: COMPETITORS

1. List and briefly describe the companies with which you will be competing directly.
2. Analyse their size, profitability and operating methods, as far as you can.
3. What are their relative strengths and weaknesses compared both with each other and with your business?
4. What, in the light of this competitive analysis, do you believe to be the critical factors for success in your business sector?
5. What is unique about your business that makes it stand out from the competition?

SUGGESTED FURTHER READING

Bagel Express, Case History, Parts A, B & C, Start-Up and Growth, video and teaching note (Reference: 595-032-1), available from the European Case Clearing House, Cranfield, Beds MK43 0AL; tel: 01234 750903; fax: 01234 751125; Web site: www.ecch.cranfield.ac.uk; e-mail: ecch@cranfield.ac.uk

Haig, Matt (2002) *If You're So Brilliant. . . How come you don't have an e-strategy?* Kogan Page, London

Porter, Michael E (1998) *Competitive Strategy: Techniques for analyzing industries and competitors,* Simon & Schuster, New York

6

A plan for market research

It is unlikely that you will already have the answers to all the important questions concerning your marketplace.

The purpose of the market research element of the workbook is to ensure you have sufficient information on customers, competitors and markets so that your market entry or expansion strategy is at least on the target, if not the bull's-eye itself. In other words, enough people want to buy what you want to sell at a price that will give you a viable business. If you miss the target completely, you may not have the resources for a second shot.

One of the sad aspects of new business starts is that often the one-in-three failure rate for businesses in the first three years of life involves someone investing a lump-sum payment received from a previous redundancy, through taking early retirement, or from an inheritance. It is one of the paradoxes of small businesses that whereas you cannot start without investing some time and money, it may be safer to have more time than money. Those with their own money frequently have less pressure from banks or financial investors to thoroughly research their ideas first, simply because they do not *have* to go to see the bank manager in the early stages to obtain support before starting. Those with *time* but inadequate resources always have to seek advice before starting, and inevitably this will include researching the market as widely as possible *before* commencing. You do not have to open a shop to prove there are *no* customers for your goods or services; frequently some modest DIY market research beforehand can give clear guidance as to whether your venture will succeed or not.

The purpose of practical DIY market research for entrepreneurs investigating or seeking to start a new business is, therefore, twofold:

1. To build *credibility* for the business idea; the entrepreneur must demonstrate first to his or her own satisfaction, and later to outside financiers, a

thorough understanding of the marketplace for the new product or service. This will be vital if resources are to be attracted to build the new venture.
2. To develop a *realistic* market entry strategy for the new business, based on a clear understanding of genuine customer needs and ensuring that product quality, price, promotional methods and the distribution chain are mutually supportive and clearly focused on target customers.

Otherwise, 'fools rush in, where angels fear to tread'; or, as they say in the army, 'time spent in reconnaissance is rarely time wasted'. The same is certainly true in starting a business, where you will need to research in particular:

1. your customers – who will buy your goods and services? What particular customer needs will your business meet? How many of them are there?
2. your competitors – which established companies are already meeting the needs of your potential customers? What are their strengths and weaknesses?
3. your product or service – how should it be tailored to meet customer needs?
4. what price should you charge to be perceived as giving value for money?
5. what promotional material is needed to reach customers; which newspapers, journals do they read?
6. where should you locate to reach your customers most easily, at minimum cost?

Research, above all else, is not just essential in starting a business, but, once launched, must become an integral part in the ongoing life of the company. Customers and competitors change; products have life cycles. Once started, however, ongoing market research becomes easier, as you will have existing customers (and staff) to question. It is important that you monitor regularly their views on your business (as the sign in the barber shop stated: 'We need your head to run our business') and develop simple techniques for this purpose (eg touch screens, questionnaires for customers beside the till, suggestion boxes with rewards for employees).

THE MORE HASTE, THE LESS SPEED

Procter & Gamble test-marketed the home dry-cleaning product Dryel on 150,000 households for more than three years before introducing the product. Contrast this with how Drugstore.com tested the water. Before its launch, the online company spent less than a week surveying only about 100 people. Around that time, market research for many online companies was reduced to slapping up a Web site and hoping for the best. Now that this practice has stopped, it seems likely that new Internet firms will have to act a bit more slowly and follow some of the old rules of marketing, while maybe at the same time speeding up these traditional practices.

With so many Internet firms, being first to market has translated into little less than being first out of it. All that Boo.com had to show for $135 million of investment when the business failed was a bid of $400,000 from Bright Station (formerly Dialog) for the technology.

There is much evidence that successful firms take marketing very seriously and use their superior knowledge to create superior growth.

THE SEVEN STEPS TO EFFECTIVE MARKET RESEARCH

Researching the market need not be a complex process, nor need it be very expensive. The amount of effort and expenditure needs to be related in some way to the costs and risks associated with the business. If all that is involved with your business is simply getting a handful of customers for products and services that cost little to put together, then you may spend less effort on market research than you would for, say, launching a completely new product or service into an unproven market that requires a large sum of money to be spent up front.

However much or little market research you plan to carry out, the process needs to be conducted systematically. These are the seven stages you need to go through to make sure you have properly sized up your business sector.

Step 1: Formulate the problem

Before embarking on your market research you should first set clear and precise objectives, rather than just setting out to find interesting general information about the market. The starting point for a business idea may be to sell clothes, but that is too large and diverse a market to get a handle on. So, that market needs to be divided into, say, clothes for men, women and children, then further divided into clothes for working, leisure, sport and social occasions. This process is known as segmenting the market. A further segment could cover special occasions such as weddings. Even once you have narrowed your idea down to, say, smart clothes for women, the definition of what is smart will differ for each age group. Most businesses end up selling to several different market segments, but when it comes to detailed market research you need to examine each of your main segments separately.

So, for example, if you are planning to open a shop selling to young fashion-conscious women, among others, your research objective could be: to find out how many women aged 18 to 28, with an income of over £25,000 a year, live or work within 2 miles of your chosen shop position. That would give you some idea whether the market could support a venture such as this.

Step 2: Determine the information needs

Knowing the size of the market, in the example given above, may require several different pieces of information. For example, you would need to know the size of the resident population, which might be fairly easy to find out, but you might also want to know something about people who come into the catchment area to work, for leisure purposes, on holiday or for any other major purpose. There might, for example, be a hospital, library, railway station or school nearby that also pulled potential customers to that particular area.

Step 3: Where can you get the information?

This will involve either desk research in libraries or on the Internet, or field research, which you can do yourself or get help in doing. These areas are covered later in this section.

Step 4: Decide the budget

Market research will not be free even if you do it yourself. At the very least there will be your time. There may well be the cost of journals, phone calls, letters and field visits to plan for. At the top of the scale could be the costs of employing a professional market research firm.

Starting at this end of the scale, a business-to-business survey comprising 200 interviews with executives responsible for office equipment purchasing decisions cost one company £12,000. Twenty in-depth interviews with consumers who are regular users of certain banking services cost £8,000. Using the Internet for Web surveys is another possibility, but that can impose too much of your agenda onto the recipients and turn them away from you.

Doing the research in-house may save costs but may limit the objectivity of the research. If time is your scarcest commodity, it may make more sense to get an outside agency to do the work. Using a reference librarian or university student to do some of the spadework need not be prohibitively expensive. Another argument for getting professional research is that it may carry more clout with investors.

Whatever the cost of research, you need to assess its value to you when you are setting your budget. If getting it wrong would cost £100,000, £5,000 spent on market research might be a good investment.

Step 5: Select the research technique

If you cannot find the data you require from desk research, you will need to go out and find the data yourself. The options for such research are described later in this section, under 'Field research'.

Step 6: Construct the research sample population

It is rarely possible or even desirable to include every possible customer or competitor in your research. So, you have to decide how big a sample you need to give you a reliable indication how the whole population will behave.

Step 7: Process and analyse the data

The raw market research data needs to be analysed and turned into information to guide your decisions on price, promotion and location, and the shape, design and scope of the product or service itself.

FIRST STEPS

There are two main types of research in starting a business:

1. desk research, or the study of published information;
2. field research, involving fieldwork in collecting specific information for the market.

Both activities are vital for the starter business.

Desk research

There is increasingly a great deal of secondary data available in published form and accessible via business sections of public libraries throughout the UK to enable new starters both to quantify the size of market sectors they are entering and to determine trends in those markets. In addition to populations of cities and towns (helping to start quantification of markets), libraries frequently purchase Mintel Reports, involving studies of growth in different business sectors. Government statistics, showing trends in the economy, are also held (Annual Abstracts for the economy as a whole, Business Monitor for individual sectors). It is important to demonstrate that your sector is growing (you have the wind behind you, like Anita Roddick with the 'green' movement behind the Body Shop's 'natural' beauty products), or if the sector is declining, you can demonstrate why your product/service will be different and will not be affected by this trend (eg although UK car manufacturing has declined, the makers of 'kit cars' have focused on a growing profitable niche of enthusiasts).

If you plan to sell to companies or shops, Kompass and Kelly's directories list all company names and addresses (including buyers' telephone numbers); the Registrar of Companies, in Cardiff, contains Extel card information on the 3,000 major quoted UK companies (£1.00 per card). Many industrial sectors are represented by trade associations, which can provide information (see *Directory of British Associations,* CBD Research), while Chambers of Commerce are good sources of reference for import/export markets. Detailed addresses and contact telephone numbers for these organisations are included in Appendix 1.

Field research

If you are contemplating opening a classical music shop in Exeter focused on the young, while desk research might reveal that out of a total population of 250,000 there are 25 per cent of under 30-year-olds, it will not state what percentage are interested in classical music or how much they might spend on classical CDs. Field research (questionnaire in street) provided the answer of 1 per cent and £2 a week spend, suggesting a potential market of only £65,000 a year (250,000 × 25% × 1% × £2 × 52!). The entrepreneurs decided to investigate Birmingham and London instead! But at least the cost had only been two damp afternoons spent in Exeter, rather than the horrors of having to dispose of the lease of an unsuccessful shop.

Fieldwork is now becoming quite big business in the UK, eg expert market research companies turned over more than £500 million in 1999. Most field-work carried out consists of interviews, with the interviewer putting questions to a respondent. We are all becoming accustomed to it, whether being interviewed while travelling on a train, or resisting the attempts of enthusiastic salesmen posing as market researchers on doorsteps ('sugging', as this is known, has been illegal since 1986). The more popular forms of interview are currently:

▪ personal (face-to-face) interview: 55% (especially for the consumer markets);
▪ telephone and e-mail: 32% (especially for surveying companies);
▪ post: 6% (especially for industrial markets);
▪ test and discussion group: 7%.

Personal interviews and postal surveys are clearly less expensive than getting together panels of interested parties or using expensive telephone time. Telephone interviewing requires a very positive attitude, courtesy, an ability not to talk too quickly and listening while sticking to a rigid questionnaire. Low response rates on postal services (less than 10 per cent is normal) can be improved by accompanying letters explaining the questionnaire's purpose and why respondents should reply, by offering rewards for completed questionnaires (small gift), by sending reminder letters and, of course, by providing pre-paid reply envelopes. Personally addressed e-mail questionnaires have secured higher response rates – as high as 10–15 per cent – as recipients have a greater tendency to read and respond to e-mail received in their private e-mail boxes. However, unsolicited e-mails ('spam') can cause vehement reactions: the key to success is the same as with postal surveys – the mailing should feature an explanatory letter and incentives for the recipient to 'open' the questionnaire.

All methods of approach require considered questions. In drawing up the questionnaire attention must be paid first to:

- Define your research objectives; what exactly is it that you need vitally to know? (Eg, how often do people buy, how much?)
- Who are the customers to sample for this information? (Eg, for DIY products, an Ideal Home Exhibition crowd might be best.)
- How are you going to undertake the research? (Eg, face to face in the street.)

When you are sure of the above, and only then, you are ready to design the questionnaire. There are six simple rules to guide this process:

1. Keep the number of questions to a minimum.
2. Keep the questions simple! Answers should be either 'Yes/No/Don't know' or offer at least four alternatives.
3. Avoid ambiguity – make sure the respondent really understands the question (avoid 'generally', 'usually', 'regularly').
4. Seek factual answers, avoid opinions.
5. Make sure at the beginning you have a cut-out question to eliminate unsuitable respondents (eg those who never use the product/service).
6. At the end, make sure you have an identifying question to show the cross-section of respondents.

The introduction to a face-to-face interview is important; make sure you are prepared, either carrying an identifying card (eg student card, Association of Market Researchers watchdog card) or with a rehearsed introduction (eg 'Good morning, I'm from Manchester University [show card] and we are conducting a survey and would be grateful for your help'). You may also need visuals of the product you are investigating (samples, photographs), to ensure the respondent understands. Make sure these are neat and accessible. Finally, try out the questionnaire and your technique on your friends, prior to using them in the street. You will be surprised at how questions that seem simple to you are incomprehensible at first to respondents!

The size of the survey undertaken is also important. You frequently hear of political opinion polls taken on samples of 1,500–2,000 voters. This is because the accuracy of your survey clearly increases with the size of sample, as the following table shows:

With random sample of . . .	95% of surveys are right within . . . percentage points
250	6.2
500	4.4
750	3.6
1,000	3.1
2,000	2.2
6,000	1.2

So, if on a sample size of 600, your survey showed that 40 per cent of women in the town drove cars, the true proportion would probably lie between 36 and 44 per cent. For small businesses, we usually recommend a minimum sample of 250 completed replies.

Remember, above all, however, that questioning is by no means the only or most important form of fieldwork. Sir Terence Conran, when questioned on a radio programme, implied that he undertook no market research fieldwork (ie formal interviews) at all. Later in the programme he confessed, nonetheless, to spending nearly 'half of his time visiting competitors, inspecting new and rival products, etc'. Visiting exhibitions and buying and examining competitors' products (as the Japanese have so painfully done, in disassembling piece by piece competitive cars, deciding in the process where cost-effective improvements could be made) are clearly important fieldwork processes.

Just as important, test marketing by selling from stalls on a Saturday, or taking part in an exhibition, gives an opportunity to question interested customers and can be the most valuable fieldwork of all. All methods are equally valid, and the results of each should be carefully recorded for subsequent use in presentation and business plans.

Mark and Harvey Wooldridge exhibited their prototype fibreglass sports car at the Stoneleigh Kit Car Show, where the previous year they had conducted detailed market research among the kit car crowd enthusiasts. Not only were orders received, but the kit car was favourably reviewed by the top four kit car magazines, enabling the brothers to begin commercial production. By 1995 Quantum Cars was producing two cars a week and had won the confidence-building 'East Midlands Small Business of the Year Award'.

A saloon version and a Mark 2 sports model have subsequently been added to the range, necessitating a move to larger premises as Quantum continues to prosper.

Once the primary market research (desk and field research) and market testing (stalls and exhibitions) are complete, pilot testing of the business should be undertaken in one location or customer segment, prior to setting targets and subsequently measuring the impact of a full regional launch.

EXAMPLE QUESTIONNAIRE

Chantal Coady was seeking to open a continental chocolate shop in the lower King's Road, London. Hesitating, because of the size of the annual rent (£7,850 pa) and premium sought for the premises (£15,000), Chantal decided to carry out some market research to see if there would be enough interested passing customers to carry these heavy costs. The questionnaire used, together with results and comments on this useful exercise, is shown below. Chantal's business is still based in the same area of London, though she opened a second shop in November 2004 and has a thriving mail order business, she now has a turnover of over £3 million a year.

Chantal Coady's 'Rococo' chocolate shop

Date: Location: Time:

1. I am interested in people buying chocolate – can you tell me how often you buy the following:

	Every day	Every week	Once a month	Special Occasions
Bars				
Boxes				
Loose chocs				

2. Where do you buy these chocolates?
    Supermarket   [ ]
    Sweet shop   [ ]
    Woolworths   [ ]
    Specialist shop   [ ]
    Other   [ ]

3. When was the last time you were given chocs as a present?

   Some people enjoy receiving chocs as a gift – where would you put yourself on this scale?

   Overjoyed   Very pleased   Pleased   Indifferent   Ungrateful

4. Do you ever buy chocs as a present for anyone?

   The last time you bought chocs for someone, who were they for?

   _____

5. Where did you buy them from? _____

6. How much did you spend?   Up to £1 [ ]   Up to £5 [ ]   Over £5 [ ]

7. Were they wrapped in the shop? (as a gift)

8. Do you have a favourite chocolate bar or box? _____

9. Any preferences for   Dark [ ]   Milk [ ]   White [ ]

10. Do you have a favourite from any particular country?

    English   French   German   Belgian   Swiss   Other

11. Some people say that the existing chocolates on the market are rather boring – would you agree?

12. If there were a shop which sold a unique range of gifts in chocolate, and high quality loose and boxed chocs, how interested would you be in buying them?

    Extremely   Very   Moderately   Indifferent   Not interested

13. *Age group*

Up to 20	[ ]
21–25	[ ]
26–30	[ ]
31–40	[ ]
41–50	[ ]
Over 50	[ ]

14. *Profession*

15. *Income bracket*

Up to £5,000	[ ]
Up to £10,000	[ ]
Up to £15,000	[ ]
Over £15,000	[ ]

Any other comments _____

_____

_____

_____

_____

OBJECTIVES AND RESULTS OF QUESTIONNAIRE

The purpose of the questionnaire was:

■ To quantify positive response to a chocolate shop at this location as a percentage of total population.
■ To establish the 'character' of the positive respondent in terms of socio-economic grading, ie profession/income bracket, their buying habits and their unfulfilled requirements (ie customer needs).
■ To clarify the problem gift area (ie product types).

The character of the target market can be split into two main parts:

■ the passing trade, of which the weekday and Saturday influx constitute different subdivisions.
■ the genuine residents, many of whom have lived in the area for generations.

I have decided to poll the residents in their own right by direct leafleting. There will be an incentive to reply (such as a reduction in the price of a box of chocolates). At the same time I shall be sampling the passing trade, by means of the questionnaire. Thus I expect to obtain information about these different market sectors.

The sample

The figures below represent the first 100 questionnaires. Early results bear out expectations that the Saturday afternoon shoppers on the King's Road are made up of a large number of under 20 year olds, groups D and E (up to £10,000 pa).

Total sample to date: 100 (50 male, 50 female).

Table 2.4 Results of the first 100 questionnaires

Age		Socio-economic grading	
30 aged up to 20	which		%
20 aged 21–25	converts	E up to £5,000	: 42
20 aged 26–30	to:	D £5,001–10,000	: 28
10 aged 31–40		C £10,001–15,000	: 11
10 aged 41–50		B £15,001–20,000	: 8
10 aged over 50		A over £20,000	: 11
___			___
100			100

General information drawn from the sample

Customers

Ninety per cent of this sample buy chocolate bars more than once a week. Sixty per cent bought boxes of chocolates for special occasions such as birthdays, Christmas, Easter, Mother's Day, or for a thank-you present. Only 10 per cent said that they never bought boxed chocolate.

When asked if they had ever bought chocolate as a gift for a particular person, 86 per cent responded positively, and the categories of people for whom the gift was bought are as follows:

Friends	44%
Mothers	26%
Relations	15%
Grandparents	8%
Wives	4%
Lovers	3%
	100%

Price

When asked how much they had spent on the last box of chocolates bought as a gift:

15% spent under £1
75% spent up to £5
10% spent over £5

Ninety-six per cent responded positively when asked if they had ever been given chocolates as a gift. Their reactions to receiving chocolates as a gift were:

– 45% were very pleased or overjoyed
– Only 3% were ungrateful: one suffered from migraine, one preferred scotch, one was on a diet
– 20% of the sample bought chocolates from specialist shops, the rest were bought in sweet shops, garages, or supermarkets.

Product

Chocolate preferred (by nationality type)

Swiss	37%
English	25%
Belgian	16%
French	7%
German	3%
American	1%
Italian	1%

Trades and professions in the sample were widely varied, including the titles:

- student;
- secretary;
- civil servant;
- teacher;
- financier;
- hotelier;
- roof tiler;
- jelly-baby maker.

The diversity of favourites showed no clear pattern, and ranged through specialist Belgian fresh-cream chocolates such as Godiva and Leonidas, standard boxes like Lindt and Bendicks, to Mars Bars and Double Deckers.

When asked if they thought the existing chocolates on the market were boring (and this was evidently a question that they had not considered):

43% said that they found them boring
57% were negative

An attempt was made to test the response to the 'Rococo' concept of fanciful product lines, without leading the respondent:

18%	were extremely interested
16%	were very interested
21%	were moderately interested
20%	were indifferent
25%	were not interested

100%

These figures show that 55 per cent responded to 'Rococo' positively.

When examined in terms of age groups and income brackets a pattern quickly became evident: the A/Bs showed a high degree of awareness, and an established buying pattern of high-quality chocolates. They were also interested in a shop which offered a service superior to that otherwise available.

Examination of the lower income brackets showed less awareness of available products and less readiness to spend money on them.

In the age groupings, the over 50s showed little desire to buy novelty chocolates, though the As, Bs and Cs aged 26–50 seemed to have a definite appetite for high-class, well-presented chocolates.

Of the positive respondents only 12 per cent had been offered a gift-wrapping service in the shop where they had bought the chocolate.

SUMMARY OF FINDINGS SO FAR

The overall habits of the chocolate-buying public (which is the majority of the population) are supported by the early findings, that is that the average Briton eats 8 oz of chocolate per head/per week. I will carry a wide range of chocolate bars for everyday consumption.

It also appears that at some time in the year, most people will buy chocolate as a gift. When chocolate is purchased, in the normal way, it would not come with a gift presentation.

The awareness of certain 'Rococo' product lines will have to be heightened by advertising in the appropriate media; for example: Chocolate Cameras in the *British Journal of Photography*.

Competition:

Other chocolate shops in London:

Charbonnel and Walker, Bond Street;
Prestats, South Molten Street;
Thornton, Covent Garden;
Elena, Hampstead, Edgware and St John's Road;
Harrods and Selfridges;
Clare's, Regent's Park;
Ackermans, Smithfield and NW6;
Bendicks, Sloane Street and Mayfair;
Richoux, Knightsbridge;
Newmans, City and Shaftesbury Avenue.

None of these shops offer the kind of service I am proposing.

Following two further Saturdays of market research, Chantal was able to tabulate the largely positive results and make successful representations to her bank for finance to lease the shop. Rococo has subsequently been a happy 'success story' in the King's Road.

DOING ONLINE QUESTIONNAIRES

Get online user feedback

To get the best out of selling online you should use your site to learn more about your customers; this will help you to tailor your offerings to their needs. You need to get information about your customers and store it in a way that allows you to use it when they visit your site again. Below are some of the ways in which you can get this user feedback.

Cookies

These are small files deposited on the hard disk of anyone visiting your site. If you have cookies set up on your site, your server will be able to read visitors' cookie files on their hard drives. The information contained in them can be related back to any information on your customer database. A cookie might contain a customer's name, the type of computer they use, their password for accessing your site and any other routine information that would otherwise have to be re-entered every time they returned to your site.

Executable programmes

Inviting customers to install an 'executable programme' is another means of getting online feedback. This will allow you to get a lot more information about the user, but is seen as intrusive by most people. In all probability, fewer than one in five users will let you install such a programme, but in some circumstances it may work well.

Personalisation

You could go a stage further and offer an intelligent Internet tool such as 'My Web', which reacts to customers' shopping habits and suggests different sites related to subjects or products in which they are interested. You can then monitor customers' reactions to these suggestions and use the information to refine your own offerings in a highly sophisticated manner.

Questionnaires

Web questionnaires can help by getting very detailed user feedback. They are similar to paper-based questionnaires, but with a few major advantages. As there are no paper or postage costs, you can 'mail' as many users as you like as often as you like. Questionnaire distribution and feedback can be very quick. Also, rudimentary analysis of feedback can be done automatically by inserting links between the questionnaire and some spreadsheets.

Julian Talbot-Brady, Cranfield MBA and qualified architect, investigated launching 'EU-architect.com', an Internet-based start-up company targeted at the UK's 30,000 registered architects. The aim was to provide a 'one-stop', all-in-one service to meet the needs of busy architects by providing easily accessible online sources for all their information needs. He designed a questionnaire to be e-mailed directly to the top 100 architectural practices in the UK, as well as to the leading 500 construction product suppliers. He chose to use Zoomerang.com, which provides a free 30-day survey clearing house service. Despite an accompanying letter (offering possible equity sharing), the resulting response rate of only 12 per cent made him realise that the potential for his service was much smaller than he had anticipated, leading him to accept a post with an industry supplier to develop a similar site for its own products.

Remember, if you are storing personal data about your customers on your site, they have a right to know what is going to happen to those data. In Europe and elsewhere, there are laws on data protection with which you will have to comply.

WORKSHEET FOR ASSIGNMENT 6: A PLAN FOR MARKET RESEARCH

1. What information do you currently have on customers, competitors, markets, etc?
2. What information do you still need to find, and why specifically do you need it?
3. What desk research will you have to carry out to answer this question?
4. What field research will you have to carry out?
5. How much time and money will be needed to carry out this market research?
6. Who will be responsible for each element of the research?
7. When will all the key market research information be available?

SUGGESTED FURTHER READING

Quantum Cars, Case History, Parts 1, 2 & 3, Start-Up and Growing the Business, teaching note (Reference: 397-115-1), available from the European Case Clearing House, Cranfield, Beds MK43 0AL; tel: 01234 750903; fax: 01234 751125; Web site: www.ecch.cranfield.ac.uk; e-mail: ecch@cranfield.ac.uk

Barrow, Colin (2002) *The Complete Small Business Guide*, 5th edn, Capstone Reference, Oxford

Brace, Ian (2004) *Questionnaire Design*, Kogan Page, London

Crimp, Margaret (1995) *The Market Research Process*, 3rd edn, Prentice Hall, Harlow

Kinnard, Shannon (1999) *Marketing with E-mail*, Maximum Press, Gulf Breeze, FL (see also www.zoomerang.com)

West, C (1999) *The Internet Market Research Audit*, Financial Times/Prentice Hall, Harlow

Wright, Len Tiu and Crimp, Margaret (2000) *The Marketing Research Process*, Longman Higher Education, Harlow

Zaltman, Jerry (2003) *How Customers Think: Essential insights into the mind of the market*, Harvard Business School Press, Boston, MA

My IT Team Ltd specialises in providing cost-effective Information Technology advisory and support services to Start Up companies and small businesses, enabling you to reduce your IT costs, and improve the reliability of your IT Infrastructure.

Providing computer support and advice, we give our clients a number of hours remote and onsite maintenance each month. Most of our support is done remotely though if that is not possible we do send out engineers to resolve any workstation or server issues you may have.

Other services we offer include Remote Monitoring and Patch Management of your computer systems, Remote Hosting of your entire IT server infrastructure, Blackberry Handheld Solutions and Anti-virus Online Data Backup Services.

Remote Monitoring.
This provides you with continuous monitoring of your IT infrastructure, including servers (e.g. disk and memory utilisation, checking logs, monitoring backups, etc.) and workstations. You would be contacted at the first sign of an issue within your systems. This service also allows us to undertake sophisticated remote access and support activities, such as remote control to your user's desktop.

Patch Management.
We can also remotely update the client's Microsoft software with the latest patches and security fixes. It allows anti- virus update deployment, operating system updates, and remote application deployment. These activities can be scheduled to run out of business hours, to minimise any disruption to your business.

Remote Server Hosting.
My IT Team Ltd will provide a server infrastructure on a managed platform hosted at a government approved hosting facility. Your company benefits from high end solutions at a fraction of the cost of an in house system. The financial rewards of remote hosting are low cost implementation as there is no up-front capital outlay on infrastructure and all monthly rentals can be written off against tax as an operating expense. There is no need to purchase hardware and software for the servers or software licences for Microsoft office.

The Blackberry Solution.

The BlackBerry Server (BES) is hosted alongside a Microsoft Exchange Server within a hosting facility. BlackBerry provides users with 'Always On, Always Connected' access to voice and data, from a single wireless device. With BlackBerry push technology, users would immediately receive up-to-date information while they're on the go. Blackberry acts as a single, integrated device for all your voice and data needs and allows wireless access to your e-mail. Blackberry 'push' technology means you don't have to retrieve your e-mail or data – it finds you. E-mail attachments can be viewed in popular document formats and there is the option of advanced security for enterprise and government organisations.

The fully managed and hosted infrastructure with Blackberry provides significant business benefits including:

Increased employee productivity by:

- providing anytime, anywhere access to their email, calendar and clientinformation from PC, laptop or Blackberry
- increasing efficiency by enabling the use of "down time" for example when waiting for meetings or travelling
- giving quick access to the information they need to make good, timely decisions allowing collaboration and file sharing
- Consolidated customer and partner information to manage and drive sales opportunities,
- Improved communication by sharing information effectively between colleagues, customers, partners and suppliers,
- Outsourced support allows the company to focus on the core business,
- Complete system access from anywhere in the world.

The support service that My IT Team Ltd provides consists of a service desk which will deal with all support calls and incident management. Desktops will be monitored using our remote management software allowing you the peace of mind to run your business effectively and successfully. My IT Team Ltd works closely with a number of other Business Support and Technology companies, in order to offer our clients a full spectrum of products and services. With our team of full-time, highly experienced staff and our methodical approach, employing the services of My IT allows you to protect yourself against unexpected IT failures and expenditure thus leaving you to focus on the business in hand.

achieving thedifference

Your markets don't stand still so neither should you.

In a world that's changing around us, how can you improve short term performance and build long term value?

We believe it's down to market focus, where achieving the difference is not only your goal, it's also the way you think.

Our practitioners bring blue chip strategic, creative and operational expertise to help your enterprise generate increased business value. From tiny details to major change, market difference builds sustainable marketing success.

Achieving the Difference LLP
customers, products, brands

27 Lansdown, Stroud GL5 1BG • 07973 200030
ask@thedifference.co.uk • www.thedifference.co.uk

A MARKET DIFFERENCE BUILDS SUSTAINABLE SUCCESS. WHAT'S YOURS?

Developing a market-based approach for your business means building a strategy based on a profound understanding of customers and markets – then looking at how you engage with your customers, manage your products and grow your reputation. Successful marketing thrives on **differentiation**. Whether this means bigger, better, smarter or faster than the competition, it all comes down to being more desirable to do business with; achieving this difference is something a truly market-focused organization will have not only as its goal, but also as the way it thinks. The reward is higher sales and profits, reduced risk and the generation of increased corporate value.

This is the view of the partners at Achieving the Difference LLP, a consultancy which recognises that businesses *can* deliver short term results as well as build long term value.

As proponents of market-driven business strategy and planning, they established a team in 2002 that could bring innovative, blue chip enterprise learning about customers, products and brands, to ambitious SMEs and large companies. With a corporate pedigree including the likes of KPMG, Smiths Industries, Orange and Canon, the consultants at Achieving the Difference know first-hand what is required and how effective a customer-focused organisation can be.

Peter Roberts, a Managing Partner at the firm, believes in the power of branding as a compelling platform for sustainable competitive advantage. "If you look at the world's top brands, you'll see a lot of things they have in common. They will be well differentiated with a clear vision and market position; they'll deliver great value *as perceived by their customers*, and this will usually be reflected in their pricing policy. They're also able to balance consistency with change – because they have to always be *relevant* to their customers."

He doesn't see branding as a corporate preserve. "These principles hold good whatever the size of your business, whatever industry you're in. The list of benefits from having a strong brand is long. What we encourage our clients to do is look hard at the strategic and operational opportunities that exist for achieving some difference of their own. Even tiny details can make a big impact, so we're not always talking about major change or huge investment."

Achieving the Difference LLP has clients in financial services, telecommunications and IT, sports & leisure, food and drink, professional services, public sector and aerospace.

ACHIEVING THE DIFFERENCE IN CUSTOMER VALUE

All good businesses strive for a profitable customer base, but not all achieve it. Why not?

Many feel that things like 'marketing' and 'branding' are not really necessary for their business; they are driving sales today, that's what matters. The rest is nice to have, but not essential, and not now. In truth, they are missing the point, and missing the profit.

"We believe a business has four fundamental tasks", says Richard Jefferies, a founding partner of the firm, "Acquire new customers, serve them, develop their propensity to buy more from you, and keep them."

It's a simple formula but one which many companies fail to implement, often because they're not sure how. That's where Achieving the Difference comes in. "We can help our clients take a closer look at the way they engage with their customers at each stage, and commercially whether the investment and return stacks up . Most are pretty good at attracting in new business, and they're getting better at providing a good quality service. But they haven't usually thought through what they can do with their customers once they have them – this is where significant value can be generated. This is about developing loyalty."

Small differences in the way a business behaves towards its customers and potential customers, can make a big difference to loyalty, and sales. So too can having the right products and services. According to Jefferies, "If a business isn't working on the new product that will knock out its own best seller, then someone else will be. In my experience, too many firms rely on what they've already got and tend to ignore what they'll need next; they don't talk to their customers, or stay up with their markets. Then they're surprised when customers jump ship for something better."

So aligning the product portfolio with existing and future needs of customers is something that every business should take seriously. Build it into your business plan process and if in doubt, you can always call the team at Achieving the Difference.

For further information:

www.thedifference.co.uk
ask@thedifference.co.uk

Or by direct phone: 07973 200030 (Peter Roberts) and 07970 256198 (Richard Jefferies)

Phase 3

Competitive business strategy

Introduction

The data you have begun to collect should enable you to formulate a competitive business strategy. This will involve explaining exactly how you intend to satisfy your target customers, with the products or service you will provide, in the face of competition.

Keith Musto, a round-the-world yachtsman, explains how he developed a winning strategy for Musto Ltd, his sailmaking business.

'We recognised that the boat clothing market was wide open. Most of it was being made by clothing manufacturers who were not sailors. We felt we could turn our sewing machines from making sails to making clothes, faster than they could learn to sail. We knew what was needed to improve clothing design to make sailors perform better. A warm, dry sailor is a safer sailor.'

Musto developed a range of designs to keep storms out, from windsurfer to round-the-world yachtsman. He used the best synthetic materials to keep the wearer comfortable in a three-layer system, which consists of 'good underwear that sucks the moisture from the skin like blotting paper; then a middle layer using fibres to trap as much warm air as possible; and a protective outer layer to keep the storms out'.

His clothing has been endorsed by leading yachtsmen. But the biggest accolade came when the company won a Duke of Edinburgh's Design Award for its latest outfit. The British and Spanish lifeboatmen wore jackets and trousers based on this design, which was rigorously tested by the RAF's Medical Research Centre at Farnborough.

'We were a long way ahead of our competitors in those tests,' says Musto. 'The Spaniards knew the RNLI and the RAF were very thorough and were happy to follow on.'

You have at your disposal a 'mix' of ingredients which, according to how they are used, can produce different end results. There will obviously have to be an internal consistency in your actions. For example, a high-quality image, supported by a prestige location and sophisticated advertising, is hardly consistent with a very low price and untidy staff.

The principal elements of this 'marketing mix', as it is frequently called, are the *product* or service you have to sell, the *price* you propose to charge, the *promotion* you will use to communicate your message, and the *place* you will operate from or the distribution channels you will use (ie where do your customers have to be for you to get at them?).

You may find when you come to tackle the assignments in this phase that you have to collect more data. This is not unusual – indeed, gathering information is a continuous activity in a healthy business. Unfortunately, this healthy search for additional data can lead to some confusion as to how eventually to formulate strategy.

The strategic framework shown in Figure 3.1 should put the whole strategic process clearly in view and help you to formulate a clear course of action.

STRATEGIC FRAMEWORK

The foundation of this process is a clear statement of the mission of your venture, your objectives and the geographic limits you have set yourself, at least for the time being. These issues were addressed in the first assignment and until they are satisfactorily resolved, no meaningful strategy can be evolved.

Market research data are then gathered on customers, competitors and the business environment, for example, to confirm that your original perception of your product or service is valid. More than likely this research will lead you to modify your product in line with this more comprehensive appreciation of customer needs. You may also decide to concentrate on certain specific customer groups. Information on competitors' prices, promotional methods and location/distribution channels should then be available to help you to decide how to compete.

No business can operate without paying some regard to the wider economic environment in which it operates. So, a business plan must pay attention to factors such as:

▪ The state of the economy and how growth and recession are likely to affect such areas as sales, for example. During a time of economic recession, start-ups sometimes benefit from increased availability of premises, second-hand equipment, etc, and find they develop sales strongly as the economy and markets recover. For example, Cranfield MBA Robert Wright developed ConnectAir at the end of the 1982 recession and was able to sell to Air Europe at the height of the Lawson boom in 1989 – a trick that he subsequently repeated for 10 times the value between 1991 and 1999!

▪ Any legislative constraints or opportunities. One Cranfield enterprise programme participant's entire business was founded solely to exploit recent laws requiring builders and developers to eliminate asbestos from existing properties. His business was to advise them how to do so.

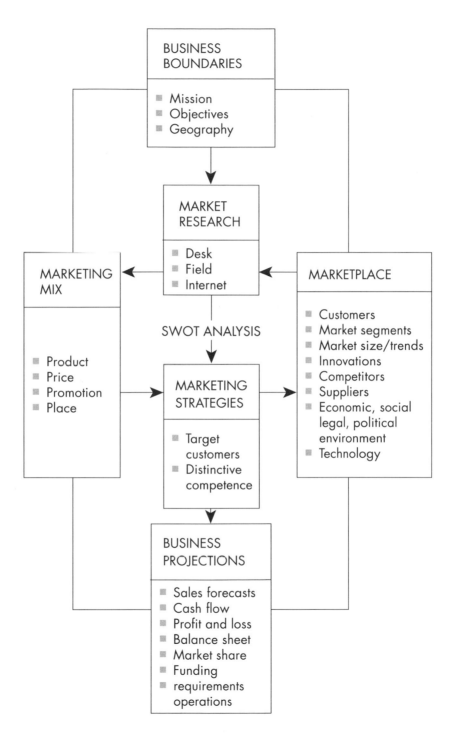

Figure 3.1 Elements of a business strategy

∎ Any changes in technology or social trends that may have an impact on market size or consumer choice. For example, the increasing number of single-parent families may be bad news at one level, but it's an opportunity for builders of starter unit housing. And the increasing trend of wives returning to work is good news for convenience food sales and restaurants.
∎ Any political pressures, either domestic or pan-European, that are likely to affect your business. An example is New Labour's law against late payment of bills. The Goverent's aim is to help small firms get paid more quickly by large firms. However, experience elsewhere, where such legislation is in force, suggests that large firms will simply alter their terms of trade. In that way all small firms could end up taking longer to collect money owed them, rather than just the unlucky or the inefficient ones.

If you sell on credit to larger firms, debtors will be an important element of your business capital base, in which case this particular political pressure could be an issue for your business. If you run a shop selling for cash to private customers this issue will be of little interest.

The process by which all these data are examined is called the SWOT analysis: your company's strengths and weaknesses are analysed and compared with the perceived environment, opportunities and threats. Its purpose is to allow you to develop a strategy using areas in which you are more able than the competition to meet the needs of particular target customer groups.

Harvard's Professor Porter has concluded that there are three distinctive marketing strategies for a company to pursue:

1. Overall cost leadership, characteristic of large companies, which are able to achieve economies of scale by major capital investment, to operate on low margins by virtue of efficient control systems and to create barriers of entry through low pricing. The major car manufacturers exemplify these traits; though Henry Ford lost money in his first year of operation with the model T, he raised his prices considerably above those of Buick in his second year of trading and was subsequently able to trim prices, from a profitable basis, in a growing market.
2. Differentiation, characterised by quality, good design and image, with high margins, based on achieving brand loyalty and unique products. If you think this is not possible for your company, just remember how Perrier has managed to sell a basic commodity, water, to the British, at the same price as Coca-Cola and even wine!
3. Focus, whereby a company serves one particular target market well, with low costs and high margins, creating barriers to entry by the very narrowness of the market and raising distribution barriers. For example, Autoglass Ltd focused simply on the replacement windscreen market in the UK (the average motorist would suffer only one broken windscreen every 20 years), too small to attract the attention of the major glass manufacturers,

and by establishing a depot network was able to build a strong windscreen distribution network, able to supply garages, small tractor cab manufacturers, etc.

Our experience with new starters at Cranfield has emphasised the importance for the small company of strategies 2 and 3, sometimes judiciously mixed, particularly bringing into play the four major elements of the marketing mix (product, price, promotion and place) to emphasise your differentiation and focus.

Many new start-ups at the turn of the millennium sought to benefit from the newly available Internet technology and vigorously pursued strategy number 1. The low margins often implicit in this strategy left little room for manoeuvre when things went awry. For example, Cranfield MBA Dexter Kirk, with 12 traditional clothing stores, noted: 'My heart is only gladdened by the final reality that has set in on dot.com apparel marketing. Funny, we old lags called it "mail order" and knew that you should allow for 30 per cent returns. When I told Boo.com that at a meeting before Christmas, they thought I was mad. I also warned my daughter who is in dot.com PR that "brown boxes" would be the problem, ie fulfilment is the most unsexy part of the job. Sure enough, one of her B2C clients delivered all their Christmas trees on January 5th!'

Needless to say, neither company survived. Hence the need to emphasise differentiation and focus with better margins in the early learning phase of start-up and business growth.

Rex Online

After his success with Goldsmiths Fine Foods, Simon Hersch was called in to help loss-making Rex Online. Its innovative Web site was designed to link recruitment agencies with job-seeking IT staff. He realised that to be successful, the company had to differentiate itself from other online recruitment companies like Stepstone and Monster.com. To this end, Rex Online was developed to include:

- broadened multi-channel access for employers and job seekers (Internet, phone and face-to-face);
- a more personalised service for employers, offering pre-screening and psychometric testing of applicants;
- a device enabling companies to buy direct links on Rex to their own Web sites;
- the creation of different Internet brands – Jobtrack.co.uk, Jobmagic.net and Gimme jobs.com – allowing specialisation through target marketing to create industry-specific databases for candidates.

Simon was able to raise £1 million from capital markets to build this differentiated strategy for a predicated higher-margin company.

The final element in this strategic framework is the business projection of the likely financial outcome of your strategic decisions. The outcome should, of course, coincide with your starting objectives.

An example of a competitive business strategy for a Cranfield enterprise programme participant is set out below.

Competitive business strategy for the Total Yoghurt Company

We plan to specialise in retailing Frozen Yoghurt, a product similar in appearance and consistency to ice cream. There all similarities end as our product is far lower in terms of calories, and is designed as a healthy and delicious snack that can be eaten throughout the year. There will be a variety of flavours, ranging from cappuccino to mandarin orange, complemented by a choice of optional toppings from fresh fruit to chocolate chip – the yoghurt and topping combined will be known as 'Frogurt'.

We are aiming at three primary segments:

- The youth market, aged 6 to 18, who will make up a small portion of our customer base. They will prefer simple flavours with sweet toppings.
- The 18 to 35 range, who, as Euromonitor's 'Healthy Food and Healthy Eating Report' provides irrefutable evidence, combine a rapidly increasing health awareness level with a growing demand for convenience foods and confectionery items. This segment will be the most adventurous, preferring fruity flavours with fresh fruit toppings.
- The 35+ age range, who, although even more health conscious than the earlier groups and with the highest disposable income, are less likely to be product innovators than either of the previous groups.

There is strong evidence that all three of these segments are already 'heavy' yoghurt users and the overall market has grown from £90 million to £281 million in the seven years prior to start-up.

There is also evidence that much of this rapid growth can be attributed to new product innovations such as Frogurt. Over the past six years the sales of fruit yoghurt have shrunk from 93 per cent of the market to 50 per cent, with children's natural, whole milk, set type, long life and very low fat yoghurt claiming the balance.

Our objectives are:

Short term – 6 months to 2 years

- To have our first frozen yoghurt outlet up and running successfully.
- To have developed a sound base of expertise upon which to build a substantial enterprise.

Long term – 2 to 7 years

- To have 3–6 retail outlets up and running, owned and managed by the Total Yoghurt Company Ltd.
- To have 15 franchised outlets opened up.
- To make Frogurt a household name.

There are currently six retailers of frozen yoghurt in London:

The Garden Store, Holborn – health food/fruit shop.
Natural Dividends, Trocadero – healthy fast foods.
Onion, Holborn – sandwich bar.
Selfridges, Oxford Street – food hall.
Harrods, Knightsbridge – food hall.
Healthy Eats, Victoria Station – healthy fast foods.

The above outlets exist only as indirect competition to the Frogurt outlet for two reasons:

▓ Frogurt will specialise in frozen yoghurt, whereas the above treat it as an additional product.
▓ Frogurt will be started in catchment areas largely unaffected by the above outlets' market-place.

Competition will arise in the form of ice cream outlets and vans, although Frogurt is not to be seen as an ice cream substitute but rather as a completely different concept of a soft-serve, low-calorie, healthy and original snack.

Marketing strategy (product, price, promotion and place)

One of our policies is to use yoghurt with natural ingredients. The frozen yoghurt mix used in the production of Frogurt contains non-fat milk solids, honey, fructose, no preservatives, no fat or salt and only natural colouring from beetroot and elderberries. The natural, healthy and low-calorie features of Frogurt will appeal to all consumers whose health awareness levels have been or are increasing. The delicious flavours and toppings coupled with the product's originality are features which will appeal to consumers regardless of their health interest.

Product. There will be five yoghurt flavours to choose from. This range of flavours will change from day to day. Complementing this variety will be 7–10 different types of topping which will be a fixed range. The on-the-spot nature of the manufacturing process means that once the outlet has closed and the machines have been cleaned out, a new flavour may be used the following day. The flavours available from our suppliers can be found in the appendix (not included here). The proposed toppings are as follows:

▓ fruit salad;
▓ crushed nut;
▓ chocolate chip;
▓ mini marshmallow;
▓ raisins or sultanas;
▓ granola;
▓ smarties.

The product will be served in small, medium and large sizes.

Price. Prices will vary according to the size of yoghurt serving. There will be one price charged for any of the toppings, which will be optional. Given a cost of approximately 20 pence for a 3.5 ounce serving and an expected gross profit margin of 75 per cent, the average price of product is 80 pence. The expected prices per serving are as follows:

small	60p
medium	80p
large	100p
toppings	20p

Further analyses of costings, projections and competitors' prices are shown in the appendix.

Promotion. These techniques and ideas are being evaluated for the promotional aspect of the business:

(a) A large emphasis will be placed on hygiene at each outlet and this will be portrayed by specifically designed fixtures and fittings.
(b) All the positive aspects of the product will be conveyed to the consumer in point of sale displays making specific claims about the product, eg non-fat. Emotive wording will be used to create the healthy image as well as to show the product's originality.
(c) All toppings will be attractively displayed within the service counter, either on a bed of ice for perishable types or in vertical compartments for non-perishables.
(d) Initially, a flyer distributed to passers-by will serve to inform consumers about the outlet, the product and its benefits. It will also serve to entice customers to try the product for free on production of the flyer – this will entail a tiny serving.
(e) Editorial coverage in local and tourist press will be sought to announce the opening of each outlet, and to describe the product, its price and the free tastings available.

Place

Location. The targeted market segments described earlier in the book show that an area must be picked to ensure the presence of the particular age groups and socio-economic classes required to form the customer base. The three main areas chosen as possible locations are:

■ busy shopping centres;
■ underground and mainline train stations;
■ international airports.

These three possible locations each have two vital characteristics:

■ High levels of consumer traffic. This means that awareness levels concerning the outlet and its product will rise quickly, as well as serving to ensure high turnover levels.
■ Captive markets. None of the above targeted locations will be exposed to the elements. This will ensure the protection of turnover levels from the harmful effects of seasonality, as well as creating the scenario for the 'impulse buy' to take place as consumers window-shop or await trains and flights.

Premises. The premises will have an area of approximately 300 square feet with as large a frontage as possible – approximately 15 feet. The frontage will act as the counter over which customers will be served; this will be transparent so that customers can see what toppings are available. There will be no seating facilities provided as the frontage will face directly on to the main concourse of the shopping centre, station or airport. The premises must have a water supply to enable washing facilities to be installed and an electricity supply to run the machinery and lighting. Fixtures and fittings will be designed to convey an exciting, new and healthy image.

The 300 square feet will be divided into:

- A service area containing washing, storage, staff and refrigeration facilities.
- The area exposed to the general public containing the machines involved in the on-the-spot manufacturing process, fixtures and fittings, the toppings and counter unit and the staff themselves.

In the next three assignments we will look more closely at the remaining key elements of the marketing mix, to build on your product/service differentiation and focus, to avoid the trap of launching too similar products into tired existing markets.

7

Pricing

The most frequent mistake made when setting a selling price for the first time is to pitch it too low. This mistake can occur either through failing to understand all the costs associated with making and marketing your product, or through yielding to the temptation to undercut the competition at the outset. Both these errors usually lead to fatal results, so in preparing your business plan you should guard against them.

These are the important issues to consider when setting your selling price.

COSTS

Make sure you have established *all* the costs you are likely to incur in making or marketing your product. Don't just rely on a 'guess' or 'common sense' – get several firm quotations, preferably in writing, for every major bought-in item. Don't fall into the trap of believing that if you will initially be working from home, you will have no additional costs. Your phone bill will rise (or you will fail!), the heating will be on all day and you'll need somewhere to file all your paperwork.

One potential entrepreneur, when challenged as to why there were no motoring expenses budgeted for in his business plan, blandly replied that he already owned his car and paid its running expenses. It had not occurred to him that the average personal mileage per annum is 12,000, whereas for the self-employed businessman that rises to nearly 30,000. Similarly, his insurance could nearly double as a business user, his service charges and petrol would increase directly with the increased mileage, and the expected useful life of his car would be reduced from six years to three. The net effect of this was to wipe out his projections for a modest profit in the first year and push his break-even out to the second year.

Also make sure you analyse the effect of changes in turnover on your costs. This can be done by breaking down your costs into direct and indirect (see Assignment 15 for an explanation of break-even analysis, as this area is sometimes referred to).

CONSUMER PERCEPTIONS

Another consideration when setting your prices is the perception of the value of your product or service to the customer. His or her opinion of value may have little or no relation to the cost, and he or she may be ignorant of the price charged by the competition, especially if the product or service is a new one. In fact, many consumers perceive price as a reliable guide to the quality they can expect to receive. The more you pay, the more you get. With this in mind, had Dyson launched his revolutionary vacuum cleaner, with its claims of superior performance, at a price below that of its peers, then some potential customers might have questioned those claims. In its literature Dyson cites as the inspiration for the new vacuum cleaner, the inferior performance of existing products in the same price band. A product at six times the Dyson price is the one whose performance Dyson seeks to emulate. The message conveyed is that, although the price is at the high end of general run-of-the-mill products, the performance is disproportionately greater. The runaway success of Dyson's vacuum cleaner would tend to endorse this argument.

COMPETITION

The misconception that new and small firms can undercut established competitors is usually based on ignorance of the true costs of a product or service, such as in the example given above; a misunderstanding of the meaning and characteristics of overheads; and a failure to appreciate that 'unit' costs fall in proportion to experience. This last point is easy to appreciate if you compare the time needed to perform a task for the first time with that when you are much more experienced (eg changing a fuse, replacing a Hoover bag, etc).

The overheads argument usually runs like this: 'They (the competition) are big, have a plush office in Mayfair, and lots of overpaid marketing executives, spending the company's money on expense account lunches, and I don't. *Ergo* I must be able to undercut them.' The errors with this type of argument are, first, that the Mayfair office, far from being an 'overhead' in the derogatory sense of the word, is actually a fast-appreciating asset, perhaps even generating more profit than the company's main products (department stores, restaurants and hotels typically fit into this category), and second, the marketing executives may be paid more than the entrepreneur, but if they don't deliver a constant stream of new products and new strategies they'll be replaced with people who can.

Clearly, you have to take account of what your competitors charge, but remember price is the easiest element of the marketing mix for an established company to vary. They could follow you down the price curve, forcing you into bankruptcy, far more easily than you could capture their customers with a lower price.

ELASTICITY OF DEMAND

Economic theory suggests that, all others things being equal, the lower the price, the greater the demand. Unfortunately (or perhaps not!), the demand for all goods and services is not uniformly elastic – that is, the rate of change of price versus demand is not similarly elastic. Some products are actually price inelastic. For example, Bristol and Bentley would be unlikely to sell any more cars if they knocked 5 per cent off the price – indeed, by losing 'snob' value they might even sell fewer. So, if they dropped their price they would simply lower profits. However, people will quite happily cross town to save 5p in the £1 on fresh vegetables and meat.

So setting your price calls for some appreciation of the relative elasticity of the goods and services you are selling.

COMPANY POLICY

The overall image that you try to portray in the marketplace will also influence the prices you charge.

However, within that policy there will be the option of high pricing to skim the market and lower pricing to penetrate. Skim pricing is often adopted with new products with little or no competition and is aimed at affluent 'innovators'. These people will pay more to be the trend setters for a new product. Once the innovators have been creamed off the market, the price can be dropped to penetrate to 'lower' layers of demand.

The danger with this strategy is that high prices attract the interest of new competitors, who see a good profit waiting to be made.

Opening up with a low price can allow you to capture a high market share initially, and it may discourage competitors. This was the strategy adopted by Dragon Lock, Cranfield enterprise programme participants (the executive puzzle makers), when they launched their new product. Their product was easy to copy and impossible to patent, so they chose a low price as a strategy to discourage competitors and to swallow up the market quickly.

BUSINESS CONDITIONS

Obviously, the overall conditions in the marketplace will have a bearing on your pricing policy. In 'boom' conditions, where products are virtually being rationed, the overall level of prices for some products could be expected to rise disproportionately. In 2000–04, house prices, for example, rose sharply ahead of general price inflation. However, during the recession of 1990–92 house prices fell rapidly, in real terms.

Seasonal factors can also contribute to changes in the general level of prices. A turkey, for example, costs a lot less on the afternoon of Christmas Eve than it does at the start of Christmas week.

CHANNELS OF DISTRIBUTION

Your selling price will have to accommodate the mark-ups prevailing in your industry. For example, in the furniture business a shop may expect to set a selling price of double that charged by its supplier. This margin is intended to cover its costs and hopefully make a profit. So, if your market research indicates that customers will pay £100 for a product bought from a shop, you, as the manufacturer selling to a shop, would only be able to charge £50.

CAPACITY

Your capacity to 'produce' your product or service, bearing in mind market conditions, will also influence the price you set. Typically, a new venture has limited capacity at the start. A valid entry strategy could be to price so high as to just fill your capacity, rather than so low as to swamp you. A housewife who started a home ironing service learnt this lesson on pricing policy to her cost. She priced her service at £5 per hour's ironing, in line with competition, but as she only had 20 hours a week to sell she rapidly ran out of time. It took six months to get her price up to £10 an hour and her demand down to 20 hours a week. Then she was able to recruit some assistance and had a high enough margin to pay some outworkers and make a margin herself.

MARGINS AND MARKETS

According to *Management Today*, nearly 80 per cent of UK companies price by reference to costs: either using a cost plus formula (eg materials plus 50 per cent) or a cost multiplier (eg three times material costs). Whatever formula you use, as accountant Brian Warnes has pointed out, you should endeavour to ensure that you achieve a gross profit margin of at least 40 per cent (sales price less the direct materials and labour used to make the article, the resulting margin expressed as a percentage of the sales price). If you do not achieve such margins, you will have little overhead resource available to you to promote and build an effective, differentiated image for your company.

Your competitive analysis will give you some idea as to what the market will bear. We suggest you complete a comparison with your competitors (Table 3.1) to give you confidence that you can match or improve upon your competitors' prices. At the very least you will have arguments to justify your higher prices to your customers and, importantly, your future employees.

Price is, after all, the element of the marketing mix that is likely to have the greatest impact on your profitability. It is often more profitable for a new company to sell fewer items at a higher price while you are getting your organisation and product offerings sorted out (remember Henry Ford); the key is to

Table 3.1 Product comparison with competitors

(Score each product factor from –5 to +5 to justify your price versus the competition)

Rating score: \\\\		Much worse	Worse	Same or nearly so	Better	Much better
Product attributes		–5	–4 –3 –2	–1 0 +1	+2 +3 +4	+5
Design						
Performance						
Packaging						
Presentation						
Appearance						
After-sales service						
Availability/ distribution						
Delivery methods/ time						
Colour/flavour						
Odour/touch						
Image/street cred.						
Specification						
Payment terms						
Other						
Total						

concentrate on obtaining good margins, often with a range of prices and quality (eg Marks & Spencer has a tiered catalogue of three main price ranges: easy, medium and upper). And if you have to increase prices? Try to combine the increase with some new feature (eg new design, colour scheme) or service improvement (eg the Post Office re-introducing Sunday collections at the same time as a 1p increase in price).

REAL-TIME PRICING

The stock market works by gathering information on supply and demand. If more people want to buy a share than sell it, the price goes up until supply and demand are matched. If the information is perfect (that is, every buyer and seller knows what is going on), the price is optimised. For most businesses this is not a practical proposition. Their customers expect the same price every time for the same product or service – they have no accurate idea what the demand is at any given moment.

However, for the Internet company, computer networks have made it possible to see how much consumer demand exists for a given product at any time. Anyone with a point-of-sale till could do the same, but the reports might come in weeks later. This means online companies could change their prices hundreds of times each day, tailoring them to certain circumstances or certain markets, and so improve profits dramatically. Easyjet.com, a budget airline operating out of Luton, does just this. It prices to fill its planes, and you could pay anything from £30 to £200 for the same trip, depending on the demand for that flight. Ryanair (Stansted) and Eurotunnel (Waterloo) have similar price ranges based on the simplest rule of discounted low fares for early reservations and full fares for desperate late callers!

Bigmack Health Food

The average mark-up by Bigmack Health Food Co's (BHFC) competition is 300 per cent. This mark-up is necessitated by the high cost of their locations and the cost of personnel. After careful analysis of the costs involved, BHFC has determined that it could use a mark-up of only 200 per cent and still make a sizeable profit. BHFC will be able to do this because:

- Its location costs will be one-third less than that of the major competition. This is due to our ability to focus on a specific market segment made up of aware customers who are prepared to buy from smaller, secondary locations (our market research has confirmed this view).
- The employee costs of BHFC will be only 20 per cent of the costs incurred by the competition. This is due to the fact that BHFC's customers will be almost entirely long-time health food devotees who will not need assistance or advice to select their

purchases. The competition, on the other hand, has a constant stream of people who are novice health food consumers or who are not interested in health food but want to purchase, on a one-time basis, a particular product. These types of people require a lot of advice and instruction and thus several employees must be working at all times.

The company will sell on credit to several health food restaurants. It will require that they pay COD for the initial order but will allow a 'net 30 day' account thereafter if their credit is adequate. All other sales will be on a cash basis.

Policy

BHFC will adopt an introductory pricing policy using a 300 per cent mark-up, offering selective new customer discounts for the first month that will bring the mark-up down to 200 per cent.

In this way we can test the market at the higher price level and only come down if we have to, and so achieve the optimum revenue.

WORKSHEET FOR ASSIGNMENT 7: PRICING

1. List all the costs you are likely to incur in making or marketing your product.
2. Refer forward to Assignment 15 and then calculate the fixed and variable costs associated with your product.
3. Using the costs as calculated above and your profit objective, calculate the optimal price you should charge.
4. What price do your competitors charge?
5. Are any of your possible market segments less price sensitive than others?
6. Does your answer to question 5 lead you to believe that there is an opportunity for a differentiated pricing policy for each market segment – so enhancing profits?

SUGGESTED FURTHER READING

Berends, William (2004) *Price and Profit: The essential guide to product and service pricing and profit forecasting*, Berends & Associates, Ontario.

Nagle, Thomas T and Holden, Reed K (2002) *The Strategy and Tactics of Pricing: A guide to profitable decision making*, Prentice Hall, New York

Warnes, Brian (1999) *The Ghenghis Khan Guide to Business Survival*, Osmosis, London

- What message will make it happen?
- What media should be used?
- How will results be checked?

What are your advertising objectives?

There is no point in informing, educating or pre-selling unless it leads to the opportunity in a significant number of instances for a sale to result. So what do potential customers have to do to enable you to make these sales? Do you want them to visit your showroom, to phone you, to write to your office, to return a card, or to send an order in the post? Do you expect them to have an immediate need to which you want them to respond now, or is it that you want them to remember you at some future date when they have a need for whatever it is you are selling?

The more you are able to identify a specific response in terms of orders, visits, phone calls or requests for literature, the better your promotional effort will be tailored to achieve your objective, and the more clearly you will be able to assess the effectiveness of your promotion and its cost versus its yield.

The more some particular promotional expenditure cannot be identified with a specific objective but is, for example, to 'improve your image' or 'to keep your name in front of the public', then the more likely it is to be an ineffective way of spending your money. Prospective financiers will be particularly wary of advertising expenditure detailed in your business plan, as this money, once spent, is gone for ever, unlike expenditure on cars, equipment or even stocks, which have at least some recoverable element.

How much is it worth to achieve your objective?

Once you know what you want a particular promotional activity to achieve, it becomes a little easier to provide for it in your business plan. In practice, four methods are most commonly used, and they each have their merits, with the exception of the first.

The 'What can we afford?' approach has its roots in the total misconception of promotional activity, which implies that advertising is an extravagance. When times are good, surplus cash is spent on advertising and when times are bad this budget is the first to be cut back. In fact, all the evidence points to the success of businesses that increase promotional spending during a recession, usually at the expense of their meaner competitors.

The 'percentage of sales' method very often comes from the experience of the entrepreneur or his or her colleagues, or from historical budgets. So, if a business spent 10 per cent of sales last year, it will plan to spend 10 per cent in the next, particularly if things went well. This method at least has some logic and provides a good starting point for preparing the overall budget.

'Let's match the competitors' becomes a particularly important criterion when they step up their promotional activity. Usually this will result in your either losing sales or feeling threatened. In either case you will want to retaliate, and increasing or varying your promotion is an obvious choice.

The 'cost/benefit' approach comes into its own when you have clear and specific promotional goals and an experience base to build on. If you have spare capacity in your factory or want to sell more out of your shop, you can work out what the 'benefit' of those extra sales is worth.

Suppose a £1,000 advertisement is expected to generate 100 enquiries for our product: If our experience tells us that on average 10 per cent of enquiries result in orders, and our profit margin is £200 per product, then we can expect an extra £2,000 profit. That 'benefit' is much greater than the £1,000 cost of the advertisement, so it seems a worthwhile investment.

In practice, you should use all of these last three methods to decide how much to spend on promoting your products.

What message will help to achieve the objectives?

To answer this question you must look at your business and its products from the customer's standpoint and be able to answer the hypothetical question, 'Why should I buy your product?' It is better to consider the answer in two stages.

1. 'Why should I buy your *product*?'
   The answer is provided naturally by the analysis of factors that affect choice. The analysis of buying motives or satisfactions is an essential foundation of promotional strategy.

2. 'Why should I buy *your* product?'
   The only logical and satisfactory answer is: 'Because it is different.' The difference can arise in two ways:

   We – the sellers – are different.
   Establish your particular niche.

   It – the product – is different.
   Each product should have a unique selling point, based on fact.

Your promotional message must be built around these factors and must consist of facts about the company and about the product.

The stress here is on the word 'fact', and while there may be many types of fact surrounding you and your products, your customers are only interested in two: the facts that influence their buying decisions, and the ways in which your business and its products stand out from the competition.

These facts must be translated into benefits. There is an assumption some-times that everyone buys for obvious, logical reasons only, when we all know of innumerable examples showing this is not so. Does a woman only buy a new dress when the old one is worn out? Do bosses have desks that are bigger than their subordinates' because they have more papers to put on them?

Having decided on the objective and identified the message, now choose the most effective method of delivering your message.

WHAT MEDIA SHOULD YOU USE?

Not all methods of communication have an equal impact. We are much more likely to be favourably influenced if a trusted and respected friend recom-mends a product or service to us, rather than a door-to-door salesman.

In practice, most new businesses should concentrate their advertising and promotional activity on the following:

Press advertising

From your market research you should have a clear idea of who your potential customers are – in terms of socio-economic classification, for example. Your business plan should detail the media you plan to use.

These associations and publications can provide information that will help you with press advertising:

Advertising Association
Institute of Practitioners in Advertising
Regional Newspapers Advertising Bureau

In practice such press advertising, like radio and TV, known in the media business as 'above-the-line' advertising, is more likely to be used effectively by major companies; there is, however, a vast array of 'below-the-line' specific items likely to be effective for targeted marketing by the small company, such as:

Below-the-line advertising
After-sales/technical service
Brochures
Business card

Business stationery
Complaints handling
Delivery service
Direct mail
Discount lists
Editorial coverage (press releases)
Exhibitions, conferences, seminars
Gifts
Giveaways
Leaflet inserts
Leaflets (loose)
Letterhead
Livery
Logo
Overalls
Packaging
Personal selling
Posters
Price lists
Product literature
Product names
Promotions, competitions
Prototypes
Samples
Telephone selling
Trade fairs
Vans
Web site
Yellow Pages

Some of the most effective promotional ideas from entrepreneurs at Cranfield have been the simplest, eg a business card for Sue Claridge, with a map on the reverse side showing how to find her restaurant. This is like the 'thank-you cards', instead of letters, sent by Wally Olins showing the design company's recently completed assignments on the face of the card (eg new designs for Suttons Seeds packs).

The *Financial Times* runs an annual competition to decide on the most consumer-effective business Christmas card; in giving the award to a humorous Ratners Jewellery card, which emphasised the company's product, the authors warned against the 'crookedest broker who often sends the most pious card!'. Given all that it costs, don't be afraid to promote your company name or product, particularly if it can be done with some taste and humour.

Leaflets/brochures and letters

These are the most practical ways for a new business to communicate with its potential customers. These forms of communication have the merits of being relatively inexpensive, simple and quick to put into operation, can be concentrated into any geographic area, and can be mailed or distributed by hand. Finally, it is easy to monitor results.

Mark Goldsmith and Simon Hersch started their catering wholesaling business while still students at Manchester University. Taking advantage of a catering strike, they began supplying the student union with portioned cakes sourced from Robert's Fridge Factory, a small London-based manufacturer known to them. Buoyed on by their initial success, they produced a single-sheet leaflet entitled 'Earning More Bread is a Piece of Cake', with a smart Goldsmith's Ltd logo, and itemising on the reverse side the various small food items they could provide. This was distributed to small snack outlets in the vicinity of the university and became their primary marketing tool and calling card. Goldsmith's (Northern) Ltd continues to provide Simon and his 40 employees with an interesting and rewarding lifestyle!

These organisations can provide information that will help you with leaflets and brochures:

British Direct Marketing Association
Chartered Institute of Marketing
British List Brokers Association

Listbroker.com
Web site: http://www.listbroker.com
This is the site of a list broker that supplies lists of all types, including consumer and business to business, mostly in the UK but some overseas. All list details, including prices, are available on the site. The database is updated daily and offers consumer and business-to-business lists with over 1.6 billion names for rental. To use the search facilities you have to register, but there is no charge. You can put in your specific requirements and see the types of list that are available. They can be useful for constructing market research survey populations.

Drawing up a new single-page sales leaflet for an exhibition can be a helpful way to rethink your marketing message: list the benefits, target the audience and let the customer know where to contact you (with a discount on the return of the leaflet to measure its effectiveness).

Public relations

This is about presenting yourself and your business in a favourable light to your various 'publics' – at little or no cost. It is also a more influential method of communication than general advertising – people believe editorials.

Chantal Coady, who founded Rococo, the unique King's Road confectioners, was 22 when she wrote the business plan that secured her £25,000 start-up capital. The cornerstone of her strategy to reach an early break-even point lay in a carefully developed public relations campaign. By injecting fashion into chocolates and their packaging, she opened up the avenue to press coverage in such magazines as *Vogue, Harpers & Queen* and the colour supplements. She managed to get over £40,000 worth of column inches of space for the cost of a few postage stamps. This not only ensured a sound launch for her venture but led to a contract from Jasper Conran to provide boxes of chocolates to coordinate with his spring collection.

To be successful, a press release needs to get attention immediately and be quick and easy to digest. Studying and copying the style of the particular journals (or other media) you want your press release to appear in can make publication more likely.

- *Layout.* The press release should be typed on a single sheet of A4. Use double spacing and wide margins to make the text both more readable and easy to edit. Head it boldly 'Press Release' or 'News Release' and date it.
- *Headline.* This must persuade the editor to read on. If it doesn't attract interest, it will be quickly 'spiked'. Editors are looking for topicality, originality, personality and, sometimes, humour.
- *Introductory paragraph.* This should be interesting and succinct and should summarise the whole story – it might be the only piece published.
- *Subsequent paragraphs.* These should expand and colour the details in the opening paragraph. Most stories can be told in a maximum of three or four paragraphs. Editors are always looking for fillers, so short releases have the best chance of getting published.
- *Contact.* List at the end of the release the name and telephone number of a contact for further information.
- *Style.* Use simple language, short sentences and avoid technical jargon (except for very specialised technical magazines).
- *Photographs.* They must be black and white, reasonably sized and well captioned. Don't staple them to the release (photographs with holes are unpublishable).
- *Follow-up.* Sometimes a follow-up phone call to see if editors intend to use the release can be useful but you must use your judgement on how often to do so.

Find out the name of the editor or relevant writer/reporter and address the envelope to him or her personally. Remember that the target audience for your press release is the professional editor; it is he or she who decides what to print. So, the press release is not a 'sales message' but a factual account designed to attract the editor's attention. Too many small companies, in their enthusiasm for their products, overlook this difference between the sales leaflet and PR release, which explains why a recent survey showed that only 6 per cent of press releases are printed; 94 per cent are not! With UK editors receiving an average of 80–90 press releases per week, make sure that you are making your latest newsworthy item public, but make sure it is free of puffery and jargon.

Web site

Many small companies start with a presence on the Web and quickly become disillusioned with it. This is partly due to reasons explained by the MD of Microsoft UK: 'So many Web sites are just online brochures – a real e-commerce solution allows customers to buy and sell products and services just as they would in a traditional supply chain.' Moving away from a static, rarely updated Web site is clearly advisable, yet, as the authors of *The Age of E-tail* point out, changing to a regularly updated shopping Web site such as that maintained by Gap can cost seven figures in Year 1 – Amazon's 'virtual shopping world' cost eight figures in Year 1!

So what can the new small company do to attract customers?

1. Good Web site design is essential, with short loading time (use graphics, not photographs), short and sweet, legible text and an attractive layout. Research indicates that 'within 3 clicks, visitors must be captivated or they will leave' (Alex Birch, Philipp Gerbert and Dirk Schneider, *The Age of E-tails*, Capstone, London, 2000). So, clear signposting is necessary, including a menu on every page so that visitors can return to the homepage or move to other sections in just one click. Also, fill the first page with 'key terms' that search engines can latch on to, as 9 out of 10 visitors reach Internet sites via a search engine or equivalent (ie AOL, Freeserve).
2. Effective banner advertising and page headings are vital, with animation and regular updates (Pedigree Petfoods in the UK has been successful with its 'catisfaction' page heading).
3. Promote your Web site by acquiring links on other commercial Web sites, using key words to ensure you can be found and by promoting outside the Internet – feature your Web site address on all products and publications. Fill your homepage with regularly updated 'success stories', give discounts to first-time buyers, ask customers to 'bookmark' your site or

add it to their list of 'favorites' on their browser. You could also try partnering with manufacturers and distributors.

Simon Hersch defied the e-commerce business model, which suggests that 30–50 per cent of turnover should be spent on marketing, as he wanted to make Rex Online profitable! With his chief operating officer, Robert Dunning, he searched for alliances and partnerships on the Web. He even went to a competitor and said: 'Let me advertise in your monthly e-newsletter for free'. Incredibly, the competitor said yes. Through alliances, Simon was able to 'piggy-back' on the marketing efforts of other sites and increased Rex's exposure. Robert Dunning compared marketing on the Web to 'the American Wild West. You know, anything goes, you just have to be creative and try things'.

Exhibitions

As a means of gathering market research data on competitors, exhibitions are extremely valuable. They are also a useful way of establishing the acceptability of your product or service quickly and relatively inexpensively, and so provide a convincing argument in support of your case for financial backing. There are hundreds of exhibitions to choose from.

Equinox, a designer furniture company, took part in its first national exhibition while its founders were on a Cranfield enterprise programme. The cost of their stand at Earls Court was £1,200. They secured £5,000 of new orders, which just recovered their exhibition costs, but more importantly they got 40 contacts to follow up. These eventually resulted in 10 further long-term customers. This whole process took two months, and transformed Equinox from the drawing board to being a bankable proposition.

UK Trade & Investment (http://www.exhibitions.co.uk/)
This Web site is sponsored by UK Trade & Investment, the UK government organisation responsible for all trade promotion and development work. It provides a comprehensive listing of all the consumer, public, industrial and trade exhibitions to be held in major venues around the UK. You can search the list by exhibition type, by exhibition date, by exhibition organiser or by exhibition venue. There is also a complete list of main subject categories and subject headings, the main UK exhibition venues, and exhibition organisers.

The site covers all exhibitions being held in the UK for two or more years ahead. The data is updated regularly twice a month.

The Direct Marketing Association UK, Haymarket House, 1 Oxendon Street, London SW1Y 4EE; tel: 020 7321 2525; fax: 020 7321 0191; Web site: www.dma. org.uk. Its members include direct-mail houses, which prepare and market lists of prospective customers.

Chartered Institute of Marketing, Moor Hall, Cookham, Maidenhead, Berkshire SL6 9HQ; tel: 01628 427500; fax: 01628 427499; Web site: www.cim.co.uk. The main professional marketing association, which includes advertising agencies.

Institute of Practitioners in Advertising (IPA), 44 Belgrave Square, London SW1X 8QS; tel: 020 7235 7020; fax: 020 7245 9904; Web site: www.ipa.co.uk. The majority of reputable advertising agents belong to the IPA, which can provide a list of members and guidelines for choosing an agency.

British List Brokers Association, Contact House, Feeder Road, St Philips, Bristol BS2 0EE; tel: 0117 916 8000; Web site: www.listbroker.com

Publications for PR

United Business Media International
Riverbank House, Angel Lane, Tonbridge, Kent TN9 1SE; tel: 01732 364422; fax: 01732 377439; Web site: www.ubminternational.com

Hollis Press & Public Relations Annual
Harlequin House, 7 High Street, Teddington, Middlesex TW11 8EL; tel: 020 8977 7711; fax: 020 8977 1133; Web site: www.hollis-pr.com

BRAD Group
33–39 Bowling Green Lane, London EC1R 0DA; tel: 020 7505 8273; fax: 020 7505 8836; Web site: www.brad.co.uk

How will the results be checked?

A glance at the advertising analysis below will show how one organisation tackled the problem.

Table 3.2 shows the advertising results for a small business course run in London. At first glance the Sunday paper produced the most enquiries. Although it cost the most, £340, the cost per enquiry was only slightly more than for the other media used. But the objective of this advertising was not simply to create interest; it was intended to sell places on the course. In fact, only 10 of the 75 enquiries were converted into orders – an advertising cost of £34 per head. On this basis the Sunday paper was between 2.5 and 3.5 times more expensive than any other medium.

Table 3.2   Measuring advertising effect

Media used	Enquiries	Cost of advertising	Cost per enquiry	Number of customers	Advertising cost per customer
		£	£		£
Sunday paper	75	340	4.50	10	34
Daily paper	55	234	4.25	17	14
Posters	30	125	4.20	10	12
Local weekly paper	10	40	4.00	4	10
Personal recommendation*	20	?	?	19	?
Total	190	739	4.35	60	18

*These are excluded from the cost calculations.

Judy Lever, co-founder of Blooming Marvellous, the upmarket maternity-wear company, believes strongly not only in evaluating the results of advertising, but in monitoring a particular media capacity to reach her customers:

'We start off with one-sixteenth of a page ads in the specialist press,' says Judy, 'then once the medium has proved itself we progress gradually to half a page, which experience shows to be our optimum size. On average there are 700,000 pregnancies a year, but the circulation of specialist magazines is only around the 300,000 mark. We have yet to discover a way of reaching all our potential customers at the right time – in other words, early on in their pregnancies.'

The Bigmack Health Food Co (BHFC)

Advertising

When BHFC started up, its founders planned only limited advertising in a few selected media. The amount of £750 was allocated to print up handbills announcing the shop's 'grand' opening. These handbills were distributed in the immediate catchment area around the shop during its first week of opening.

The amount of £75 a month was also allocated for local advertising. Other media were to be kept under review.

Promotion

BHFC put together a 'Health Food Weekend' programme that consisted of a weekend hike in the West Country. The outing included health food meals, nightly entertainment and leisurely hikes during the day. The event was open to the public and free.

BHFC also considered other promotional techniques, including a radio series of short messages on health foods, a speaker's bureau for groups interested in learning about health foods, and a newsletter to be distributed to customers, suppliers and others.

WORKSHEET FOR ASSIGNMENT 8: ADVERTISING AND PROMOTION

1. Prepare a leaflet describing your product/service to your main customers.
2. Write a press release announcing the arrival of your business on to the market. List the media to which you will send the release.
3. Prepare an advertising and promotional plan for the upcoming year, explaining:
   (a) what you want to happen as a result of your advertising;
   (b) how much it's worth to you to make that happen;
   (c) what message(s) you will use to achieve these results;
   (d) what media you will use and why;
   (e) how the results of your advertising will be monitored;
   (f) how much you will spend.
4. If you have already done some advertising or promotional work, describe what you have done and the results you have achieved. Has your work on this assignment given you any pointers for future action?

SUGGESTED FURTHER READING

Daws, Nick (2000) *Advertising for the Small Business*, 2nd edn, Otter Publications, Chichester

Farley, A D (2002) *How to Produce Successful Advertising*, Kogan Page, London

Goldsmith's Fine Foods, Case History, Parts 1, 2 & 3, Start-Up and Growth, teaching note (Reference: 596-025-1), available from the European Case Clearing House, Cranfield, Beds MK43 0AL; tel: 01234 750903; fax: 01234 751125; Web site: www.ecch.cranfield.ac.uk; e-mail: ecch@cranfield.ac.uk

Pricken, Mario (2004) *Creative Advertising: Ideas and techniques from the world's best campaigns*, Thames & Hudson, London

Zeff, Robbin and Aronson, Brad (1999) *Advertising on the Internet*, Wiley, Chichester

9

Place and distribution

'Place' is the fourth 'P' in the marketing mix. In this aspect of your business plan you should describe exactly how you will get your products to your customers.

If you are a retailer, restaurateur or garage proprietor, for example, then your customers will come to you. Here, your physical location will most probably be the key to success. For businesses in the manufacturing field it is more likely that you will go out to 'find' customers. In this case it will be your channels of distribution that are the vital link.

Even if you are already in business and plan to stay in the same location, it would do no harm to take this opportunity to review that decision. If you are looking for additional funds to expand your business, your location will undoubtedly be an area prospective financiers will want to explore.

LOCATION

From your market research data you should be able to come up with a list of criteria that are important to your choice of location. Here are some of the factors you need to weigh up when deciding where to locate:

1. Is there a market for the particular type of business you plan? If you're selling a product or service aimed at a particular age or socio-economic group, analyse the demographic characteristics of the area. Are there sufficient numbers of people in the relevant age and income groups? Are the numbers declining or increasing?
2. If you need skilled or specialist labour, is it readily available?
3. Are the necessary back-up services available?
4. How readily available are raw materials, components and other supplies?

5. How does the cost of premises, rates and utilities compare with other areas?
6. How accessible is the site by road, rail, air?
7. Are there any changes in the pipeline that might adversely affect trade, eg a new motorway bypassing the town, changes in transport services, closure of a large factory?
8. Are there competing businesses in the immediate neighbourhood? Will these have a beneficial or detrimental effect?
9. Is the location conducive to the creation of a favourable market image? For instance, a high fashion designer may lack credibility trading from an area famous for its heavy industry but notorious for its dirt and pollution.
10. Is the area generally regarded as low or high growth? Is the area pro-business?
11. Can you and your key employees get to the area easily and quickly?

You may even have spotted a 'role model' – a successful competitor, perhaps in another town, who appears to have got his or her location spot on.

Using these criteria you can quickly screen out most unsuitable areas. Other locations may have to be visited several times, at different hours of the day and week, before screening them out.

Chantal Coady, founder of Rococo, stated in her business plan:

'Location is crucial to the success or failure of my business, therefore I have chosen the World's End section of the King's Road, Chelsea, at the junction of Beaufort Street. This is conveniently located for the Chelsea/Knightsbridge clientele. There is a good passing trade, and a generally creative ambience on this road, and no other specialist chocolate shop in the vicinity.'

World's End was not chosen on a whim; it was the subject of a most careful study. While Chantal was confident that her 'Rococo' concept was unique, she was enough of a realist to recognise that at one level it could be seen as just another upmarket chocolate shop. As such, her shop needed its own distinctive catchment area. She drew up a map of chocolate shops situated in central London, which verified her closest competitors to be in Knightsbridge – in central London terms, another world.

A further subject of concern was the nature of the passing trade in the vicinity of the proposed World's End shop. The local residents could be polled by direct leafleting, but she decided to find out more about the passing trade by means of a questionnaire. About half the people questioned responded favourably to the 'Rococo' concept.

When writing up this element of your business plan keep these points in mind:

1. Almost every benefit has a cost associated with it. This is particularly true of location. Make sure that you carefully evaluate the cost of each

prospective location against the expected benefits. A saving of a couple of hundred pounds a month in rent may result in thousands of pounds of lost sales. On the other hand, don't choose a high-rent location unless you are convinced that it will result in higher profits. Higher costs do not necessarily mean greater benefits.

2. Choose the location with the business in mind. Don't start with the location as a 'given'. You may think it makes sense to put a bookshop in an unused portion of a friend's music shop since the marginal cost of the space is zero. The problem with this approach is that you force the business into a location that may or may not be adequate. If the business is 'given' (ie already decided upon), then the location should not also be given. You should choose the best location (ie the one that yields the most profit) for the business. 'Free' locations can end up being very expensive if the business is not an appropriate one.

   On the other hand, if you have a 'given' location, you should try to find the right business for the location. The business should not also be predetermined. What business provides the highest and best use of the location?

   Andrew Purves assessed 15 different locations in central London before deciding on a Tottenham Court Road site for his new 'high-end contemporary furniture' store. It was critical to get a site in London because furniture is not a frequently bought item, and outside London the choice of merchandise is limited. To be noticed, a new furniture store has to be in an area well known for furniture trading. The site was directly opposite Heals and Habitat, which he perceived as the most likely competitors for his target customers. For Andrew, the advantage was that 'we won't have to advertise to attract our customers, Heals opposite us will already be doing that for us'.

3. When you write your business plan as a financing tool, you often may not have the specific business location selected prior to completion of the business plan. This is fine, since there is no point in wasting time deciding on a location until you know you will have the money to start the business. Besides, even if you do select a location before obtaining the money, it is very possible that the location will already be gone by the time you get through the loan application process and have the business firm enough to sign a lease or purchase agreement. Another consideration is that you may wear out your welcome with an estate agent if you make a habit of withdrawing from deals at the last minute, due to lack of funds.

   It will suffice if you are able to explain exactly what type of location you will be acquiring. Knowing this, you will be able to make a good attempt at cost and sales estimates, even though the specific location has yet to be determined.

PREMISES

In your business plan you will need to address these issues with respect to premises:

1. Can the premises you want be used for your intended business? The main categories of 'use' are retail, office, light industrial, general industrial and special categories. If your business falls into a different category from that of a previous occupant you may have to apply to the local authority for a 'change of use'.

    An unhappy illustration of this came from a West Country builder who bought a food shop with living accommodation above. His intention was to sell paint and decorative products below and house his family above. Within three months of launching his venture he was advised that as his shop stock was highly flammable, the house would need fire retardant floors, ceilings and doors – at a cost of £20,000, even doing the work himself. The business was effectively killed off before it started.

    There are many regulations concerning the use of business premises. You should contact the Health & Safety Executive to ensure that whatever you plan to do is allowed. Two useful leaflets to refer to are PLM54 and INDG220, available from:

    Health & Safety Executive (www.hse.gov.ulc) Tel: 01787 881165

2. Will you be making any structural alterations? If so, planning permission may be needed and building regulations must be complied with. Both take time and should be allowed for in your cash-flow projections.
3. Are the premises the appropriate size? It is always difficult to calculate just how much space you'll require, since your initial preoccupation is probably just surviving. Generally, you won't want to use valuable cash to acquire unnecessarily large premises. However, if you make it past the starting post you will inevitably grow, and if you haven't room to expand, you'll have to begin looking for premises all over again. This can be expensive, not to say disruptive.

    Equinox, whose founder attended a Cranfield enterprise programme, got over this problem by renting a Beehive unit from English Industrial Estates. These units are ready to use with all services connected and are available on quarterly agreements. Equinox started in a 500-square-foot unit, expanded into next door to make 1,000 square feet of space, and at the start of its third year moved over the road into 3,000 square feet. Removal costs and disruption were thus kept to a minimum.

    One other possible solution is to take larger premises than you initially require and sublet the surplus accommodation on a short-term lease (provided the landlord agrees). If this isn't possible, it's more prudent to think small and gauge your requirements by where your business plan suggests you'll be in two or three years' time.

To calculate your space requirements, prepare a layout that indicates the ideal position for the equipment you will need, allowing adequate circulation space. Shops require counters, display stands, refrigeration units, etc. In a factory, machinery may need careful positioning and you may also have to consider in great detail the safe positioning of electricity cables, waste pipes, air extractors, etc.

Make cut-out scale models of the various items and lay these on scaled drawings of different-sized premises – 400 square feet, 1,000 square feet, etc.

By a process of trial and error you should arrive at an arrangement that is flexible, easy to operate, pleasant to look at, accessible for mainte-nance, and comfortable for both staff and customers. Only now can you calculate the likely cost of premises to include in your business plan.

Andrew Purves's new shop was a ground- and basement-floor property, some 2,000 square feet in all, at only £19 per square foot, directly opposite Heals. Within 14 months of its opening, a larger shop unit sized 7,000 square feet became available two doors down from his current site and with the advantage of corner shop visibility. With Sunday trading about to become legal, Andrew rented the additional store, clearly dividing the two stores between furniture and 'small ticket' gift items. Within three years Andrew had a successful and profitable double store and was offered a newly refurbished store sized 20,000 square feet some 500 yards further down Tottenham Court Road — on the same side as Heals. At a time when many experts were claiming that 'the future of shopping is online', Andrew bravely decided to relocate, while still investing in his mail-order and Web site business.

4. Will the premises conform with existing fire, health and safety regulations? The Health & Safety at Work Act (1974), the Factories Act (1961), the Offices, Shops & Railway Premises Act (1963) and the Fire Precautions Act (1971) set out the conditions under which most workers, including the self-employed and members of the public at large, can be present. (The Health & Safety Commission (www.hse.gov.aboutus/hsc/; tel: 01787 881165) can advise).

5. If you plan to work from home, have you checked that you are not prohib-ited from doing so by the house deeds, or whether your type of activity is likely to irritate the neighbours? This route into business is much in favour with sources of debt finance as it is seen to lower the risks during the vulnerable start-up period. Venture capitalists, on the other hand, would probably see it as a sign of 'thinking too small' and steer clear of the proposition. Nevertheless, working from home can make sound sense.

For example, Peter Robertson, aged 20, who founded Road Runner Despatch, started out running his business as a very domestic affair operated from his home in

Brightlingsea, Essex. His mother answered the telephone and frequently his father used the family car to make collections. Within two years he was employing 10 full-time motorcycle riders. Only at this stage did Robertson put together a plan, which involved raising £100,000 capital, to open an office on a central site, complete with a state-of-the-art radio-telephone system.

6. Will you lease or buy? Purchasing premises outright frequently makes sense for an established, viable business as a means of increasing its asset base. But for a start-up, interest and repayments on the borrowings will usually be more than the rental payments. But leasing itself can be a trap; eg a lease rental of £5,000 a year may seem preferable to a freehold purchase of say £50,000. But remember, as the law currently stands, if you sign and give a personal guarantee on a new 21-year lease (which you will be asked to do), you will remain personally responsible for payments over the whole life of the lease. Landlords are as reluctant to allow change in guarantors as they are to accept small business covenants. You could then be committing yourself, in these circumstances, to a minimum £105,000 outlay! Some financiers feel that your business idea should be capable of making more profit than the return you could expect from property. On this basis you should put the capital to be raised into 'useful' assets such as plant, equipment, stocks, etc.

However, some believe that if you intend to spend any money on converting or improving the premises, doing so to leased property is simply improving the landlord's investment and wasting your (their) money. You may even be charged extra rent for the improvements, unless you ensure that tenant improvements are excluded from the rent reviews.

In any event, your backers will want to see a lease long enough to see your business firmly established and secure enough to allow you to stay on if it is essential to the survival of your business. Starting up a restaurant in short-lease premises, for example, might be a poor investment proposition, but, as Bob Payton proved (page 39), it might actually be a sensible way to test your business at minimum risk. The ideal situation, which can sometimes be obtained when landlords are in difficulties, would be to negotiate a short lease (say 1–2 years) with an option to renew on expiry. All leases in Singapore and Malaysia are for 2 years, with options to renew at prevailing rates, which might seem much more helpful to encourage new business start-ups. It may be best for you to brief a surveyor to help you in your search and negotiation (their charge is normally 1 per cent, with payment only by result).

7. If appropriate, you could consider locating in a sympathetic and supportive environment. For example, universities and colleges often have a Science Park on campus, with premises and starter units for high-tech ventures. Enterprise agencies often have offices, workshops and small industrial units attached. In these situations you may have access to a

telex, fax, computer, accounting service and business advice, on a pay-as-you-use basis. This would probably be viewed as a plus point by any prospective financial backer.

8. What opening/works hours do you plan to keep, and why? Many new retailers survive by working very long hours; be careful with many of the new shopping 'malls', where hours of opening are strictly controlled, thereby preventing you 'being different' by having unusual operating hours.

CHANNELS OF DISTRIBUTION

If your customers don't come to you, then you have the following options in getting your product or service to them. Your business plan should explain which you have chosen and why.

- *Retail stores.* This general name covers the great range of outlets from the corner shop to Harrods. Some offer speciality goods such as hi-fi equipment, where the customer expects professional help from the staff. Others, such as Marks & Spencer and Tesco, are mostly self-service, with customers making up their own mind on choice of product.
- *Wholesalers.* The pattern of wholesale distribution has changed out of all recognition over the past two decades. It is still an extremely important channel where physical distribution, stock holding, finance and breaking bulk are still profitable functions.
- *Cash and carry.* This slightly confusing route has replaced the traditional wholesaler as a source of supply for smaller retailers. In return for your paying cash and picking up the goods yourself, the 'wholesaler' shares part of his or her profit margin with you. The attraction for the wholesaler is improved cash flow and for the retailer a bigger margin and a wide product range. Hypermarkets and discount stores also fit somewhere between the manufacturer and the marketplace.
- *Mail order.* This specialised technique provides a direct channel to the customer, and is an increasingly popular route for new small businesses.

Paul Howcroft, who built his clothing 'casuals with toughness and durability' business, Rohan, from modest beginnings when he had just £60 in the bank, to a £7 million business in less than a decade, puts much of his success down to changing distribution channels. For the first two years most of his sales were to retail shops, which either wouldn't take enough produce or didn't pay up when they did. He set up his mail-order branch, using his box of enquiries and letters built up over the years as a mailing list. He moved a year's sales in two months, getting all the cash in up front.

Other direct from 'producer to customer' channels include:

▮ *Internet.* There is no really accurate way of measuring the number of people who use the Internet, but pulling together the facts from various quarters shows a world total in excess of 200 million. Online sales in Britain alone are estimated at £10 billion in 2001. Everything from shares and books, to cigar humidors and flowers can be bought at the click of a mouse. In just three years the Oxford-based Internet Bookshop grew from start-up to a stock market value of £8 million. Seattle-based Amazon Co, which started at about the same time as the Oxford firm, was worth over £300 million within the same time period.

A Cornish company won a £150,000 order from South Africa for high-tech equipment just over 12 months after it was established. Liberty means freedom but not for thousands of criminals in an African prison soon to be secured by a locking system supplied by Liberty Control Networks. David and Sharon Parker established their firm just over a year ago at St Austell, in mid-Cornwall, and gained the big order in South Africa via their Web site. A prison management team thousands of miles away was 'surfing the Net' to find someone who could supply a state-of-the-art jail locking system. Liberty Control Networks was one of four companies to respond to the challenge, with the Parkers providing the best solution. Mr Parker said: 'As with any new company, long hours are expected, and at about 11.30 pm one Friday evening in January, I finished work by checking my e-mails before going to bed. I found this enquiry from South Africa. They were asking for 500 of this, 100 of that and so on. Needless to say, I didn't go to bed but put together our proposal.' Burning the midnight oil produced a bumper dividend, resulting in the first of what hopefully will be a series of orders, each in excess of £150,000.

   – *Search engines.* The key to selling on the Internet is to have an effective site and let people know how to find it. One fact that no Internet business should be unaware of is how deeply dissatisfied most people are with their online experiences. A recent study by BCG (Boston Consulting Group) found that 65 per cent of all virtual 'shopping carts' are abandoned. When did you last see a real shopping cart abandoned (except maybe outside a block of flats where someone had dumped it after a particularly heavy shopping trip)? Getting the site right means making it attractive, easy to use, quick to open and simple to navigate. Major turn-offs include complicated registration procedures and too many advertisements.

   Any business Web site should be registered with as many search engines as possible so that people can quickly and easily find a product or service. A search engine is a type of software index agent that searches registered sites and provides results based on the words a person keys in.

   Search engines are designed to 'crawl' the Internet, moving from site to site. When visiting a site, they record the text of every page and then continue to visit any external links. Search engines are a quick and easy way to find information on the Internet. For this reason, it is worth spending a little to ensure you are accessible.

Registering your site with search engines can be done in two ways:

- Your Internet service provider will sometimes offer (for a fee) registration with a set number of search engines. This means you do not have to worry about contacting hundreds of search engines to register; it also means you are free to focus on other ways to promote your site.
- Register your site yourself. Visit www.altavista.co.uk, www.excite. co.uk, www.hotbot.lycos.com and www.uk.yahoo.com; these are some of the most common places where you can register. You should fill in the online form for the main page of your Web site, but be aware that registering in this way can be rather time-consuming.

Ensure that your site is seen by search engines. Before you think about registering your site, you should ensure that you have included the appropriate text and strategies to enable the engines to best identify you. These strategies are targeted towards the way in which search engines work:

- *Keywords* – because each search engine looks at different elements of your site pages, try to ensure that you use keywords in the title of your document, making it as descriptive as possible.
- *Meta tags* – the <Meta> tag is often found at the top of an HTML document between the </title> and the </head> tag. It has many uses, but one of the most common is the client-pull function, which can be used to either reload or redirect pages after a specified amount of time (you can also use the tag to convey information about your document that can't be found anywhere within it).

Tags allow you to submit more details to the search engine about your Web site, yet are not visible to the reader. While not all search engines use these tags, the act of adding them to your pages will make them more accessible to the search engines that do use them.

Other factors to consider include:

- Do you have the time to register with the search engines yourself? If not, ask your Internet service provider how much it charges for this service and how many engines it will register you with.
- Many search engines take time to list a site, so if you are having trouble finding your site listed, you should re-submit your URL to the search engines that do not have your listing. It can take more than one submission to get the best results.

The best pages to submit are your major topic pages or pages that describe a specific product or service that you are providing.

- *Door-to-door selling*. Traditionally used by vacuum cleaner distributors and encyclopaedia companies, this is now used by insurance companies, cavity-wall insulation firms, double-glazing firms and others. Many use hard-sell techniques, giving door-to-door selling a bad name. However, Avon Cosmetics has managed to sell successfully door-to-door without attracting the stigma of unethical selling practices.
- *Party plan selling*. This is a variation on door-to-door selling that is on the increase, with new party plan ideas arriving from the United States. Agents enrolled by the company invite their friends to a get-together where the products are demonstrated and orders are invited. The agent gets a commission. Party plan has worked very well for Avon and other firms that sell this way.

  On a more modest scale, one man turned his hobby of making pine bookcases and spice racks into a profitable business by getting his wife to invite neighbours for coffee mornings where his wares were prominently displayed.
- *Telephone selling*. This too can be a way of moving goods in one single step, from 'maker' to consumer. Few products can be sold easily in this way; however, repeat business is often secured via the phone.

Selecting distribution channels

These are the factors you should consider when choosing channels of distribution for your particular business:

1. *Does it meet your customers' needs?* You have to find out how your customers expect their product or service to be delivered to them and why they need that particular route.

   TWS, a window systems manufacturer, wanted to increase its sales. A customer survey was commissioned which revealed that 80 per cent of TWS customers did not have forklift trucks, resulting in manual offloading of deliveries by customer tradesmen. The TWS solution was to order delivery vehicles, complete with their own fork-lift, facilitating unloading at customer premises in 15 minutes instead of 2 hours, giving faster turnaround time and requiring no customer assistance. This, in turn, did not waste the valuable time of customer tradesmen and encouraged extra orders from existing TWS customers as well as opening up new customer possibilities.

2. *Will the product itself survive?* Fresh vegetables, for example, need to be moved quickly from where they are grown to where they are consumed.

3. *Can you sell enough this way?* 'Enough' is how much you *want* to sell.

Atrium, a £5 million annual turnover company whose executives attended Cranfield's Business Growth Programme, uses an actively managed Web site to have periodic sales. The company sells modern furniture, mostly via architects who have been retained to build or refurbish business premises. Atrium has products on display in its London showroom, and from time to time these have to be sold off to make way for new designs. But having hundreds of people milling around looking for bargains in a sale is not quite the atmosphere that is conducive to an architect and his or her client reviewing plans for a new project.

So, 'sale' products are displayed and sold on Atrium's Web site saleroom. 'Enough' products are sold with no disruption to the normal showroom activity.

4. *Is it compatible with your image?* If you are selling a luxury product, then door-to-door selling may spoil the impression you are trying to create in the rest of your marketing effort.

5. *How do your competitors distribute?* If they have been around for a while and are obviously successful, it is well worth looking at how your competitors distribute and using that knowledge to your advantage.

6. *Will the channel be cost-effective?* A small manufacturer may not find it cost-effective to sell to retailers west of Bristol because the direct 'drop' size – that is, the load per order – is too small to be worthwhile.

7. *Will the mark-up be enough?* If your product cannot bear at least a 100 per cent mark-up, then it is unlikely that you will be able to sell it through department stores. Your distribution channel has to be able to make a profit from selling your product too.

8. *Push–pull.* Moving a product through a distribution channel calls for two sorts of selling activity. 'Push' is the name given to selling your product in, for example, a shop. 'Pull' is the effort that you carry out on the shop's behalf to help it to sell your product out of that shop. That pull may be caused by your national advertising, a merchandising activity or the uniqueness of your product. You need to know how much push and pull are needed for the channel you are considering. If you are not geared up to help retailers to sell your product, and they need that help, then this could be a poor channel.

Historical Connections, a new company established to market educational wall charts, faced conflicting distribution issues. Its products had to be securely and economically packed in such a way that the charts could be unrolled, crease free, by the end user; at the same time the product had to occupy an acceptable amount of shelf space in a crowded gift shop, for example.

A cardboard tube was the obvious answer to these problems; however, that rendered the true 'value' of the product invisible to shoppers. This problem was overcome by providing retailers with a framed chart, positioned by Historical Connections' salespeople, when the account was opened.

This simple 'point of sale' display was an elegant and cost-effective 'pull'.

9. *Physical distribution*. The way in which you have to move your product to your end customer is also an important factor to weigh up when choosing a channel. As well as such factors as the cost of carriage, you will also have to decide about packaging materials. As a rough rule of thumb, the more stages in the distribution channel, the more robust and expensive your packaging will have to be.

10. *Cash flow*. Not all channels of distribution settle their bills promptly. Mail-order customers, for example, will pay in advance, but retailers can take up to 90 days or more. You need to take account of this settlement period in your cash-flow forecast.

WORKSHEET FOR ASSIGNMENT 9: PLACE AND DISTRIBUTION

1. What type and size of premises are required for your business?
2. Describe the location.
3. Why do you need this type of premises and location? What competitive advantage does it give you?
4. If freehold:
   Value   _____
   Mortgage outstanding   _____
   Monthly repayments   _____
   Mortgage with whom   _____
5. If leasehold:
   Unexpired period of lease   _____
   Is there an option to renew? _____
   Present rent payment   _____
   Date of rent payment   _____
   Date of next rent review   _____
6. What rates are payable on your business premises?
7. What are the insurance details?
   Amount   _____
   Premium   _____
8. Are these premises adequate for your future needs? If not, what plans do you have?
9. If you have not found your premises yet, what plans do you have to find them?
10. What channels of distribution are used in your field; which do you plan to use and why?

SUGGESTED FURTHER READING

Purves & Purves, Case History, Parts A, B, C & D, Start-Up and Expansion, video and teaching note (Reference: 500-031-1), available from the European Case Clearing House, Cranfield, Beds MK43 0AL; tel: 01234 750903; fax: 01234 751125; Web site: www.ecch.cranfield.ac.uk; e-mail: ecch@cranfield.ac.uk

Bird, Drayton (2000) *Commonsense Direct Marketing*, 4th edn, Kogan Page, London

Planning IT and Communications (ICT) as a vital element of your overall business strategy in the era of convergence

by Chris Windley

About the author:

Chris is the Chairman and CEO of Comz4biz, a national company established in 2002 to provide effective ICT advice and solutions to start-ups and SME's.

As an investor and business angel to a number of high-tech companies Chris has built and seen many business plans.

About Comz4biz:

Comz4biz believes that in the era of convergence it is necessary to look at ICT in an overall rather than an isolated way.

Since the Directors of start-ups and SME's are often not technical advice should be given in plain English.

ICT Planning as part of the overall business plan

ICT and the Internet are vital tools in all areas of the business, from carrying out market and competitive research, setting pricing, marketing and distribution strategies and building financial plans to controlling the business once up and running.

Although ICT is the foundation of a business it is often not given the level of attention that it deserves. In a typical SME the ICT role is given to one of the Directors, for example the Financial Director or, in some cases, whoever will take it.

Comz4biz takes clients overall business plans and strategies and builds an ICT strategy to fit them.

What you need to do

The first thing you need is a business strategy and someone that can and will articulate it.

Secondly you either need to have the required records or allow us to compile them. The effort involved in providing this information is more than outweighed by the benefits that will be achieved.

You should avoid making decisions on isolated elements of the system without considering the overall objectives.

Viewing ICT strategically

ICT systems that are being built or upgraded now are happening in the era of convergence.

This is a time when all types of communications, voice, data and video will run over a common network or infrastructure – the Internet Protocol (I.P.) network – which should not be confused with The Internet. It is also a time when applications should connect seamlessly over this common network.

Finally, it is a time when telephone numbers and databases are merging together over this network.

It is no longer appropriate to think about ICT components, like telephone systems, in an isolated way with separate departments or people controlling them.

ICT Audits

When building a converged ICT system it is vital to have a robust, suitably performing network and also to understand the capabilities of the devices attached to the network such as, for example, the PC's and servers.

We are in a time where massive cost savings can be made on, for example, line rentals, call costs, maintenance, support and consumables. This is a result of deregulation, standardization and innovation.

Over time companies will have redundant system components and standards that were set early on will have started to break down.

The savings can be used to reduce initial and ongoing capital expenditure and yet still acquire systems that meet the business's objectives.

Mobility and work/life balance

Directors of SME's are usually very mobile and yet need to be in control of the business. They work long hours yet need to have some sort of work/life balance

Therefore access to central systems while out on the road or while working from home is vital.

The technology is available but it needs to be planned in to the system design.

Comz4biz Process

We understand the business; audit the existing ICT; produce a plan for change; manage and implement these changes and monitor and review regularly.

Whilst doing this we are looking at the overall ICT picture and thinking in a converged way.

Conclusion

We believe that ICT is a vital part of the start-up business plan and deserves a section which shows how ICT will assist in achieving the overall business objectives.

We also believe that existing companies should review their ICT in a strategic way. Systems should support mobility and the achievement of a work/life balance.

We have proven time and time again that companies can acquire new ICT systems, that meet their business objectives, at no effective cost to the business.

What is required is a plan, some information and an open mind.

Phase 4

Operations

10

The operations plan

Operations is the general name given to all the activities required to implement strategy. So, for example, once you have decided what to sell, to whom and at what price, you may still need to find someone to make your product, sell it and deliver it. You may also need to take out insurance, draw up contracts of employment, print stationery and recruit staff, for example.

Of necessity, the emphasis you put on each element of this assignment will depend entirely on the nature of your business.

Your business plan need not show the complete detail as to how every operational activity will be implemented. Clearly, you and your colleagues will need to know, but for the business plan it is sufficient to show that you have taken account of the principal matters that concern your venture, and have a workable solution in hand.

The following are some of the most important operational issues to be addressed in your business plan.

SELLING AND SALES MANAGEMENT

Anyone considering backing your business will look long and hard at how you plan to sell. Unbelievably, it is an area often dismissed in a couple of lines in a business plan. That error alone is enough to turn off most investors. Your business plan should provide answers to these questions:

■ Who will conduct the selling for your business, and have they been professionally trained to sell?

Howard Fabian's business was designing and selling greetings cards. His main market was London and the South-East, where there were 120 important shops to be sold to. He planned to sell to these accounts himself. This meant visiting all the outlets once at the outset. He could make four to five calls a day, so it would take between four and five weeks to cover the ground. After that he would visit the most important 30 every month, the next 30 every two months, and he would phone or visit the remainder from time to time, and send samples of new designs in the hope of encouraging them to order. While on an enterprise programme at Cranfield he took a professional selling skills course.

Outside London and the South-East, Howard proposed to appoint agents, based in the principal provincial cities. To recruit these he planned to use the trade press and the Manufacturers Agents Register. Each appointment would be made on a three-month trial basis, and he had an agency contract explaining this business relationship drawn up. He proposed to set each agent a performance target based on the population in this catchment area. Sales within 25 per cent of target would be acceptable; outside that figure he would review the agent's contract.

Initially he was looking for 10 agents, whom he would visit and go out with once a quarter.

As selling time in a shop was short, it was important that he and his agents should have a minimum set agenda of points to cover, and a sales presenter to show the range quickly and easily from the standing position.

▪ **What selling methods will you employ? For example, telephone selling, cold calling, following up leads from mailshots and advertising, etc.**

When Graham Davy started his Equinox designer furniture business, his principal potential customers were furniture retailers. This was too large and widespread a target audience to sell to without some specific focus.

First, he boxed in an area bounded by Bristol, London and St Albans – effectively the wedge between the M4 and M40 motorways. He felt this was a large enough area of affluent users to support his modest production capacity. From desk research he identified the names and addresses of 250 prospective customers. He mailed his brochure to every one of these and then called on the 40 or so most likely firms. In the meantime his partner telephoned the remaining firms to gauge reaction and see if they were 'worth' visiting.

In the first six months they got five customers, two of which had given repeat business and were prepared to place orders by phone.

The next year they attended an exhibition, which resulted in 25 potential customers completing enquiry slips on their stand. These were followed up and a further six customers were secured. By the third year, Equinox had 23 customers, all of which had placed repeat business.

▪ **If you plan to sell to retailers, what point-of-sale material will you use to attract purchasers?**
▪ **Who will direct, monitor and control your sales effort and what experience/ skills do they have?**
▪ **What sales volume and activity targets, such as calls per day, etc, have you set for each salesperson or selling method?**
▪ **What selling aids such as leaflets, brochures, videos, technical back-up, etc, will you provide? Include also any details on in-house sales support, such as technical service, telesales, etc.**

■ How do you plan to impart full 'product' knowledge to your sales team?

Paul Howcroft, who took his Rohan clothing company from a standing start to a £7 million business within a decade, put much of that success down to the fact that all his staff were trained so that they could talk sensibly about the products with any of their 300,000 customers.

■ What objections do you anticipate from prospective customers, and what arguments do you have to meet these?

■ Who exactly makes the buying decision, and which other people can influence that decision?

■ How long is the process from becoming aware of your product or service to making the buying decision, receiving the product or service and finally paying for it?

This will have an important bearing on your cash flow and initial sales forecast, as the examples that follow will illustrate.

Medsoft was set up to sell dedicated microcomputer systems to hospital consultants. The business concept grew out of a chance meeting at a computer exhibition between Richard Kensall, then a successful department store owner and slightly disillusioned computer dealer, and an up-and-coming young doctor with a love of computers.

The doctor's problem was that he had too large a volume of patient data to classify and analyse. Some 16,000 consultants had a need to record details on 35 million patient attendances and 5 million in-patients per annum. For each patient a record had to be generated containing all details concerning the patient, his or her clinical history and indications, clinical tests, results, diagnoses, operations, complications and follow-up care. In 1980, almost all such patient records were generated and maintained manually.

So, for Medsoft the market opportunity was substantial and with some further development their product range was proven. The only problem was the time taken to get a decision made as to whether to buy or not, and then to get the cash in.

Capital investment decisions such as this follow a long and complex procedure in the UK hospital service. From finding a consultant who wants to buy, to encouraging him or her to write out a project proposal, getting that proposal through the hospital committee, on to endorsement from the district management team and then finally to approval by the Regional Scientific Officer, could take up to nine months. Even when over all these hurdles, a project could fail if the region had insufficient funds to pay for all the properly approved proposals. To add insult to injury, under these circumstances all proposals start again at the bottom of the pile.

With this process in mind, Medsoft's business plan had to anticipate zero sales revenue for the first nine months at least, and only modest sums thereafter until well into the second year. Their resultant cash-flow forecast looked very sick indeed over this period, but in their business plan they were able to provide a satisfactory argument for this situation occurring.

Fortunately, while investigating the decision-making process they uncovered four types of potential customer who could 'buy' within six months. Newly appointed hospital consultants were unofficially awarded £30,000 for capital expenditure on appointment; some hospitals had their own trust funds; some consultants had close ties with pharmaceutical companies who would support their 'pet' projects; and some consultants had experience of getting government grants from such organisations as the RDA (Regional Development Authority). These people were to be the focus of all sales effort for the first six months of Medsoft's life.

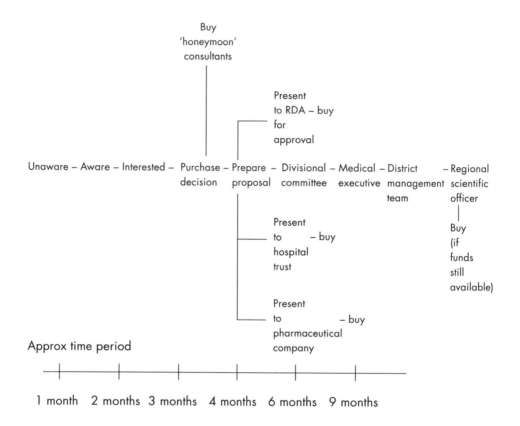

Figure 4.1 Medsoft decision-making process

▮ What incentives are there for people to meet targets and how will you motivate them to do so?
▮ What value of orders are currently on hand, or are expected in the immediate future, and from whom?
▮ What procedures do you have for handling customer complaints?

MANUFACTURING

If your business involves making or constructing products, then you should address the following issues in the business plan:

▪ Will you make the product yourself, or buy in either ready to sell, or as components for assembly? One Cranfield graduate enterprise programme had these examples of different types of operation:

Jenny Row designed her knitwear herself, but had it made up by outworkers. In this way she could expand or contract output quickly, paying only the extra cost of materials and production, for more orders. It also left her free to design new products to add to her existing range.

Tim Brown sold computer systems tailor-made to carry out solicitors' conveyancing work. He commissioned software writers to prepare the programs, bought in computers from the manufacturer and selected a range of printers to suit individual customers' requirements. His end product was a total system, which he bought in 'kit' parts from his various sub-contractors. Apart from IBM and a handful of giants, no one company could produce all these elements in-house.

Graham Davy designed and manufactured his own range of furniture. He rented a Beehive workshop and bought in cutting, turning and polishing tools, and a finish spraying room. He bought in wood, worked on it himself, producing batches of three or four of each design. The equipment needed for design and prototype work was also sufficient for small-batch production.

▪ You should also explain why you have chosen your manufacturing route. Describe the manufacturing process to be used, and if appropriate explain how your principal competitors go about their manufacturing.

Jon Newall's company Escargot Anglais Ltd was set up to breed and market edible snails in the UK. The production system he adopted had already been used with some considerable success at one of the world's largest snail ranches in California. The stages of production are as follows:

1. *Commencing production*. Breeding snails will be fed on a compound with the essential requirements of a low copper content (below 13–14 mg/kg) and no anticoccidiostat, but with an appropriate calcium content for good shell disposition.
2. *Growing young snails*. These are grown in 25-litre buckets in batches of 150.
3. *Fattening and finishing*. At three months the snails will have attained market weight. They are then processed and frozen on site. For this, boiling and freezing equipment is needed, costing around £2,500 per line packaging. Finally, snails will be packaged in batches of six in a moulded aluminium foil dish, covered in shrink-wrap, with promotional material on the front and recipes on the back. Equipment for packaging will cost around £2,000.

▪ What plant and equipment will you need and what output limits will they have (see Table 4.1)?
▪ Provide a rough sketch of the layout of your manufacturing unit, showing the overall size of facility needed, the positioning of equipment, etc, and the path of materials and finished goods.
▪ What engineering support, if any, will you need?
▪ How will you monitor and control quality?

Table 4.1 Example showing goods needed, their purpose and cost

Plant/ equipment	Process (what does it do?)	Maximum volume	Cost	Do you already own it?

There are a number of well-regarded quality standards that may help you monitor and control your quality. The BS/ISO 9000 series are perhaps the best-known standards. They can ensure that your operating procedure will deliver a consistent and acceptable standard of products or services. If you are supplying to large firms they may insist on your meeting one of these quality standards, or on 'auditing' your premises to satisfy themselves.

The British Standards Institution (389 Chiswick High Road, London W4 4AL; tel: 020 8996 9000; fax: 020 8996 7400; Web site: www.bsi-global.com) can provide details of these standards.

A number of commercial organisations will provide user-friendly guidelines and systems to help you reach the necessary standard. Searching the Web using key words such as 'quality standards' (or 'measurement') will bring you some useful sites.

MATERIALS AND SOURCES OF SUPPLY

Your business plan should also explain what bought-in materials you require, who you will buy them from, and how much they will cost.

To return to Escargot Anglais Ltd: Jon Newall explained in his business plan how he chose his main source of supply:

'The breeding snails were at first fed on vegetable waste obtained free in abundance from local greengrocers. While at first this seemed a very attractive proposition which I have seen work well in France and elsewhere, local supplies were unsatisfactory. The high water content led to difficulties in disposing of waste matter, but, most importantly, residual pesticides, particularly in the more succulent leafy matter, led to a high snail fatality rate.

'After much experimenting I found a chicken feed, "Pauls Traditional 18", that has all the essential ingredients. It can be bought from the local wholesaler for £4.60 per 25-kilogram bag. My original budgets were based on the assumption that free vegetable waste would be used; this is no longer valid and all feeding stuffs will have to be bought in. This will increase costs by about £7,000 per annum and so reduce gross profits. However, apart from capital expenditure on boiling, freezing and packaging equipment (total £4,500), the only non-labour cost apart from feeding stuffs is for packaging materials, butter and garlic. These will be bought in, locally at first; however, I am looking at the possibility of purchasing cheap EEC butter surplus.'

■ What major items of bought-in materials or services will you require?
■ Who could supply those and what are the terms and conditions of sale?
■ Why have you chosen your supplier(s)?

Keep stock cards so that you can identify fast- and slow-moving stock.

BUYING ONLINE

Businesses can save money by buying online – it means they can cast their nets wider, buying from abroad if necessary. Many products and services can already be bought online and it seems likely that most standard company requirements will soon be available online. It may save you time and money, though you have to balance lower prices against the extra hassle of dealing with someone you do not know. It may even be worth running a credit check on your supplier.

Business-to-business e-commerce is one of the fastest-growing areas. Supplies of non-production equipment – from paper clips to furniture – are moving online so fast that the Web may quickly become the standard purchase channel for many categories of goods. Suppliers are already geared up for direct delivery – it is not difficult to add a Web 'front end' to take orders. From the customer's point of view, the Web is an efficient way of choosing from a large catalogue. It combines the visual advantage of a print catalogue (easy to choose – you are unlikely to make a mistake) with the speed of a phone or fax. You can buy from an exclusively Internet-based company or from the e-commerce wing of an established name, as brand may not be so important on the Net.

Try out suppliers with small orders at first until you have confidence in them. You will need to keep shopping around the Net in much the same way as you do already. There are now super search systems that will search out the cheapest supplier of many standard items sold on the Internet, but price is not everything. If a company's delivery or back-up service is unsatisfactory, buying cheap could be an expensive experiment.

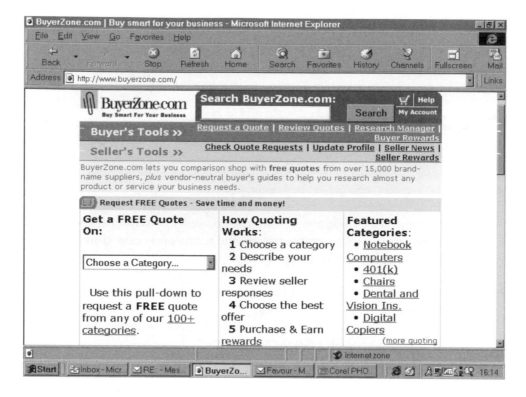

Figure 4.2 Example of an online business buyers' site

An example of an online business buyers' site is shown in Figure 4.2.

PEOPLE

People are the most important element of any business venture. However good or innovative the business idea, or competitive the strategy, absolutely nothing can get done without people.

For F International, the consultancy business, people are the business. The cost flexibility that comes from having a workforce that consists primarily of part-time freelance staff – working mothers – provides F International's key competitive advantage. It can respond to market changes without having to hire or fire large numbers.

The company's backbone consists of a pool of over a thousand freelance (hence the F) computer programmers, supplemented by a core of full-time and part-time managerial and administrative staff. This high ratio of management to staff workers underlines the degree of organisation required to run such a decentralised group, who for the most part work from home.

'The office is no more than a bit of glue that holds us together,' says Steve Shirley, who founded F International when she was 28 years old.

Your business plan should explain which people are important to your venture and should provide answers to the following questions.

■ Have you written job descriptions for each key position in your business? A summary of responsibilities should appear in your business plan.

Michael Golder, who grew the £65 million a year Kennedy Brooks business from a single restaurant in just seven years, gives each of his 4,000 employees a 'staff handbook'. This contains every detail of their duties, right down to having clean fingernails.

■ The Employment Protection (Consolidation) Act 1978 requires you to issue every employee who works more than 16 hours per week with a written statement of the main terms and conditions of their employment. Apart from being good practice to provide job descriptions, it is a legal obligation to do so, no later than 2 months after the start of their job. As well as describing the work, pay and holidays, company rules and disciplinary procedures also need to be covered.

This job description may also help should you have cause to dismiss anyone later on. Claims for unfair dismissal are currently running at a rate in excess of 100,000 per annum. Successful claims are about 12 per cent of this total, down from 17 per cent 10 years ago.

■ Are all key positions filled? If not, how do you plan to recruit and select these people?

Carolyn Lowing made this entry in her business plan to raise £120,000 for the Oriental, a Cambridge-based martial arts centre:

'Initially I shall be responsible for setting up the enterprise. Before opening the centre a part-time assistant will be taken on to help with administration and the day-to-day matters, leaving me free to concentrate on promoting the centre and attracting clients, as well as organising the first few courses and the opening event. Further part-time assistants will be employed when the workload gets such that individual posts can be justified. This stage should be reached about three months after opening.

'The first assistant will be responsible for secretarial and administrative duties as well as acting as receptionist and bar staff. These responsibilities will later be mainly administration and office duties as extra staff are taken on as reception and bar staff and for general duties.

'An outside contractor may be employed for the cleaning of the centre following this expansion in staff requirements.

'The local Cambridge paper will be a suitable place to advertise for all these appointments. I have two people in mind for my first part-time assistant, both of whom have wide, relevant experience and are available now.'

New companies traditionally recruit family and friends, as they are often assumed to be 'cheap and loyal'. Yet one person can destroy a small business. 'Expert' skills may be less important than the way people 'fit' in your organisation. So, do not recruit technicians you do not like. You may think you cannot afford a suitable expert, but while you cannot match big-company salaries, sometimes small amounts of equity shares (generally 1 or 2 per cent) can be tempting, particularly if you are building a quality company needing quality employees.

■ What wage and salary levels have you set for employees? How do these compare with those of other similar employers in the area?

■ What arrangements have you made to handle Pay As You Earn, National Insurance and pensions?

■ Health and safety at work are a legal responsibility of employers. Are you aware of the terms and conditions of the various Acts of Parliament, and their likely cost implication for your business?

■ Training, from induction to job training, are also factors to be considered at the outset, and their costs allowed for in your business plan. You may be eligible for subsidised instruction from one of the various government agencies responsible for this.

Debra Turkington, a Californian who established her business, the California Cake & Cookie Company, in Govan, Scotland, incorporated her ideas on training into her business plan. With her belief in the value of 'investing in people', Debra recognised from the outset that as the business grew, she needed to train her managers if she was to make the business run profitably:

'Never underestimate the ability and potential of your staff. If I could understand what a balance sheet meant there was no reason why they shouldn't and as a result of the training they had a much better grasp of what made the company work. That meant they could help the company to move forward more effectively.'

Debra's training programme for her young managers saw her gross margin increase. The quality of the product rose as well. What's more, the quality of the product has risen as well, with the result that her company is among the fastest growing in the West of Scotland.

■ What back-up do you have if you or any other key person is ill, or absent for any reason?

The reasons for absence can be quite obscure, as one new business founder recently discovered. He became one of the 400,000 or so people in the UK who annually receive a summons to do compulsory but unpaid jury service. The libel trial he was called to attend lasted approximately three weeks, which he remarked set him back nearly six months! He could have insured against such an event and received sufficient funds either to buy in help or to compensate for loss of profits.

■ Do you expect your employees to dress in a particular style for work, or to wear uniform?

■ How will you make it easy for employees to 'make a difference' in your business (eg reward suggestions, provide opportunities for employees to learn)?

■ Do you want non-executive directors? They are a useful addition to a young team, but they need to have relevant experience or be able to open doors and do deals. They need to be interested in you and your business and able to offer insights into how things really work in your industry.

Finally, keep personnel information on all your employees in an orderly way (eg previous employment, telephone numbers to contact in an emergency). Many companies supply personnel envelope files, including Oyez House, 16 Third Avenue, Bletchley, Milton Keynes MK1 1TE. Tel: 01908 837 1111.

LEGAL AND INSURANCE ISSUES

Every venture will have to address some legal and insurance issues. Certain insurance, such as motor insurance and employers' and public liability cover, is compulsory for all businesses and there are certain forms of insurance that are compulsory in law for specific businesses. All other forms of insurance are voluntary.

As far as your business plan is concerned, these issues will always be raised by potential backers:

■ What will your terms and conditions of sale be and are they printed on your order acceptance stationery?

> One unfortunate entrepreneur felt that his business, a management training consultancy, had got off to a good start when his first client, a major American computer company, booked him for three courses. Just three weeks prior to the first of these courses, and after he had carried out all the preparatory work and prepared relevant examples, handouts, etc, the client cancelled the order. The reason given was a change in 'policy' on training dictated by the overseas parent company.
>
> If this entrepreneur had included in his standard terms and conditions a cancellation clause, then he would have received adequate compensation. In fact, he was operating on a 'wing and a prayer', had no terms of trade, and wasn't even aware there was an industrial 'norm'. Most of his competitors charged 100 per cent cancellation fee for cancellations within three weeks, 50 per cent within six weeks, 25 per cent within eight weeks, and for earlier cancellations no charge.

■ Are your premises, equipment and stocks adequately insured? You should cover yourself against items that could 'wipe you out'. By way of illustrating the need to take professional advice in these matters, the following incident was related to the enterprise programme class at Cranfield:

> Those in charge of a newly established business, planning to expand its activities economically, sought and found a specialist supplier of second-hand reconditioned woodworking machinery – lathes, turners, bandsaws, etc. After inspecting the

machinery in Yorkshire, they arranged for it to be transported by the vendor under his own goods in transit insurance cover to their factory in the West Country.

While a particularly heavy piece was being unloaded, it fell from the transporter on to the ground immediately outside their factory, and was damaged beyond repair. Their own insurance only covered machinery inside their workshop, the vendor's only while the goods were on the transporter. The gap in between was an insurance 'no man's land', where neither party had cover. As a result, the entrepreneur lost £3,000 but learnt a lot about the value of taking professional advice.

■ Have you arranged for employers' liability cover and public liability and product liability cover?
■ If you are offering expert advice, are you protected against claims for negligence from your clients?
■ If your business is one of the hundred or so that require licensing before they can operate, what steps have you taken to obtain a licence?

WORKSHEET FOR ASSIGNMENT 10: THE OPERATIONS PLAN

Describe briefly the main operational aspects that are involved in ensuring that your strategy is successfully implemented. In particular, you should consider:

1. Who will sell for you?
2. What selling methods will they employ?
3. Will you use point-of-sale material – leaflets, brochures or videos, for example?
4. Who will manage, monitor and control your sales effort and how will they do so?
5. Describe the selling process leading from an unaware prospect to a converted client, covering identification of decision makers, overcoming objections, gaining agreement, etc.
6. Will you make your product yourself or buy it in – and why?
7. If you are making a product, describe the production process; also explain how your principal competitors go about manufacturing.
8. What plant and equipment will you need, what can it do, how much will it cost and where will you get it from?
9. What bought-in materials and/or services will you need, where will you buy them from and how much will they cost?
10. What employees will you need in your business? If they are not already recruited, how will you go about finding them?
11. What arrangements have you made for contracts of employment, job descriptions, wages and salary levels, training, payroll processing, etc?

12. What back-up do you have if you or any other key staff are absent?
13. Have you examined any likely legal issues that might affect your venture, such as conditions of sale?
14. Have you examined any likely insurance issues that might affect your venture, such as employers', public or product liability cover, or premises, equipment and stock insurance?

SUGGESTED FURTHER READING

De Winter, Chris (2000) *30 Minutes to Improve Telesales Techniques*, Kogan Page, London
Elliott, Alan (2000) *Getting Started in Internet Auctions*, Wiley, Chichester
Waters, Donald (1999) *Operations Management*, Kogan Page, London

Phase 5

Forecasting results

Introduction

Once you have formulated a basic or new strategy for your business, you will have to make some forecast of the likely results of your endeavours. These projections are essential to show how much cash you will need and how much profit you could make, and to chart a safe financial strategy. This is the part of your business plan of greatest interest to potential investors and lenders.

11

The sales forecast

'The precision of numbers often bears no relation to the facts.'

Denis Healey, former Chancellor of the Exchequer

The sales forecast is perhaps the most important set of numbers to come out of the business planning process. How much stock to hold, how many staff to employ, how much material to buy, are all decisions that hinge on the sales forecast. These sales figures are also are used to predict the cash-flow forecast and hence the funding requirements of the business.

These projections are also the key to valuing the business, so they will determine whether or not bankers will lend and investors invest. Furthermore, they will give some guidance as to how much of an enterprise investors expect in exchange for funding.

Naturally enough, potential backers do not accept a sales forecast unchallenged as, in their experience, new ventures nearly always miss the target by a wide margin.

The Millennium Dome

How could a forecast of 12 million visitors have been made for the number of visitors to the Millennium Dome in Greenwich?

Pierre-Yves Gerbeau, the French MBA brought in to stabilise the situation, explained:

'Few business plans show you can break even in Year 1. Yet the forecast was based on costs. How many visitors do we need to balance the books, was the question asked? The answer was 12 million! I am convinced now, half-way through the year, that we can reach 6 million. But with a 2 per cent of turnover marketing budget only (compared with an 8–12 per cent average in the attractions industry), don't shoot the Frenchman if we don't make it!'

While forecasts may turn out to be wrong, it is important to demonstrate in your business plan that you have thought through the factors that will have impact on performance. You should also show how you can deliver satisfactory results even when many of these factors may be working against you. Backers will be measuring the downside risk to evaluate the worst scenario and its likely effects, as well as looking towards an ultimate exit route.

Here are some guidelines to help you make an initial sales forecast:

▪ Check how others have fared. Your overall projections will have to be believable. Most lenders and investors will have an extensive experience of similar business proposals. Unlike yourself, they will have the benefit of hindsight, and are able to look back several years at other ventures they have backed to see how they fared in practice compared with the ventures' initial forecasts. You could gather some useful knowledge on similar businesses yourself by researching filed company accounts and trade magazines, or by talking with the founders of such ventures who will not be your direct competitors.

Scoops

Edmund Bradley estimated that in its first year of trading, Scoops would generate £50,000 worth of sweet sales. The projection was based upon observation of the numbers of purchases made by a competitor's outlet in Bath, Confetti, over a one-week period. The number of customers per hour varied between 34 (during rainy weather) and 140 (when sunny), with an average expenditure per purchase of £1. Discussions with confectionery-shop owners revealed that the summer months of June, July and August, plus Christmas (December), accounted for half of the years' sales. In other months, purchases made on Saturdays accounted for half the weekly sales.

Based on a different town population (Taunton is half the size of Bath), Edmund estimated that Scoops would only attract half the customers of Confetti and would require an average of 25 customers per hour to reach his sales target. As well as working there himself, he planned to employ one full-time assistant, part-time help on Saturdays and student part-timers in the summer and Christmas vacations.

▪ Work out market share: how big is the market for your product or service? Is it growing or contracting? At what rate and percentage per annum? What is its economic and competitive position? These are all factors that can provide a market-share basis for your forecasts.

An entry market share of more than a few per cent would be most unusual. In spite of all the hype, after a decade of hard work the Internet booksellers still account for less than 2 per cent of all books sold, and Amazon is just one of a score of major players. But beware of turning this argument on its head.

Many sales forecasts are made on the premise that 'If we capture just 1 per cent of the potential market, we'll be a great success.' This statement is made so that no time is wasted in doing basic market research – after all, the business only has to sell to this tiny percentage of possible buyers! In fact, this type of thinking leads to more business failures than any other single factor. If the market is so huge as to make 1 per cent of it very profitable, then inevitably there are large and established competitors. For a small firm to try to compete head on in this situation is little short of suicidal. It can be done, but only if sound research has clearly identified a market niche. No investor will be impressed by unsubstantiated statements such as 'In a market of £1 billion per annum, we can easily capture 1 per cent – £1 million a year.'

■ Think about your customers: how many customers and potential customers do you know who are likely to buy from you, and how much might they buy? You can use many types of data on which to base reasonable sales projections: you can interview a sample of prospective customers, issue a press release or advertisement to gauge response and exhibit at trade shows to obtain customer reactions.

Werner Herker

Having arranged UK suppliers and fixed teams to install Victorian conservatories in Germany, qualified engineer and Cranfield MBA Werner Herker formed a company and placed a tiny advertisement in the leading German television-programme listings magazine. With over 15 replies, and knowing that an average fitted installation costs at least £5,000, Werner was able to accurately forecast his first year's sales and accordingly launched a successful company.

■ Be aware of order cycles and timescales. If your product or service needs to be on an approved list before it can be bought, then your forecast should confirm you have that approval.

■ Look at seasonality. You should consider seasonal factors that might cause sales to be high or low in certain periods of the year. For example, 80 per cent of toys are sold in just three months of the year, leaving nine very flat months. If you were selling toys, this would have a significant effect on cash-flow projections.

■ Use rules of thumb where possible. For some businesses, there are rules of thumb that can be used to estimate sales. This is particularly true in retailing, where location studies, traffic counts and population density are all known factors.

Using rules of thumb – Tim Brown

When Tim Brown founded his second restaurant, Alamo, in Los Angeles, with substantial backing from private investors, he used one such rule. In his experience, once a restaurant has served 25,000 clients it can expect sufficient repeat business to break even. In his first eight months of operation he had achieved 20,000.

■ Work out your desired income. Forecasts will accommodate the realistic aims of the proprietor. You could even say that the whole purpose of strategy is to ensure that certain forecasts are achieved. This is more likely to be the case in a mature company with proven products and markets than with a start-up. Nevertheless, an element of 'How much do we need to earn?' must play a part in forecasting, if only to signal when a strategy is not worth pursuing.

Working out desired income – Jane Jenkins

Jane Jenkins set up her business 18 months after finishing a college degree. At first she was not sure what business to start, but a friend with whom she lived wanted to set up a craft studio to teach students how to slip-cast (an ancient method of making pottery using liquid clay poured into a mould). Jane visited a number of potteries and discovered people with this skill. 'Their mug shapes were revolting, though. So I drew my own. I found, doing so, that all my frustration evaporated just like that. Suddenly I knew what I wanted to do.'

The next few months were spent driving around the country, staying in hotels normally frequented by travelling salesmen. She equipped herself with sponges and colours so that she could apply her designs to her mugs in the factories.

'At first people thought I was mad and were sceptical but helpful.' However, she soon won her first order, worth £600, from the General Trading Company and within two months she joined a lot of 'hysterical stall-holders with lavender bags' at a trade fair.

Jane Jenkins was of the opinion that if she could not earn at least £40,000 per annum in the second year of her new business, she would not want to start up. Her predicted profit margin was 40 per cent, so this 'objective' called for a sales forecast of £100,000. She used her market research and the resultant strategies to satisfy herself (and her backers) that this was a realistic goal.

■ Relate the sales forecast to activity. However they are arrived at, sales figures will convince no one unless they are related back to the specific activities that will generate business. For example, if, in your business, salespeople have to make visits to generate orders, then knowing how many calls need to be made to get one order and what the average order size could be are essential pieces of information to include in your sales forecast.

Making the sales forecast – Exploration Works

For the past two years, Anthea Cody has run a very successful outdoor clothing shop called Exploration Works.

The business took on an agency from Asian Adventure Holidays, one of the largest and most respected tour operators in the market. With virtually no marketing effort, some 200 adventure holidays were sold in six months, netting £40,000 in commissions. Sales of insurance policies and other services added to this total and could potentially add much more.

When making her sales forecast, Anthea estimated that her enquiry-to-sale conversion rate on adventure travel holidays sold within the outdoor clothing shop to date had been 33 per cent. However, she revised her estimate downward in order to be conservative, assuming that only 20 per cent of enquiries would actually result in an adventure holiday being booked.

She expects a steady build-up of clients coming to the clothing shop to talk about holidays (see Table 5.1). She also thinks the number of new enquiries generated by promotional activity will build up during the year, gradually overtaking enquiries from the clothes shop. This is a trend she expects to continue. Based on the projection below, she is forecasting to sell 660 adventure travel holidays next year at an average price of £2,125.

Once insurance and other service sales are added, she can expect to generate an income of £160,948 over 12 months.

Table 5.1 Sales forecast projection

	Q1	Q2	Q3	Q4	Year total
Enquiries generated through promotion	200	425	425	750	1,800
Adventure shop enquiries	300	300	450	450	1,500
Total enquiries	**500**	**725**	**875**	**1,200**	**3,300**
Holidays sold	100	145	175	240	660
Average holiday's cost (£)	2,000	2,000	2,250	2,250	–
Commission received (£)	20,000	29,000	43,312	59,136	151,448
Commission on insurance & other services received (£)	1,000	2,000	3,000	3,500	9,500
Total commission & fees earned (£)	**21,000**	**31,000**	**46,312**	**62,636**	**160,948**

■ Finally, how far ahead should you forecast? Opinions are divided between three and five years ahead. However, financiers we have talked to, while often asking for a five-year view, only pay serious attention to the first three years.

The arguments for looking this far ahead are twofold. First, most new ventures are at their greatest risk in the first few years, so investors and lenders want to see that the proprietors have a well thought out strategy to cover this period. Second, venture capitalists in particular want to look forward to the time when they can realise their investment and move on. Typically their exit route has to materialise between years 3 and 5 – hopefully during the earlier of the two.

The first two years of the sales forecast should be made on a monthly basis, and the remaining three years on a quarterly basis.

The examples below provide a flavour of the range of possible outcomes for the first few years of a new venture's life.

Graham Brown founded Oasis in Oxford a year after completing his economics degree, and two years later his second opened in Brighton. Finding that running two shops was very different from running one, he took on a partner, Andrew Thomas, who had learnt his retailing at Debenhams and Habitat. Two years later they raised £100,000 to open their Guildford store and four years further on their Covent Garden flagship was opened. This cost £65,000 for shopfitting alone. Within a decade of starting up, turnover was up to £3.5 million a year.

Blooming Marvellous, a mail order company providing stylish and imaginative maternity clothes, is the brainchild of two successful businesswomen, Judy Lever and Vivienne Pringle. Started on a shoestring with £750 and only two dresses on offer, within two and a half years Blooming Marvellous had built up to an annual turnover of £120,000.

Brian Davies – a former sales manager – and his wife Anne bought the Rothesay, a middle-market 23-bedroomed private hotel at Llandudno, North Wales. They spent the summer of that year learning the ins and outs of the hotel trade under the guidance of the previous owners. Total turnover for their first year was £37,925.

The following year Brian introduced a new sales strategy and cold-called on coach tour companies to drum up new business. This succeeded in raising turnover for that year to £54,134.

The third year saw Brian making improvements to the decor and restaurant facilities, but several coach cancellations left total revenue for the year at £60,816.

By year 4 they consolidated past strategies and turnover rose to £64,844, but, with some cost savings, profits grew faster than turnover.

The strategy for their fifth year in business was to extend the season from its previous 17 weeks into the 20–22 range. Unfortunately, unusually bad weather reduced the casual trade by 12 per cent but coach party sales were a record. The resultant sales level peaked at £73,950.

Maureen Davy and her husband Graham, a former Naval officer, the founders of Equinox designer furniture company, took £6,000 in revenue in their first year, £20,150 in their second, £63,280 in their third and £111,050 in their fourth year.

Former stockbroker David Stapleton was 40 when he bought Pinneys, a sleepy salmon-smoking business in the Scottish borders, for £20,000. Three years later Pinneys made its first real breakthrough, when it secured Marks & Spencer as a customer. It was a gamble for M & S, which at that time had never stocked products costing more than £3 per pound on its shelves before. But it paid off for both of them. Within 10 years of starting up, Stapleton had taken Pinneys' sales to £50 million pa and an estimated net worth of £15 million.

Former advising executive John Nettleton borrowed £1,800 from his four-year-old daughter's building society and set up his business in a tumble-down shed in Richmond. His company, MicroScent, uses micro-encapsulation technology to trap bubbles of fragrant oil on paper. Scratching or rubbing releases the scent over time. The principal application is scented drawer lining paper.

His first year's turnover amounted to £30,000 with a nominal £1,000 loss. A friendly bank manager, enthused by the venture's prospects, advanced £70,000 for proper manufacturing equipment on the basis of a business plan and £10,000 collateral on his house. In his second year turnover was £204,000 with profits at £45,000; the third year turnover was £369,000; in his fourth year turnover rose to £680,000 with profits forecast at £130,000.

WORKSHEET FOR ASSIGNMENT 11: THE SALES FORECAST

1. Provide details of any firm orders on hand.
2. Provide details of all customers you expect to sell to over the forecast period, and how much you expect to sell to each.
3. Give market research data that support or verify these forecasts. This is particularly important for ventures in the retail field, for example, when names of customers are not necessarily known in advance.
4. Prepare a sales forecast by value and volume for each major product group (eg for a hotel: bedrooms, restaurant, off-licence) throughout the whole period of the business plan – eg up to five years (monthly for years 1 and 2 and quarterly thereafter).
5. Support your forecast with examples from other similar ventures started recently, and drawing from company accounts and other sources.
6. Give an estimate of the likely market share that these forecasts imply.

SUGGESTED FURTHER READING

Mentzer, John T and Bienstock, Carol C (1998) *Sales Forecasting Management*, Sage Publications, Thousand Oaks, CA

Powell, Rodney (2004) *Excel Sales Forecasting for Dummies*, Wiley, New York

12

Pro forma balance sheet

Before we look in detail at the balance sheet, it will be useful to see why financial data are such an important element of the business plan, and what sort of information on financial performance is needed.

The sales forecasts are the essential input from which financial projections contained in a business plan are made. These projections are not the business plan; rather they should be viewed as the financial consequences of pursuing a particular course of action. Every business plan should contain them. If additionally you can demonstrate a sound grasp of financial matters, you will be talking the same language as financiers, which has to be an advantage in any negotiation for funds. But more importantly, the financial reports used for planning the business are also used for monitoring results and controlling events once the venture is under way.

Liquidators, who ought to know why businesses fail if anyone does, have at the top of their reasons for failure 'lack of reliable financial information'. Many failed entrepreneurs believe accounting to be a bureaucratic nuisance carried out for the benefit of the Inland Revenue alone. These same people, who would never drive a car without a fuel gauge, speedometer or oil pressure indicator, frequently set off at breakneck speed running their business with only a 'gut feel' or perhaps the annual accounts to guide them. For them the end of the first year is often the end of the business. Financiers recognise this syndrome only too well, which is one reason why they take the 'financials' so seriously. The other reason is that it's *their* money that is at stake.

To take the analogy further, the motorist must also plan ahead to arrive successfully at his or her goal – to reach his or her destination safely and on time.

The success of any journey, particularly a long one, depends very much on the care taken at this stage. The preparation must centre around three distinct areas:

- *The car.* Making sure it is serviced, filled with fuel, and generally in a fit state to make the journey.
- *The route.* Choosing one that takes account of other traffic, possible road-works, and *en route* facilities such as petrol, refreshments, etc. You should also choose the route that is both the shortest practical route, and one with which you are familiar.
- *The travellers.* Ensuring that everyone is prepared for the journey. This may mean seeing that the children have been to the loo, and that some games and toys have been packed to keep them occupied on the journey. It will also mean ensuring that the luggage is packed and loaded into the car, and the house is left secured.

If this stage is accomplished with reasonable care and attention, the travellers and their vehicle have a very good chance of success in the next phase, which is the journey itself.

The soundest approach to any journey is to calculate how far the distance to be travelled is, determine an average travelling speed that is maintainable and safe, and from these two determine the time needed to travel this distance. Working back from when you want to arrive at your destination and allowing a margin of safety for petrol stops, refreshments, etc, you can calculate when you should set off.

The rest of the journey, given that Phase 1 has been carried out properly, should be plain sailing provided you follow your plan, follow the map correctly, and take account of the warning signs along the route. In all probability you will arrive at your destination safely and on time.

There are many parallels between the planning, information needs and decisions made by the safe motorist and the successful entrepreneur's business plan, as the financial reports described below will illustrate.

BALANCE SHEET (ASSIGNMENT 12)

Entrepreneurs need a method of periodically measuring the growth and development of their venture. The balance sheet is this 'snapshot', which shows where the money came from to fund the business and where it was spent at a fixed point in time, usually at yearly intervals. The 'where it came from' will usually include share capital, the profit generated to date, and loans received to date (both long and short term). The 'where it went to' will usually include fixed assets, stocks, debtors, plus the cash left in the bank. The comparison with motoring would be the milometer, which measures the absolute distance the car has travelled, as opposed to the relative or changing performance measurement offered by the speedometer.

PROFIT-AND-LOSS STATEMENT
(ASSIGNMENT 13)

This is like a moving picture of how well the business is doing in terms of sales, costs and profitability, usually prepared on a monthly basis but covering an accounting period of one year. This can be compared to the speedometer in the car, which constantly changes as the car progresses on its journey. The profit-and-loss account monitors the day-to-day performance of the business and gives the entrepreneur the information needed to identify the areas where corrective action needs to be taken – the equivalent of slowing down and taking notice of the road signs.

CASH-FLOW STATEMENT (ASSIGNMENT 14)

Yet another moving picture of how well the business is doing, but this time in terms of cash-flow generation. It bears a very close resemblance to the profit-and-loss account but reflects the effect that credit taken from suppliers and given to customers has on cash flow. Profit does not always equal cash. Here, the comparison with the car is particularly apt: a car needs petrol to run and the petrol gauge shows how much there is in the tank; a business needs cash to survive and the cash-flow statement shows how much there is in the business's 'tank'.

BREAK-EVEN ANALYSIS (ASSIGNMENT 15)

With the information contained in the above financial statements the entrepreneur will know if the business has made a profit or loss in the past, but may not know whether it is still making a profit. The break-even analysis will show the level of sales required to generate sufficient gross profit to cover the overheads of the business, and thereby break even. The entrepreneur can now be confident that if the business trades at above this break-even level of sales it will be operating profitably, barring any changes in the level of gross profit and overheads. In car terms, the driver knows that in order to arrive at the destination on time the car has to average so many miles per hour, say 50. If it averages less than 50 miles per hour, then the driver will be late, and if it exceeds it for any length of time the driver will arrive early. In business terms arriving early equals making a profit, and arriving late equals making a loss. The 50 miles per hour is the break-even point.

ASSUMPTIONS UNDERPINNING
FINANCIAL FORECASTS

These financial statements form a significant part of any business plan. However, they can only be produced once the sales forecast has been arrived at. Their believability (as well as their construction) will also to a large extent depend upon the validity of the assumptions made along the way.

An example of these assumptions is given in the extract from a business plan below:

Celtic Carveries will set up and operate a small chain of carvery restaurants in Scotland. These will provide traditional food in a relaxed atmosphere offering value-for-money food in the middle-price market.

The carvery is already a proven concept in parts of England, serving roast meals on a quick throughput basis but without the 'fast food' image. Labour costs are low and with a limited menu, waste is avoided and cooking processes simplified. These factors reduce operating costs, which in turn makes value for money possible.

One carvery has been in operation for six months in Stirling, so the following assumptions have been drawn partly from experience and partly from market research.

Profit-and-loss assumptions

(a)　*Sales*
　　　Carveries in operation will be:
　　　year 1 – 2
　　　year 2 – 4
　　　year 3 – 7
　　　year 5 onwards – 10
　　　Opening six days per week, meal sales will be:
　　　year 1 – 40 per day
　　　year 2 – 50 per day
　　　year 3 onwards – 60 per day
　　　Sales value per meal will be:
　　　food – £6.50
　　　drink – £2.50
(b)　*Cost of sales per meal*
　　　food　　　£1.75
　　　drink　　　£1.00
　　　labour　　£2.70
　　　　　　　　‾‾‾‾‾
　　　　　　　　£5.45
　　　This equals 61 per cent of sales
(c)　*Wages*. Each carvery will employ seven staff at a cost of £42,600 pa (labour costs = 30 per cent of sales, which compares favourably with a general restaurant's 40 per cent)

(d) *Directors*. Paid £15,000 in first year, rising to £20,000 from year 3
(e) *Administrative staff*. Needed mainly from year 2. Costs will rise from £5,000 to £40,000 over seven years
(f) *Rent and services*. £30,000 per carvery per annum
(g) *Alterations, equipment and decoration*. £40,000 per carvery
(h) *Advertising*. £2,000 per carvery per annum
(i) *Inflation*. All income and expenditure is stated at current prices

Cash-flow assumptions

(a) No debtors – all meals paid for in cash
(b) Salaries and wages paid monthly
(c) Purchases paid monthly
(d) Rent paid half-yearly
(e) Rates paid monthly
(f) Loan interest paid quarterly from month 1
(g) Overdraft interest paid quarterly from month 3
(h) Sales spread evenly over each month of year (sensitivity analysis described later shows how this assumption can be varied)

Balance-sheet assumptions

(a) *Closing stock*. Building up to six weeks' sales
(b) *Depreciation of fixed assets*. Improvements and office – 20 per cent per annum; fixtures and fittings – 25 per cent per annum
(c) *Creditors*. Equivalent to one month's cost of sales

Let's now look at each account in more detail, showing how it can be prepared for inclusion in your business plan. We will start with the balance sheet.

PRO FORMA BALANCE SHEET

A personal experience

This example looks at the finances of Terry Brown. She has become a little confused by the complexity of her financial affairs and has decided to get things sorted out. In short, she wants to know where she stands.

If you were to summarise your present financial position it would contain at least some elements of the example in Table 5.2. This information tells us something of Terry's circumstances, but until we organise the information we cannot really understand her true financial position.

Terry believes that in money matters, things divide neatly into two: things you have and things you owe, with the latter usually exceeding the former. So, using this concept and slightly different words, we could show the same

Table 5.2 Example showing simple financial position

Terry Brown – financial position today (28 March)

	£
Cash	50
House	50,000
Mortgage	45,000
Money owed by sister (Jackie)	135
Overdraft	100
Car	1,000
Credit cards	50
Jewellery and paintings	350
Hire purchase (on various goods)	500
Furniture	500

information in the following manner (Table 5.3). On the right-hand side we have made a list of Terry's *assets:* what she has done with the money she has had. On the left is listed where she got the money from to pay for these assets: the *liabilities and claims* against her.

Table 5.3 Example showing assets balanced against liabilities and claims

Terry Brown – financial position today (28 March)

Liabilities and claims (where I got the money from)	£	Assets (what I have done with the money)	£
Overdraft	100	Cash	50
Mortgage	45,000	House	50,000
Hire purchase	500	Car	1,000
Credit cards	50	Jewellery and paintings	350
		Money owed by sister	135
Total claims by other people	45,650	Furniture	500
My capital	6,385		
Total of my and other people's capital	52,035	My assets	52,035

You may even have got a little lost towards the bottom of the left-hand column. This is simply because we have to try to show the complete picture of Terry's financial affairs. She has acquired £52,035 worth of assets and must have provided an identical sum from one source or another. We can find only £45,650 owed to other people. The only reasonable assumption is that Terry herself must have put her past salary or wages towards buying the assets.

Now, while Terry might be happy with the help we have given her so far, it is unlikely she will be completely satisfied. Like the rest of us, she probably considers events as long or short term in nature. Even though we have shown a fairly dazzling picture of £52,000+ of assets, she knows she is short of cash for day-to-day living. So once again we could restructure the information on her financial position to give a clearer picture (Table 5.4).

For example, we can now see that her short-term financial position is dominated by the money her sister owes her. If that is safe, then all current liabilities can be met. If it is not safe and the money is unlikely to be repaid quickly, the position is not so good. There is an accounting convention according to which 'current' liabilities are those that we will have to pay within a year. Similarly, 'current' assets will turn into cash within a year.

Table 5.4 Example showing assets balanced against liabilities and claims

Terry Brown – financial position today (28 March)

Liabilities (long term) (where I got the money from)	£	*Assets* (long term) (what I have done with the money)	£
Mortgage	45,000	House	50,000
Hire purchase	500	Car	1,000
My capital	6,385	Jewellery and paintings	350
		Furniture	500
	51,885		51,850
Current liabilities (short term)		*Current assets* (short term)	
Overdraft	100	Money owed by sister	135
Credit cards	50	Cash	50
	150		185
Total liabilities	52,035	Total assets	52,035

We are getting very close to having a *balance sheet* of Terry's financial position. One further adjustment will reveal all. It is vital that both the long- and short-term financial positions are readily visible to the examiner. Terry's day-to-day assets and liabilities need to be clearly highlighted. What we are looking for is the net position: how much she currently owes, subtracted from how much she has.

By redrafting the financial position, we shall see the whole picture much more clearly: £51,850 is tied up in *fixed assets* and £135 is tied up in *net current assets*. All these assets have been *financed by* £6,385 of Terry's capital and £45,500 provided by a mortgage and a hire purchase company.

The structure of the business balance sheet

The balance sheet of a business has many similarities to the personal account we have just examined. However, some of the terms used may be new to you. Returning to Celtic Carveries, let's see how a business balance sheet is con- structed as shown in Table 5.5.

First, you will notice the date at the top. This is essential, as the balance sheet is a picture of the business at a particular moment in time. The picture could look quite different tomorrow if, for example, more money was spent on fixtures. That would cause the fixed assets to rise – and the overdraft in all probability.

You can also see that some different terms are used for the account cat- egories. Before we look at the main elements of this balance sheet it will be useful to describe the key terms, 'assets' and 'liabilities'.

Assets

Assets are 'valuable resources owned by a business'. You can see that there are two key points in the definition:

1. To be valuable the resource must be cash, or of some use in generating current or future profits. For example, a debtor (someone who owes a business money for goods or services provided) usually pays up. When he or she does, the debtor becomes cash and so meets this test. If there is no hope of getting payment, then you can hardly view the sum as an asset.
2. Ownership, in its legal sense, can be seen as being different from posses- sion or control. The accounting use of the word is similar but not identical. In a business, possession and control are not enough to make a resource an asset. For example, a leased machine may be possessed and controlled by a business but be owned by the leasing company. So it is not an asset, but a regular expense appearing on the profit-and-loss account.

Table 5.5 A business balance sheet

Celtic Carveries
Balance sheet at 31 October

	Year 1	Year 2	Year 3	Year 4	Year 5
<u>Net assets employed</u>					
Fixed assets					
Improvements	48,000	86,400	141,120	184,896	147,916
Fixtures and office	30,500	43,900	83,015	97,051	85,631
	78,500	130,300	224,135	281,947	233,547
Current assets					
Stock	1,887	38,425	72,819	109,250	109,250
Cash	0	2,366	2,029	10,863	120,641
	1,887	40,791	74,848	120,113	229,891
<u>less</u>					
Current liabilities					
Creditors	11,383	25,617	48,546	72,833	72,833
Overdraft	6,063	27,919	60,974	45,656	0
Tax	0	4,000	25,000	58,000	80,000
	17,446	57,536	134,520	176,490	152,833
= Net current assets	(15,559)	(16,745)	(59,672)	(56,378)	77,058
Total assets less current liabilities	62,941	113,545	164,463	225,569	310,605
Financed by:					
Share capital					
Owners	15,000	15,000	15,000	15,000	15,000
Other directors	10,000	10,000	10,000	10,000	10,000
New venture capital	20,000	90,000	120,000	150,000	150,000
Profit/loss for year	(24,317)	(28,455)	(8,557)	25,569	85,036
Retained earnings/ reserves	–	–	–	–	25,569
	20,683	86,545	136,443	200,569	285,605
Loan capital					
Long term	25,000	25,000	25,000	25,000	25,000
Medium term	17,258	2,000	3,000	–	–
	42,258	27,000	28,000	25,000	25,000
TOTAL	62,941	113,545	164,463	225,569	310,605

Liabilities

These are the claims by people outside the business. In this example only creditors, overdraft and tax are shown, but they could include such items as accruals, deferred income, etc. The 'financed by' section of our example balance sheet is also considered in part as liabilities.

Current

This is the term used with both assets and liabilities to show that they will be converted into cash, or have a short life (under one year).

Now let's go through the main elements of the balance sheet.*

Net assets employed

This is the 'what have we done with the money?' section. A business can only do three things with funds:

1. It can buy *fixed assets*, such as premises, machinery and motor cars. These are assets that the business intends to keep over the longer term. They will be used to help to make profits, but will not physically vanish in the short term (unless sold and replaced, like motor cars, for example).
2. Money can be tied up in *working capital*, that is, 'things' immediately involved in the business's products (or services), that will vanish in the short term. Stocks get sold and are replaced; debtors pay up, and creditors are paid; and cash circulates. Working capital is calculated by subtracting the current liabilities from the current assets. This is the net sum of money that a business has to find the working capital. In the balance sheet this is called the *net current assets*, but on most other occasions the term 'working capital' is used.
3. Finally, a business can put money aside over the longer term, perhaps in local government bonds or as an investment in someone else's business venture. In the latter case this could be a prelude to a takeover. In the former it could be a cash reserve for future capital investment. The account category is called *investments*. It is not shown in this example as it is a fairly rare phenomenon in new or small businesses, which are usually cash hungry rather than rich.

---

*The precise layout of a balance sheet according to the Companies Act rules is slightly different. However, this is not relevant for business planning purposes.

Financed by

This section of the balance sheet shows where the money came from. It usually has at least two subheadings, although larger companies can have many more.

1. *Share capital.* This is the general name given to the money put in by various people in return for a part share in the business. If the business is successful they may get paid a dividend each year, but their principal reward will come from the expected increase in the worth of the business and the consequent rise in value of their share (more on this subject in Assignment 16).

   The profit or loss for each year is added to or subtracted from the shareholders' investment. Eventually, once the business is profitable, it will have some money left each year to plough back into reserves. This term conjures up pictures of sums of cash stored away for a rainy day. It is important to remember that this is not necessarily so. The only cash in a business is that shown under that heading in the current assets. The reserves, like all the other funds, are used to finance a business and are tied up in the fixed assets and working capital.

2. The final source of money to finance a business is long- or medium-term *loans* from outside parties. These loans could be in the form of debentures, a mortgage, hire purchase agreements or long-term loans from a bank. The common features of all such loans are that businesses have to pay interest on the money and eventually repay the capital, whether or not the business is successful. Conversely, if the business is a spectacular success the lenders, unlike the shareholders, will not share in the extra profits.

Some ground rules

These ground rules are generally observed by accountants when preparing a balance sheet.

1. *Money measurement.* In accounting, a record is kept only of the facts that can be expressed in money terms. For example, the state of your health, or the fact that your main competitor is opening up right opposite in a more attractive outlet, are important business facts. No accounting record of them is made, however, and they do not show up on the balance sheet, simply because no objective monetary value can be assigned to these facts.

   Expressing business facts in money terms has the great advantage of providing a common denominator. Just imagine trying to add typewriters and motor cars, together with a 4,000-square-foot workshop, and arriving at a total. You need a common term to be able to carry out the basic arithmetical functions, and to compare one set of accounts with another.

2. *Business entity.* The accounts are kept for the business itself, rather than for the owner(s), workers, or anyone else associated with the firm. If an owner puts a short-term cash injection into his or her business, it will appear as a loan under current liabilities in the business account. In his or her personal account it will appear as an asset – money he or she is owed by someone else. So depending on which point of view you take, the same sum of money can be an asset or a liability. And as in this example the owner and the business are substantially the same person, the possibilities of confusion are considerable.

This source of possible confusion must be cleared up and the business entity concept does just that. The concept states that assets and liabilities are always defined from the business's viewpoint.

3. *Cost concept.* Assets are usually entered into the accounts at cost. For a variety of reasons, the real 'worth' of an asset will probably change over time. The worth, or value, of an asset is a subjective estimate on which no two people are likely to agree. This is made even more complex and artificial because the assets themselves are usually not for sale. So, in the search for objectivity, the accountants have settled for cost as the figure to record. It means that a balance sheet does not show the current worth, or value, of a business. That is not its intention. Nor does it mean that the 'cost' figure remains unchanged for ever. For example, a motor car costing £6,000 may end up looking like the one in Table 5.6 after two years.

Table 5.6 Example showing changing value of an asset

	Year 1	Year 2
Fixed assets:		
Motor car	6,000	6,000
less cumulative depreciation	1,500	3,000
Net assets	4,500	3,000

The depreciation is how we show the asset 'consumed' over its working life. It is simply a bookkeeping record to allow us to allocate some of the cost of an asset to the appropriate time period. The time period will be determined by such factors as how long the working life of the asset is. The Inland Revenue does not allow depreciation as a business expense but it does allow tax relief on the capital expenditure.

Other assets, such as freehold land and buildings, will be revalued from time to time, and stock will be entered at cost, or market value, whichever is the lower, in line with the principle of conservatism (explained later).

4. *Going concern.* Accounting reports always assume that a business will continue trading indefinitely into the future, unless there is good evidence to the contrary. This means that the assets of the business are looked at simply as profit generators and not as being available for sale.

Look again at the motor car example above. In year 2 the net asset figure in the accounts, prepared on a 'going concern' basis, is £3,000. If we knew that the business was to close down in a few weeks, then we would be more interested in the car's resale value than its 'book' value; the car might fetch only £2,000, which is quite a different figure.

Once a business stops trading, we cannot realistically look at the assets in the same way. They are no longer being used in the business to help to generate sales and profits. The most objective figure is what they might realise in the marketplace. Anyone who has been to a sale of machinery will know the difference between book and market value!

5. *Dual aspect.* To keep a complete record of any business transaction we need to know both where money came from, and what has been done with it. It is not enough simply to say, for example, that someone has put £1,000 into their business. We have to show how that money has been used to buy fixtures, stock in trade, etc.

WORKSHEET FOR ASSIGNMENT 12: PRO FORMA BALANCE SHEET

Using the format on the pro forma balance sheets:

1. Construct a balance sheet for your business as it might look on the day *before* you start trading. This should be done now.
2. List and explain the assumptions underpinning your financial forecasts.
3. Construct a balance sheet at the end of years 1, 2, 3, 4 and 5 assuming you achieve the level of sales in your sales forecast. These should be done after you have completed the pro forma profit-and-loss account (Assignment 13) and pro forma cash-flow forecast (Assignment 14).

Remember you should produce years 1 and 2 (quarterly) and years 3, 4 and 5 (annually) using the pro forma sheets (Table 5.7) with this assignment.

SUGGESTED FURTHER READING

Barrow, Colin (2001) *Financial Management for the Small Business*, 5th edn, Kogan Page, London

Barrow, Colin (2004) *Business Accounting for Dummies*, Wiley, New York

Table 5.7 Pro forma balance sheet by year

Business name: ....

	Year 1 (20XX)			
	Qtr 1	Qtr 2	Qtr 3	Qtr 4
Fixed assets				
Cost	____	____	____	____
Accum depreciation	____	____	____	____
Net book value	____	____	____	____
Current assets				
Stock & WIP	____	____	____	____
Debtors	____	____	____	____
Bank & cash	____	____	____	____
Current liabilities				
Trade creditors	____	____	____	____
Bank overdraft	____	____	____	____
Short-term loan	____	____	____	____
Net current assets				
Total assets less current liabilities	____	____	____	____
Net assets	____	____	____	____
Financed by				
Called-up shares	____	____	____	____
Accum profits (deficit)	____	____	____	____
Loan capital	____	____	____	____

Years ended:

Year 2 (20XX)			
Qtr 1	Qtr 2	Qtr 3	Qtr 4

Table 5.8 Pro forma balance sheet summarising yearly performance

Business name: ....

	Opening	(20XX) Year 1
Fixed assets		
Cost	_____	_____
Accum depreciation	_____	_____
Net book value	_____	_____
Current assets		
Stock & WIP	_____	_____
Debtors	_____	_____
Bank & cash	_____	_____
	_____	_____
	_____	_____
Current liabilities		
Trade creditors	_____	_____
Bank overdraft	_____	_____
Short-term loan	_____	_____
	_____	_____
	_____	_____
	_____	_____
Net current assets	_____	_____
Total assets less current liabilities		
Net assets	========	========
Financed by		
Called-up shares	_____	_____
Accum profits (deficit)	_____	_____
Loan capital	_____	_____
	========	========

Summary of years 1 to 5
Years ended:

(20XX) Year 2	(20XX) Year 3	(20XX) Year 4	(20XX) Year 5

13

Pro forma profit-and-loss statement

The balance sheet shows the financial position of a business at a particular moment in time. Over time that picture will change, just as pictures of you, first as a baby, then as a teenager and lastly as an adult, will all be different – but nevertheless true likenesses of you. The 'ageing' process that changes a business's appearance is an event called a transaction. This takes place when anything is done that can be represented in money terms. For example, if you buy in stock, sell out to a customer or take credit, these are all events that can be expressed in money.

DEALING WITH TRANSACTIONS

Let us take a very simple example. On 6 April a new business called High Finance Limited is started. The initial share capital is £10,000 and on day 1 this money is held in the company's bank. The balance sheet would look something like Table 5.9.

Table 5.9   Example showing initial share capital

Balance sheet for High Finance Ltd at 6 April 20XX

Assets employed	£
Cash at bank	10,000
Financed by	
Share capital	10,000

Not very profound, but it does show the true picture at that date. On 7 April things begin to happen.

High Finance borrows £5,000 on an overdraft from another bank, taking the money out immediately in cash. This event is an accounting transaction and the new balance sheet is shown below.

Table 5.10 Example showing net assets

Balance sheet for High Finance Ltd at 7 April 20XX

Assets employed	£	£
Current assets		
Cash at Bank A and in hand	15,000	
Less current liabilities		
Overdraft (Bank B)	5,000	
Net current assets		10,000
Financed by		
Share capital		10,000

You can see that the asset, 'cash', has gone up, while the liability, 'overdraft', has also risen. Any financial event must have at least two effects on the balance sheet.

On 8 April, High Finance buys in stock for resale, at a cost of £2,000, paying cash (Table 5.11).

The working capital has been changed, not in total, but in content. Cash has been reduced to pay for stock. However, a new asset, stock, has been acquired.

On 9 April, High Finance sells for £300 cash, stock that cost it £200.

In this case cash has been increased by £300, the money received from a customer. Stocks have been reduced by £200, the amount sold. Finally, a 'profit' has been made and this can be shown, at least in this example, as retained earnings (or reserves) (see Table 5.12).

The residual effect of *all* trading transactions is an increase or decrease in the worth of the business to the owners (shareholders in this case). Income from sales tends to increase the worth of a business. Expenses incurred in generating sales tend to decrease the worth. These events are so vital to the business that they are all monitored in a separate accounting report, the profit-and-loss account.

So, to summarise: the balance sheet shows the financial picture of a business at a particular moment in time. The profit-and-loss account monitors income and expenditure over a particular period of time. The time intervals can be a week, a month, an accounting period or a year. While we are very interested

Table 5.11 Example showing breakdown of current assets

Balance sheet for High Finance Ltd at 8 April 20XX

Assets employed	£	£
Current assets		
Cash at bank and in hand	13,000	
Stock	2,000	
	15,000	
Less current liabilities		
Overdraft	5,000	
Net current assets		10,000
Financed by		
Share capital		10,000

Table 5.12 Example showing retained earnings

Balance sheet for High Finance Ltd at 9 April 20XX

Assets employed	£	£
Current assets		
Cash at bank and in hand	13,300	
Stock	1,800	
	15,100	
Less current liabilities		
Overdraft	5,000	
Net current assets		10,100
Financed by		
Share capital	10,000	
Retained earnings (reserves)	100	
		10,100

in all the components of income and expense, it is the result, the net profit (or loss), that we are most interested in. This shows the increase (or decrease) in the business's worth over the time in question.

SOME MORE GROUND RULES

Before we look at the structure of the profit-and-loss account, it would be helpful to look at the accounting concepts that apply to it. These are numbered 6 and 7 to follow on from the five concepts given in Assignment 12.

6. *The realisation concept.* A particularly prudent entrepreneur once said that an order was not an order until the customer's cheque had cleared, he or she had consumed the product, had not died as a result, and, finally, had shown every indication of wanting to buy again.

    Most of us know quite different people who can 'anticipate' the most unlikely volume of sales. In accounting, income is usually recognised as having been earned when the goods (or services) are dispatched and the invoice sent out. This has nothing to do with when an order is received, or how firm an order is, or how likely a customer is to pay up promptly.

    It is also possible that some of the products dispatched may be returned at some later date – perhaps for quality reasons. This means that income, and consequently profit, can be brought into the business in one period and have to be removed later on. Obviously, if these returns can be estimated accurately, then an adjustment can be made to income at the time.

    So the 'sales income' figure that is seen at the top of a profit-and-loss account is the value of the goods dispatched and invoiced to customers in the period in question.

7. *The accrual concept.* The profit-and-loss account sets out to 'match' income and expenditure to the appropriate time period. It is only in this way that the profit for the period can be realistically calculated. Suppose, for example, that you are calculating one month's profits when the quarterly telephone bill comes in. The picture might look like this:

Table 5.13 Example showing mismatched account

Profit-and-loss account for January 20XX

	£
Sales income for January	4,000
Less telephone bill (last quarter)	800
Profit	3,200

This is clearly wrong. In the first place, three months' telephone charges have been 'matched' against one month's sales. Equally wrong is charging anything other than January's telephone bill against January's income. Unfortunately, bills such as this are rarely to hand when you want the accounts, so in practice the telephone bill is 'accrued' for. A figure (which may even be absolutely correct if you have a meter) is put in as a provision to meet this liability when it becomes due.

With these two additional concepts we can now look at Celtic Carveries' profit-and-loss account in its business plan (Table 5.14).

Table 5.14 Example profit-and-loss account

Celtic Carveries – Profit-and-loss account for the year to 31 October

£000	Year 1	Year 2	Year 3	Year 4	Year 5	Year 6	Year 7
Sales income	224	504	955	1,432	1,600	1,685	1,685
Cost of goods sold	137	307	583	874	976	1,028	1,028
Gross profit	87	198	372	558	624	657	657
Expenditure							
Administration	5	28	30	30	40	40	40
Rent	24	48	84	120	120	120	120
Rates	6	12	21	30	30	30	30
Advertising	4	8	14	20	20	20	20
Overheads	30	60	105	150	150	150	150
Depreciation	22	38	61	77	63	50	39
Total	91	194	315	427	423	410	399
PBIT (profit before interest and tax)	–4	3	57	131	201	247	258
Interest	7	8	18	26	11	10	0
Taxation	–1	5	28	55	80	92	95
Directors' emoluments	15	18	20	25	25	25	25
Profit after tax	–24	–28	–9	26	85	120	138

The date at the top of the profit-and-loss account shows the period over which income and expenditure have been measured, in this case a year. For your business plan the earlier years should be shown in greater detail, either quarterly or preferably monthly for year 1 at any rate.

SALES INCOME

The sales income shows the value of goods and services provided by Celtic in each year. In this example all customers have paid up at the end of their meal. If Celtic had some business clients with accounts it is quite possible that some would owe money for meals provided prior to 31 October. This sum would be included in the year's sales income (refer back to the realisation concept if you are unsure about this).

COST OF GOODS SOLD

You may consider that everything you have spent in the business has gone into 'making' the product, but to calculate the cost of goods sold, only costs strictly concerned with making are considered. These will include the cost of all materials and the cost of manufacturing labour.

Blowing up the cost of the goods sold section of Celtic Carveries' profit-and-loss account, it could look like Table 5.15.

Table 5.15 Example showing cost of goods sold

	£	£	£
Sales			224,000
Manufacturing costs:			
Opening stock (wine and food)	0		
Purchases in period	85,519		
	85,519		
Less closing stock	17,075		
Cost of materials used		68,444	
Direct labour cost (cooks, bar staff, etc)		65,156	
Cost of goods sold			133,600
Gross profit			£90,400

This is not a complete list of items we would find in the cost of goods sold section of a manufacturer's profit-and-loss account. For example, work in progress, plant depreciation, etc, have been ignored to keep the example clear enough for the principle to be established.

GROSS PROFIT

The difference between sales income and cost of goods sold is the gross profit. This is a measure of the efficiency (or otherwise) of the 'manufacturing' aspect of a business. The sum is what is left to market, administer, pay financing costs, provide for future growth – and leave a profit.

EXPENDITURE

Expenditure or 'expenses' is the general term given to all the operating costs such as rent, rates, advertising, overheads and depreciation that are incurred in the process of running the business.

PROFIT BEFORE INTEREST AND TAX (PBIT)

PBIT is arrived at by deducting the total expenditure from the gross profit. After that, interest charges on loans are deducted and tax is paid on the taxable profits. Directors' emoluments, as approved by the shareholders, are then deducted and the residual sum, 'profit after tax', belongs to the shareholders.

SENSITIVITY ANALYSIS

While you have been realistic in preparing your forecasts of sales and related costs, it is highly probable that during year 1 especially, your actual performance will not be as expected. This could be for one or more reasons, such as resistance to innovation (if a new product), overestimate of market size, change in consumer demand, slow take-up of product, etc. All these could mean that sales forecasts are significantly wrong. It is advisable to pre-empt any potential investor's question, such as 'What happens if your sales are reduced by 20 per cent?', by asking yourself the question first and quantifying the financial effects in your business plan. You need not go into any great detail – it is sufficient to outline one or two scenarios.

Celtic Carveries' sensitivity analysis

'In arriving at sales forecasts, estimates were made by comparison with the accounts of X Ltd, which has a similar operation. If, however, these estimates were incorrect and our sales were 20 per cent lower, then turnover would be £180,000 with costs of sales falling to £110,000 and the company would still produce a gross profit at the end of year 1 of

£70,000. Given a fixed cost of £90,000, our first-year loss would be extended from £4,000 to £20,000. This position could be largely offset by cutting the directors' pay for that year!'

SUMMARY OF PERFORMANCE RATIOS

When you have completed your pro forma profit-and-loss accounts for years 1–5, together with your pro forma balance sheets for years 1–5, you should prepare a summary of your business's performance in certain 'key' areas. This summary will help both yourself and any potential outside investor to compare your business's performance:

1. One year against the next, eg has gross profit grown or declined between years 1 and 5?
2. Against other similar businesses, eg does your business give as good a return on investment as others?
3. The ratios can be used as an aid in making future financial projections. For example, if you believe it prudent to hold the equivalent of a month's sales in stock, once you have made the sales forecast for future years the projections for stock in the balance sheet follow logically.

This summary of key ratios should include:

Sales. Actual sales, to be used as the base figure for all other calculations.
Cost of goods sold. Expressed as a percentage of sales to highlight any increase/decrease in this key area over the period.
Gross profit. Expressed as a percentage of sales to show if this has improved or declined over the period.
Profit before tax. Expressed as a percentage of sales to show how well sales have been converted to 'bottom-line profit'. Perhaps the key measure of operational performance (add back tax to profit after tax; eg on Celtic Carveries' accounts for year 1 this is (24) + 1 = (23)).

BALANCE-SHEET RATIOS

Net worth. This is actual 'investment' in the business, ie share capital plus reserves, which on its own gives a valuable measure of absolute growth.

Return on net worth. This is also referred to as return on investment (ROI), and is undoubtedly the key measure of profitability used by outsiders to compare your business with others. It is calculated by taking your net profit (after tax and before dividends) and dividing this by the average value of your share capital and reserves.

Debt to equity. Frequently referred to as 'gearing', this is calculated by taking total borrowings (both long and short term) divided by total capital and reserves (net worth) and expressing the result as a percentage. This ratio is, however, a two-edged sword in that if your gearing is high (mainly financed by borrowings), potential investors will see high rewards, assuming your business performs well, *but* if you are asking a bank or similar institution for interest-bearing funds, then they will normally expect to see low gearing, to show a certain level of your commitment, expressed as share capital, to reduce the risk of their not being able to recover their loans.

Net current assets. This is calculated by subtracting current liabilities from current assets, thereby giving creditors an indication of your liquidity or ability to meet current liabilities when they fall due.

Current ratio. This is calculated by dividing current assets by current liabilities and expressing the result as a ratio, thereby giving an indication of your ability to meet short-term obligations as they become due. It is often refined to include only those current assets 'quickly' convertible to cash (ie excluding stocks) and all current liabilities repayable within 12 months. In this form it is known as a 'quick ratio'.

Three other useful working capital ratios that both reveal the strength of financial control in a business plan and can be used in financial forecasting are:

$$\text{Average debtor collection period} = \frac{\text{Debtors}}{\text{Sales}} \times 365$$

This gives a guide as to how long you expect to take (or have taken) getting money owed to you back in.

$$\text{Days stock held} = \frac{\text{Stock (or inventories)}}{\text{Cost of goods sold}} \times 365$$

This shows the stock level held, in proportion to your sales. This is more useful than comparing figures alone, as you would expect levels to change with increases or decreases in sales.

$$\text{Average credit period taken} = \frac{\text{Creditors}}{\text{Purchases}} \times 365$$

Table 5.16 Pro forma profit-and-loss statement by month

Business name: ....

	Month 1	Month 2	Month 3	Month 4	Month 5
Income					
Sales					
Misc income					
Total income					
Cost of goods sold					
Gross profit					
Expenses					
Total expenses					
Profit before tax					
Tax					
Profit after tax					

Year ended:

Month 6	Month 7	Month 8	Month 9	Month 10	Month 11	Month 12	Total for year
——	——	——	——	——	——	——	[——]
——	——	——	——	——	——	——	[——]
——	——	——	——	——	——	——	[——]
——	——	——	——	——	——	——	[——]
——	——	——	——	——	——	——	[——]
——	——	——	——	——	——	——	[——]
——	——	——	——	——	——	——	[——]
——	——	——	——	——	——	——	[——]
——	——	——	——	——	——	——	[——]
——	——	——	——	——	——	——	[——]
——	——	——	——	——	——	——	[——]
——	——	——	——	——	——	——	[——]
——	——	——	——	——	——	——	[——]
——	——	——	——	——	——	——	[——]
——	——	——	——	——	——	——	[——]
——	——	——	——	——	——	——	[——]
——	——	——	——	——	——	——	[——]
——	——	——	——	——	——	——	[——]
——	——	——	——	——	——	——	[——]
——	——	——	——	——	——	——	[——]
——	——	——	——	——	——	——	[——]
——	——	——	——	——	——	——	[——]
——	——	——	——	——	——	——	[——]
——	——	——	——	——	——	——	[——]
——	——	——	——	——	——	——	[——]
——	——	——	——	——	——	——	[——]
——	——	——	——	——	——	——	[——]

Table 5.17 Pro forma profit-and-loss statement by year

Business name: ....

	Year . . . (20XX)			
	Qtr 1	Qtr 2	Qtr 3	Qtr 4
<u>Income</u>				
Sales	————	————	————	————
Misc income	————	————	————	————
	————	————	————	————
Total income	————	————	————	————
Cost of goods sold	————	————	————	————
Gross profit	————	————	————	————
<u>Expenses</u>				
————————	————	————	————	————
————————	————	————	————	————
————————	————	————	————	————
————————	————	————	————	————
————————	————	————	————	————
————————	————	————	————	————
————————	————	————	————	————
————————	————	————	————	————
————————	————	————	————	————
————————	————	————	————	————
————————	————	————	————	————
————————	————	————	————	————
————————	————	————	————	————
————————	————	————	————	————
————————	————	————	————	————
Total expenses	————	————	————	————
Profit before tax	————	————	————	————
Tax	————	————	————	————
Profit after tax	————	————	————	————

Year . . . (20XX)

Total for year	Qtr 1	Qtr 2	Qtr 3	Qtr 4	Total for year
[_____]	_____	_____	_____	_____	[_____]
[_____]	_____	_____	_____	_____	[_____]
[_____]	_____	_____	_____	_____	[_____]
[_____]	_____	_____	_____	_____	[_____]
[_____]	_____	_____	_____	_____	[_____]
[_____]	_____	_____	_____	_____	[_____]
[_____]	_____	_____	_____	_____	[_____]
[_____]	_____	_____	_____	_____	[_____]
[_____]	_____	_____	_____	_____	[_____]
[_____]	_____	_____	_____	_____	[_____]
[_____]	_____	_____	_____	_____	[_____]
[_____]	_____	_____	_____	_____	[_____]
[_____]	_____	_____	_____	_____	[_____]
[_____]	_____	_____	_____	_____	[_____]
[_____]	_____	_____	_____	_____	[_____]
[_____]	_____	_____	_____	_____	[_____]
[_____]	_____	_____	_____	_____	[_____]
[_____]	_____	_____	_____	_____	[_____]
[_____]	_____	_____	_____	_____	[_____]
[_____]	_____	_____	_____	_____	[_____]
[_____]	_____	_____	_____	_____	[_____]
[_____]	_____	_____	_____	_____	[_____]
[_____]	_____	_____	_____	_____	[_____]
[_____]	_____	_____	_____	_____	[_____]
[_____]	_____	_____	_____	_____	[_____]
[_____]	_____	_____	_____	_____	[_____]
[_____]	_____	_____	_____	_____	[_____]

Table 5.18 Pro forma profit-and-loss statement summarising yearly performance

Business name ....

	(20XX) Year 1	(20XX) Year 2
<u>Income</u>		
Sales		
Misc income	———	———
Total income	———	———
Cost of goods sold	———	———
Gross profit	———	———
<u>Expenses</u>		
———————————	———	———
———————————	———	———
———————————	———	———
———————————	———	———
———————————	———	———
———————————	———	———
———————————	———	———
———————————	———	———
———————————	———	———
———————————	———	———
———————————	———	———
———————————	———	———
———————————	———	———
———————————	———	———
———————————	———	———
———————————	———	———
———————————	———	———
Total expenses	———	———
Profit before tax	———	———
Tax	———	———
Profit after tax	———	———

Summary of years 1 to 5:
Years ended:

(20XX) Year 3	(20XX) Year 4	(20XX) Year 5

Table 5.19 Summary of key ratios

Business name ....

	(20XX) Year 1		(20XX) Year 2	
<u>Operating</u>				
Sales	_____	%	_____	%
Cost of sales	_____	%	_____	%
Gross profit	_____	%	_____	%
Total expenses	_____	%	_____	%
Profit before tax	_____	%	_____	%
<u>Balance sheet</u>	_____		_____	
	_____		_____	
Net worth	_____		_____	
Return on net worth	_____	%	_____	%
Debt to equity	_____	%	_____	%
Net current assets	_____		_____	
Current ratio	_____		_____	

This shows how much credit you are taking from your suppliers. As a rough guide, if you are allowing your customers 30 days to pay, then you should be looking for that credit period yourself.

Table 5.20 Summary of Celtic Carveries' performance ratios

Year	1 %	2 %	3 %	4 %	5 %
Gross profit	39	39	39	39	39
Total expenditure	41	38	33	30	26
Profit before tax	(10)	(5)	2	6	10
ROI	–	–	–	13	30
Gearing	67	24	17	11	8

Summary of years 1 to 5:
Years ended:

(20XX) Year 3		(20XX) Year 4		(20XX) Year 5	
_____	%	_____	%	_____	%
_____	%	_____	%	_____	%
_____	%	_____	%	_____	%
_____	%	_____	%	_____	%
_____	%	_____	%	_____	%
_____		_____		_____	
_____		_____		_____	
_____		_____		_____	
_____	%	_____	%	_____	%
_____	%	_____	%	_____	%
_____		_____		_____	
_____		_____		_____	

WORKSHEET FOR ASSIGNMENT 13:
PRO FORMA PROFIT-AND-LOSS STATEMENT

Using the format on the pro forma profit-and-loss account sheets:

1. Construct a profit-and-loss account for years 1, 2, 3, 4 and 5, assuming you achieve the level of sales in your sales forecast.
2. Construct a summary of your profit-and-loss accounts for the full five years (annually).

   Do not forget to state the key assumptions that you have made in arriving at your figures; the reader of your business plan will not be impressed by figures plucked out of thin air!

   Remember you should produce years 1 and 2 (monthly) and years 3, 4 and 5 (quarterly) using the pro forma sheets with this assignment.
3. Carry out a sensitivity analysis noting by how much each of the following must change seriously to affect the apparent viability of your business plan:

(a) Sales lower by x per cent
(b) Fixed costs higher by x per cent
(c) Cost of goods sold higher by x per cent
4. Construct a summary of your key ratios over the five-year period using the summary of key ratios sheet.

SUGGESTED FURTHER READING

Barrow, Colin (2001) *Financial Management for the Small Business*, 5th edn, Kogan Page, London
Barrow, Colin (2004) *Business Accounting for Dummies*, Wiley, New York

14

Pro forma cash-flow statement

CASH FLOW/PROFIT

Your business plan must show your clear appreciation that profit is not cash and cash is not profit. In the short term, a business can survive even if it is not making a profit as long as it has sufficient cash reserves, but *it cannot survive* without cash even though it may be making a profit. The purpose of the cash-flow projection is to calculate how much cash a business is likely to need to accomplish its objectives, and when it will need it in the business.

These projections will form the basis of negotiations with any potential provider of capital.

Let us look at the following example to illustrate this point.

Kensington Quick Fit

The Kensington Quick Fit Exhaust Centre has just started up, employing a young apprentice. It has to stock a basic range of spares for most European and Japanese cars. In January it fitted 100 exhaust systems at an average cost of £75 each to the customer, making total sales for the month of £7,500. These exhausts have cost Kensington on average £35 each to buy, and its total wages bill was £300. The company's position is as follows:

	£
Materials	3,500
Labour	300
Total direct cost	3,800

The gross profit in the month is £3,700 and, after making provision for other business costs of £500 for heat, light, rates, insurance, etc, Kensington Quick Fit has made a profit of £3,200.

However, the proprietor is a little concerned that although he is making a good profit, his bank balance is not so healthy; in fact it is worse than when he started. An examination of his operations reveals that when he buys in his exhaust systems his suppliers impose a minimum order quantity of 150 units, and since he needs two suppliers – one for the European car systems and one for the Japanese cars – he has to buy in 300 units at a time. He does, however, make sure that he has sufficient cash for his other outgoings before ordering these 300 units.

At the end of the month he has spent the following cash sums to meet his January sales:

	£
Materials	10,500
Labour	300
Total direct cost	10,800

During the month he has received cheques for £7,500 and made a profit of £3,500 *but* his cash at the bank has gone down by £3,300, and he still owes £500 for the other business expenses. He does have 200 exhaust systems in stock at a cost of £7,000, which accounts for his poor cash position, but these can only be converted into cash when they are fitted to customers' cars.

Kensington's proprietor was aware of the situation as he closely monitored the timing of the outflow of cash from the business and the inflow of cash from his customers, and he knew that the temporary decrease in his bank balance would not stop his business surviving. However, there was no escaping the fact that although his business made a profit in the month of January, the most immediate result was that his bank balance went down!

THE BARE ESSENTIALS

In practical terms, the cash-flow projections and the profit-and-loss account projections are parallel tasks that are essentially prepared from the same data. They may be regarded almost as the 'heads' and 'tails' of the same coin – the profit-and-loss account showing the owner/manager the profit/loss based on the assumption that both sales income and the cost of making that sale are 'matched' together in the same month; and the cash-flow statement looking at the same transactions from the viewpoint that in reality the cost of the sale is incurred first (and paid for) and the income is received last, anywhere between one week and three months later.

Obviously, the implications for a non-cash business of this delay between making the sale and receiving the payment and using a service/buying goods and paying for them are crucial, especially in the first year of the business and when your business is growing quickly.

Celtic Carveries' cash-flow projection for year 1 is shown in Table 5.22 (on pages 240–41). Cash inflows are at the top and outflows below, with the net monthly and cumulative position to date shown at the bottom of the sheet. From this we can deduce that despite a fairly hefty injection of funds, they expect to end up with an overdraft of £6,063 at the year end, and a worst cash position in month 1 of £17,046. An overdraft facility of around £20,000 should be included in the business plan proposal.

PRE-TRADING CASH-FLOW FORECAST

Celtic Carveries' cash-flow projections were made on the assumption that the business was operating at optimum efficiency from the outset. This in all probability is a simplistic view. New businesses will have a period when set-up costs are being incurred but no revenue from sales is coming in. Under these circumstances your business plan should include a pre-trading cash-flow forecast, as Frogurt did in theirs (see Table 5.21).

Table 5.21 Frogurt: Pre-trading cash-flow forecast

£ Month:	1	2	3	TOTAL
Cash inflows				
Capital introduced	12,000	–	–	12,000
Loans	–	30,500	–	30,500
Total inflows	12,000	30,500	0	42,500
Cash outflows				
Fixtures and fittings	6,000	7,000	7,000	20,000
Stock	–	–	4,500	4,500
Machine purchases	–	17,000	–	17,000
Total outflows	6,000	24,000	11,500	41,500
Outflows – inflows	6,000	6,500	–11,500	1,000
Balance brought forward		6,000	12,500	
Balance carried forward	6,000	12,500	1,000	1,000

WORKSHEET FOR ASSIGNMENT 14: PRO FORMA CASH-FLOW STATEMENT

Using the format on the pro forma cash-flow statement sheets:

1. Construct a cash-flow statement for the pre-trading period leading up to 'opening' day.
2. Construct a cash-flow statement for years 1, 2, 3, 4 and 5 assuming that you achieve the level of sales in your sales forecast.

Table 5.22 Celtic Carveries: Year 1 cash flow

	1	2	3	4	5
Inflow					
Sales of meals	18,667	18,667	18,667	18,667	18,667
Owners' capital introduced	15,000				
Other capital introduced	30,000				
Loan capital	42,258				
	105,925	18,667	18,667	18,667	18,667
Outflow					
Capital expenditure	90,000				
Food and wine	5,703	5,703	5,703	5,703	5,703
Wages, cooks, etc	5,680	5,680	5,680	5,680	5,680
Rent	12,000				
Rates	500	500	500	500	500
Advertising	4,000				
Overheads	2,500	2,500	2,500	2,500	2,500
Administration	400	400	400	400	400
Drawings	1,250	1,250	1,250	1,250	1,250
Loan interest	938			938	
Overdraft medium-term loan interest			891		
	122,971	16,033	16,924	16,971	16,033
Net inflow (outflow)	(17,046)	2,634	1,743	1,696	2,634
Cumulative in (out) flow	(17,046)	(14,412)	(12,669)	(10,973)	(8,339)

From sales

6	7	8	9	10	11	12	TOTAL
18,667	18,667	18,667	18,667	18,667	18,667	18,667	224,000
							15,000
							30,000
							42,258
18,667	18,667	18,667	18,667	18,667	18,667	18,667	311,258
							90,000
5,703	5,703	5,703	5,703	5,703	5,703	5,703	68,436
5,680	5,680	5,680	5,680	5,680	5,680	5,680	68,160
	12,000						24,000
500	500	500	500	500	500	500	6,000
							4,000
2,500	2,500	2,500	2,500	2,500	2,500	2,500	30,000
400	400	400	400	400	400	400	4,800
1,250	1,250	1,250	1,250	1,250	1,250	1,250	15,000
	938			938			3,750
707				881		696	3,175
16,740	28,971	16,033	16,914	16,971	16,033	16,729	317,321
1,927	(10,304)	2,634	1,753	1,696	2,634	1,938	(6,063)
(6,412)	(16,716)	(14,082)	(12,329)	(10,633)	(7,999)	(6,061)	

Table 5.23 Pro forma cash-flow statement by month

Business name: ....

	Month 1	Month 2	Month 3	Month 4	Month 5
Inflow					
_____	_____	_____	_____	_____	_____
_____	_____	_____	_____	_____	_____
_____	_____	_____	_____	_____	_____
_____	_____	_____	_____	_____	_____
_____	_____	_____	_____	_____	_____
Total inflow	_____	_____	_____	_____	_____
Outflow					
_____	_____	_____	_____	_____	_____
_____	_____	_____	_____	_____	_____
_____	_____	_____	_____	_____	_____
_____	_____	_____	_____	_____	_____
_____	_____	_____	_____	_____	_____
_____	_____	_____	_____	_____	_____
_____	_____	_____	_____	_____	_____
_____	_____	_____	_____	_____	_____
_____	_____	_____	_____	_____	_____
_____	_____	_____	_____	_____	_____
_____	_____	_____	_____	_____	_____
_____	_____	_____	_____	_____	_____
_____	_____	_____	_____	_____	_____
_____	_____	_____	_____	_____	_____
Total outflow	_____	_____	_____	_____	_____
Net inflow (outflow)	_____	_____	_____	_____	_____
Cumulative in(out)flow	_____	_____	_____	_____	_____

Year . . . (20XX)

Month 6	Month 7	Month 8	Month 9	Month 10	Month 11	Month 12	Total for year
——	——	——	——	——	——	——	[_____]
——	——	——	——	——	——	——	[_____]
——	——	——	——	——	——	——	[_____]
——	——	——	——	——	——	——	[_____]
——	——	——	——	——	——	——	[_____]
——	——	——	——	——	——	——	[_____]
——	——	——	——	——	——	——	[_____]
——	——	——	——	——	——	——	[_____]
——	——	——	——	——	——	——	[_____]
——	——	——	——	——	——	——	[_____]
——	——	——	——	——	——	——	[_____]
——	——	——	——	——	——	——	[_____]
——	——	——	——	——	——	——	[_____]
——	——	——	——	——	——	——	[_____]
——	——	——	——	——	——	——	[_____]
——	——	——	——	——	——	——	[_____]
——	——	——	——	——	——	——	[_____]
——	——	——	——	——	——	——	[_____]
——	——	——	——	——	——	——	[_____]
——	——	——	——	——	——	——	[_____]
——	——	——	——	——	——	——	[_____]
——	——	——	——	——	——	——	[_____]
——	——	——	——	——	——	——	[_____]
——	——	——	——	——	——	——	[_____]
——	——	——	——	——	——	——	[_____]
——	——	——	——	——	——	——	[_____]
——	——	——	——	——	——	——	[_____]
——	——	——	——	——	——	——	[_____]

Table 5.24   Pro forma cash-flow statement by year

Business name ....

	Year . . . (20XX)			
	Qtr 1	Qtr 2	Qtr 3	Qtr 4
Inflow				
_____	____	____	____	____
_____	____	____	____	____
_____	____	____	____	____
_____	____	____	____	____
	____	____	____	____
Total inflow	____	____	____	____
Outflow	____	____	____	____
_____	____	____	____	____
_____	____	____	____	____
_____	____	____	____	____
_____	____	____	____	____
_____	____	____	____	____
_____	____	____	____	____
_____	____	____	____	____
_____	____	____	____	____
_____	____	____	____	____
_____	____	____	____	____
_____	____	____	____	____
_____	____	____	____	____
_____	____	____	____	____
_____	____	____	____	____
_____	____	____	____	____
_____	____	____	____	____
Total outflow	____	____	____	____
Net inflow (outflow)	____	____	____	____
Cumulative in(out)flow	____	____	____	____

Year . . . (20XX)

Total for year	Qtr 1	Qtr 2	Qtr 3	Qtr 4	Total for year
[_____]	_____	_____	_____	_____	[_____]
[_____]	_____	_____	_____	_____	[_____]
[_____]	_____	_____	_____	_____	[_____]
[_____]	_____	_____	_____	_____	[_____]
[_____]	_____	_____	_____	_____	[_____]
[_____]	_____	_____	_____	_____	[_____]
[_____]	_____	_____	_____	_____	[_____]
[_____]	_____	_____	_____	_____	[_____]
[_____]	_____	_____	_____	_____	[_____]
[_____]	_____	_____	_____	_____	[_____]
[_____]	_____	_____	_____	_____	[_____]
[_____]	_____	_____	_____	_____	[_____]
[_____]	_____	_____	_____	_____	[_____]
[_____]	_____	_____	_____	_____	[_____]
[_____]	_____	_____	_____	_____	[_____]
[_____]	_____	_____	_____	_____	[_____]
[_____]	_____	_____	_____	_____	[_____]
[_____]	_____	_____	_____	_____	[_____]
[_____]	_____	_____	_____	_____	[_____]
[_____]	_____	_____	_____	_____	[_____]
[_____]	_____	_____	_____	_____	[_____]
[_____]	_____	_____	_____	_____	[_____]
[_____]	_____	_____	_____	_____	[_____]
[_____]	_____	_____	_____	_____	[_____]
[_____]	_____	_____	_____	_____	[_____]
[_____]	_____	_____	_____	_____	[_____]
[_____]	_____	_____	_____	_____	[_____]
[_____]	_____	_____	_____	_____	[_____]

Remember you should produce years 1 and 2 (monthly) and years 3, 4 and 5 (quarterly) using the pro forma sheets with this assignment.

Do not forget to state the key assumptions that you have made in arriving at your figures.

SUGGESTED FURTHER READING

Barrow, Colin (2001) *Financial Management for the Small Business*, 5th edn, Kogan Page, London

Barrow, Colin (2004) *Business Accounting for Dummies*, Wiley, New York

15

Break-even analysis

CALCULATING YOUR BREAK-EVEN POINT

While some businesses have difficulty raising start-up capital, paradoxically one of the main reasons small businesses fail in the early stages is that too much start-up capital is used to buy fixed assets. While some equipment is clearly essential at the start, other purchases could be postponed. This may mean that 'desirable' and labour-saving devices have to be borrowed or hired for a specific period. This is obviously not as nice as having them to hand all the time, but if, for example, computers, word processors, photocopiers and even delivery vans are brought into the business, they become part of the fixed costs.

The higher the fixed-cost plateau, the longer it usually takes to reach break-even and then profitability. And time is not usually on the side of the small new business: it has to become profitable relatively quickly or it will simply run out of money and die. The break-even analysis is an important tool to be used both in preparing a business plan and in the day-to-day running of a business.

Difficulties usually begin when people become confused by the different characteristics of costs. Some costs, for instance, do not change, however much you sell. If you are running a shop, the rent and the rates are relatively constant figures, quite independent of the volume of sales. On the other hand, the cost of the products sold from the shop is completely dependent on volume. The more you sell, the more it 'costs' to buy stock. The former of these costs is called 'fixed' and the latter, 'variable', and you cannot add them together to arrive at total costs until you have made some assumptions about sales.

BREAKING EVEN

Let's take an elementary example: a business plans to sell only one product and has only one fixed cost, the rent.

In Figure 5.1 the vertical axis shows the value of sales and costs in £000 and the horizontal axis the number of 'units' sold. The second horizontal line represents the fixed costs, those that do not change as volume increases. In this case it is the rent of £10,000. The angled line running from the top of the fixed costs line is the variable costs. In this example we plan to buy in at £3 per unit, so every unit we sell adds that much to our fixed costs.

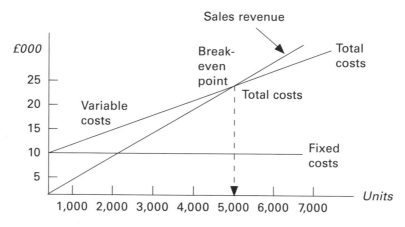

Figure 5.1 Graph showing break-even point

Only one element is needed to calculate the break-even point – the sales line. That is the line moving up at an angle from the bottom left-hand corner of the chart. We plan to sell out at £5 per unit, so this line is calculated by multiplying the units sold by that price.

The break-even point is the stage at which a business starts to make a profit. That is when the sales revenue begins to exceed both the fixed and variable costs. The chart shows our example break-even point as 5,000 units.

A formula, deduced from the chart, will save time for your own calculations.

$$\text{Break-even point} = \frac{\text{Fixed costs}}{\text{Selling price} - \text{Unit variable cost}}$$

$$\frac{10{,}000}{£5 - £3} = 5{,}000 \text{ units}$$

CAPITAL INTENSIVE VS 'LEAN AND MEAN'

Look at these two hypothetical new small businesses. They are both making and selling identical products at the same price, £10. They plan to sell 10,000 units each in the first year.

The owner of Company A plans to get fully equipped at the start. His fixed costs will be £40,000, double those of Company B. This is largely because, as well as his own car, he has bought such things as a delivery van, new equipment and a photocopier. Much of this will not be fully used for some time, but will save some money now. This extra expenditure will result in a lower unit variable cost than Company B can achieve, a typical capital-intensive result.

Company B's owner, on the other hand, proposes to start up on a shoestring. Only £20,000 will go into fixed costs, but of course his unit variable cost will be higher, at £4.50. The variable cost is higher because, for example, he has to pay an outside carrier to deliver, while A uses his own van and pays only for petrol.

So the break-even charts will look like this:

Company A: Capital intensive

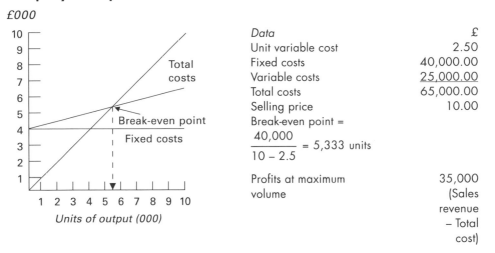

Data	£
Unit variable cost	2.50
Fixed costs	40,000.00
Variable costs	25,000.00
Total costs	65,000.00
Selling price	10.00

Break-even point =

$$\frac{40,000}{10 - 2.5} = 5,333 \text{ units}$$

Profits at maximum volume 35,000 (Sales revenue – Total cost)

Figure 5.2 Example break-even chart for a capital-intensive company

From the data on each company you can see that total costs for 10,000 units are the same, so total possible profits, if 10,000 units are sold, are also the same. The key difference is that Company B starts making profits after 3,636 units have been sold. Company A has to wait until 5,333 units have been sold, and it may not be able to wait that long.

Company B: Lean and mean

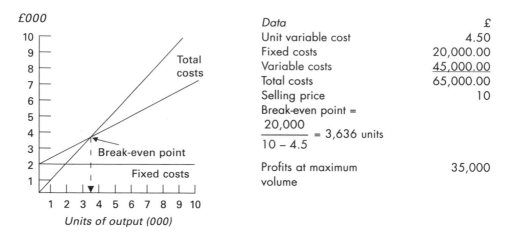

Data	£
Unit variable cost	4.50
Fixed costs	20,000.00
Variable costs	45,000.00
Total costs	65,000.00
Selling price	10

Break-even point =

$$\frac{20,000}{10 - 4.5} = 3,636 \text{ units}$$

	£
Profits at maximum volume	35,000

Figure 5.3 Example break-even chart for a 'lean and mean' company

This was only a hypothetical case. But the real world is littered with the corpses of businesses that spend too much too soon. The marketplace dictates the selling price and your costs have to fall in line with that for you to have any hope of survival.

PROFITABLE PRICING

To complete the break-even picture we need to add one further dimension – profit. It is a mistake to think that profit is an accident of arithmetic calculated only at the end of the year. It is a specific and quantifiable target that you need at the outset.

Let's go back to our previous example. You plan to invest £10,000 in fixed assets in a business, and you will need to hold another £5,000 worth of stock too – in all say £15,000. You could get £1,500 profit just leaving that money in a bank or building society, so you will expect a return of say £4,000 (equal to 27 per cent)* for taking the risks of setting up on your own. Now let's see when you will break even.

The new equation must include your 'desired' profit, so it will look like this:

---

*The UK average is around 18 per cent; high flyers aim for 35 per cent.

$$\text{Break-even profit point} = \frac{\text{Fixed costs} + \text{Profit objective}}{\text{Selling price} - \text{Unit variable cost}}$$
(BEPP)

$$= \frac{10{,}000 + 4{,}000}{5 - 3} = 7{,}000$$

We know that to reach our target we must sell 7,000 units at £5 each and have no more than £10,000 tied up in fixed costs. The great strength of this equation is that each element can be changed in turn on an experimental basis to arrive at a satisfactory and achievable result. For instance, suppose you decide that it is unlikely that you can sell 7,000 units, but that 6,500 is achievable. What would your selling price have to be to make the same profit?

Using the BEPP equation you can calculate the answer:

$$\text{BEPP} = \frac{\text{Fixed costs} + \text{Profit objective}}{\text{Selling price} - \text{Unit variable costs}}$$

$$6{,}500 = \frac{10{,}000 + 4{,}000}{6{,}500} = £2.15$$

$$£x = £2.15 + 3 = £5.15$$

If your market will bear a selling price of £5.15 as opposed to £5, all is well; if it won't, then the ball is back in your court. You have to find ways of decreasing the fixed and/or variable costs, or of selling more, rather than just accepting that a lower profit is inevitable.

FROM THE PARTICULAR TO THE GENERAL

The example used to illustrate the break-even profit point model was of necessity simple. Few if any businesses sell only one or two products, so a more general equation may be more useful if your business sells hundreds of products, as, for example, a real shop does.

In such a business, to calculate your break-even point you must first establish your gross profit. If you are already trading, this is calculated by deducting the money paid out to suppliers from the money received from customers. If you are not yet trading, then researching your competitors will give you some indication of the sort of margins you should aim for.

For example, if you are aiming for a 40 per cent gross profit, your fixed costs are £10,000 and your overall profit objective is £4,000, then the sum will be as follows:

$$\text{BEPP} = \frac{10,000 + 4,000}{0.4*} = \frac{14,000}{0.4}$$

$$= \text{£35,000}$$

So, to reach your target you must achieve a £35,000 turnover. (You can check this out for yourself: look back to the previous example where the BEPP was 7,000 units, and the selling price was £5 each. Multiplying those figures out gives a turnover of £35,000. The gross profit in that example was $2/5$, or 40 per cent, also.)

If you find that you need help in transposing the facts and figures of your business on to a break-even chart or any of the other financial statements, contact a qualified accountant.

Wavendon Plumbing: 6-month financial projection

1. Calculate your gross profit
   Projected sales   £75,000

   – Direct costs:
   Purchases (material costs)   £32,500
   Labour costs   £20,000
   = Gross profit   £22,500   (A)

2. Calculate your gross profit margin

   $$\frac{\text{Gross profit (A) £22,500}}{\text{Sales} \qquad \text{£75,000}} \times 100$$

   = Gross profit margin   30% (B)

   Note: For simplicity all figures shown are exclusive of VAT.

3. Calculate your overheads
   Indirect costs:
   Business salaries
   (including your own drawings)   £ 6,000
   + Rent   £ 2,000
   + Rates   £   500
   + Light/heating   £   500
   + Telephone/postage   £   500
   + Insurance   £   500
   + Repairs   £ 2,000
   + Advertising   £ 1,500
   + Bank interest/HP   £ 1,500

+ Other expenses	£	1,500
(eg depreciation of fixed assets)	£	
	£	
	£	
	£	
	£	
= Overheads	£16,500 (C)	

4. Calculate your actual turnover required to break even

$$\frac{\text{Overheads (C)} \quad £16,500}{\text{Gross profit margin (B)} \quad 30\%} \times 100$$

= Break-even sales   £55,000 (D)

5. Calculate the monthly target to break even

$$\frac{\text{Break-even sales (D) £55,000}}{6}$$

= Monthly break-even sales   £9,167

6. Profits accumulate in favour of the business once the break-even point has been reached. As overhead costs have been provided for in the break-even calculation, profits accumulate at a rate of 30 per cent (ie the gross margin percentage) on projected sales over and above the break-even figure.

In the case of the example, this is:

Projected sales	£75,000
– Break-even sales (D)	£55,000
× Gross profit margin (B)	30%
= Profit (for 6 months)	£6,000

These figures can be affected by:

- ▪ actual level of sales achieved;
- ▪ increase/decrease in gross margin;
- ▪ increase/decrease in overheads.

Returning to our earlier example of Celtic Carveries, the following analysis was included in their business plan.

Celtic Carveries break-even analysis

	£
Average price per meal =	9.00
Cost of food, drink and direct labour =	5.45
Therefore, contribution per meal =	3.55
Fixed costs per carvery in year 1 =	45,000
Therefore break-even point (in meals)	

$$= \frac{45,000}{3.55} = 12,676 \text{ meals per annum}$$

$$= 41 \text{ meals per day}$$

Every additional £1 spent per meal lowers the break-even point by four meals per day.

Every £1 per day saved on fixed costs lowers the break-even point by one meal per day.

Achieving both of the above would turn the first year's projected loss into a profit of around £5,000.

WORKSHEET FOR ASSIGNMENT 15: BREAK-EVEN ANALYSIS

Using the format on the break-even analysis sheet opposite:

1. Construct a break-even analysis for year 1 of your business, using the figures from your pro forma profit-and-loss account as the basis.
2. Estimate the effect of the following events on your break-even point for each year:
    (a) a 10 per cent rise/fall in sales volume;
    (b) a 10 per cent rise/fall in unit selling price;
    (c) a 10 per cent rise/fall in variable costs per unit of sale, eg a meal;
    (d) a 10 per cent rise/fall in fixed costs;
    (e) a requirement for achieving your profit objective by year 1 – now what 'volume' of product must you sell to break even?
3. Look back to Assignment 7, Pricing, and review your proposed selling price in the light of work/research carried out during this assignment.

WORKSHEET FOR BREAK-EVEN ASSIGNMENT

Using the above example, calculate the figures for your own business in the space provided opposite.

1. Calculate your gross profit

   Projected sales   £

   – Direct costs:
   Purchases (material costs)   £
   Labour costs   £
   = Gross profits   £   (A)

2. Calculate your gross profit margin

$$\frac{\text{Gross profit (A) £}}{\text{Sales} \quad £} \times 100$$

   = Gross profit margin   % (B)

   Notes:

3. Calculate your overheads

   Indirect costs:

   Business salaries
   (including your own drawings)   £
   + Rent   £
   + Rates   £
   + Light/heating   £
   + Telephone/postage   £
   + Insurance   £
   + Repairs   £
   + Advertising   £
   + Bank interest/HP   £
   + Other expenses
   (eg depreciation of fixed assets)   £
                                                      £
                                                      £
                                                      £
                                                      £
   = Overheads   £   (C)

4. Calculate your actual turnover required to break even

$$\frac{\text{Overheads (C)} \quad £}{\text{Gross profit margin (B)} \quad \%} \times 100$$

   = Break-even sales   £   (D)

5. Calculate the monthly target to break even

$$\frac{\text{Break-even sales (D) £} \underline{\hspace{3cm}}}{6}$$

= Monthly break-even sales £ _____

6. Calculate your estimated profit

Projected sales	£	
– Break-even sales (D)	£	
+ Gross profit margin (B)		%
= Profit (for 12 months)	£ _____	

SUGGESTED FURTHER READING

Barrow, Colin (2001) *Financial Management for the Small Business*, 5th edn, Kogan Page, London

Barrow, Colin (2004) *Business Accounting for Dummies*, Wiley, New York

16

Financing requirements

Your business plan may look very professional, showing that you have a very high probability of making exceptional returns, but it will fall at the first hurdle if your funding requirements have not been properly thought out and communicated to potential lenders and investors. It is not sufficient for you to look at your pro forma cash-flow statement and, taking the maximum overdraft position, say:

> The management require £150,000 to commence business, which may come either from bank loans or a share capital injection. The cash-flow projections show that if the funding was by way of a loan it would be repaid within three years. If the funding came from an issue of share capital an excellent return would be available by way of dividends.

Such a statement leaves many questions unanswered, such as:

- Why do you need the money?
- What type of money do you need?
- When will you need it?
- What deal are you offering your investors?
- What exit routes are open to your investors?

Let's examine each of these questions in turn, as your business plan will have to include answers to them.

WHY DO YOU NEED THE MONEY?

You probably have a very good idea of why you need the funds that you are asking for, but unless readers of your business plan have plenty of time to spare (which they have not) and can be bothered to work it out for themselves (which they can't), you must clearly state what you will use the funds received for.

An example might be: A net investment of £150,000 is required, which will be used as follows:

	£
To purchase:	
Motor vehicle	5,000
Plant and equipment	100,000
To provide:	
Working capital for first 6 months	75,000
Total requirement	180,000
Less investment made by (you)	30,000
Net funding requirement	150,000

This statement clearly tells the reader how the funds will be used and gives clear pointers as to appropriate funding routes and timing of the funding requirements.

Tourists visiting Bath, Windsor, Stratford-upon-Avon or London's Regent Street may mistake the English Teddy Bear Company for a small business, but it actually has sales revenues of nearly £6 million, according to managing director Jonty Crossick. That's an awful lot of teddy bears and teddy-related paraphernalia: mugs, hats, teddy clothes, and so on.

However, outside of those locations, there isn't a retail presence and the tourists, who form three-quarters of the million customers who walk through the company's doors each year, can't easily be sold additional teddy-bear gear once they return home.

Hence the attractions of a Web site. Its first launch withered and died in the following two years. The site required highly skilled IT people to create and maintain it, and the cost of employing specialists every time a new product was introduced was prohibitive. Fortunately, the company was recently able to relaunch its site with the help of 'Shopcreator', a two-year-old Yorkshire-based Web-start-up company that is partly funded by a loan from a Department of Trade and Industry scheme.

Shopcreator builds and operates easy-to-use Web retail outlets – its prices for setting up a shop on the Internet start below £200. It was just what Crossick had been looking for. Instead of recruiting hi-tech staff to maintain the site, his existing employees could simply scan in images of new products, changing and amending prices from their keyboard without any specialised training.

Crossick says the initial payment to Shopcreator was about £1,000, and there's a further annual fee payable to the company that is again around £1,000. He's also spent several hundred pounds on training and a further £1,500 on design work for the new site – chiefly to give its design an extra edge and to reuse some of the concepts used in the first attempted Web site.

Marketing costs were effectively nil. The Web address has been introduced to the company's bags, cards and boxes as fresh print runs have been requested, as well as featuring on posters dotted around the shops. Also, there are Web links from a couple of specialised gift idea sites.

Sales were £1,000 per week – well ahead of expectations – after just six weeks online. The venture was 'in the black' within months. Crossick, who claims he is able to predict a shop's likely turnover by sniffing around the location, is delighted, and the contrast with the earlier Web site venture couldn't be greater. Crossick claims: 'Within two years, we expect online sales to be between a third and a half of our turnover.'

WHAT TYPE OF MONEY DO YOU NEED?

There are many sources of funds available to independent businesses. However, not all of them are equally appropriate to all firms at all times. These different sources of finance carry very different obligations, responsibilities and opportunities for profitable business. The differences have to be understood to allow an informed choice.

Most small and medium-sized firms confine their financial strategy to bank loans, either long term or short term, viewing the other financing methods as either too complex or too risky. In many respects the reverse is true. Almost every finance source other than banks will to a greater or lesser extent share some of the risks of doing business with the recipient of the funds.

The great attraction of bank borrowings lies in the speed with which facilities can usually be arranged. Most small businesses operate without a business plan, so most events that require additional funds, such as sudden expansion or contraction, come as a surprise, either welcome or unwelcome. It is to this weakness in financial strategy that banks are ultimately appealing, so it is hardly surprising that many difficulties arise.

Lenders and investors compared

At one end of the financing spectrum lie shareholders: either individual business angels, or corporates such as venture capital providers. These share all the risks and vagaries of the business alongside the founder, and expect a proportionate share in the rewards if things go well. They are not especially concerned with a stream of dividends, which is just as well, as few small companies ever pay them. Instead they hope for a radical increase in the value of their investment. They expect to realise this value from other investors who want to take their place for the next stage in the firm's growth cycle, rather than from any repayment by the founder.

Investors in new or small businesses do not look for the security of buildings or other assets to underpin their investment. Rather they look to the founder vision and the core management team's ability to deliver results.

At the other end of the financing spectrum are the banks, which try hard to take no risk, but expect some reward irrespective of performance. They want interest payments on money lent, usually from day one. While they too hope the management is competent, they are more interested in securing a charge against any assets the business or its managers may own. At the end of the day (and that day can be sooner than the borrower expects), a bank wants all its money back – no more and certainly no less. It would be more prudent to think of banks as people who will help you turn a proportion of an illiquid asset such as property into a more liquid asset such as cash at some discount.

Understanding the differences in expectation between lenders, who provide debt, and investors, who provide equity, or share capital, is central to determining who to approach for funding. In a nutshell, lenders are risk averse, want security cover for any loan, expect to receive interest and for it to be paid on time, and want their money back in a predetermined period of time. Investors, on the other hand, have an appetite for risk, do not expect any payment until the business has grown substantially or has been sold, and rely on the founder's vision and business plan for their confidence in the proposal.

In between the extremes of shareholders and the banks lie a myriad of other financing vehicles that have a mixture of lending and investing criteria. A business needs to keep its finances under constant review, choosing the most appropriate mix of funds for the risks it plans to take and the economic climate ahead. The more risky and volatile the road ahead, the more likely it is that taking a higher proportion of risk capital will be appropriate. In times of stability and low interest, higher borrowings may be more acceptable.

Bank loans

Banks are the principal, and frequently the only, source of finance for 9 out of every 10 new and small businesses. Small firms in the UK have borrowed nearly £45 billion from the banks, a substantial rise over the past few years, but not especially high taking a longer-term view. When this figure is compared with the £38 billion that small firms have on deposit at any one time, the net amount borrowed is around £7 billion.

Bankers, and indeed any other sources of debt capital, are looking for asset security to back their loan and provide a near-certainty of getting their money back. They will also charge an interest rate that reflects current market conditions and their view of the risk level of the proposal.

Bankers like to speak of the 'five Cs' of credit analysis, factors they look at when they evaluate a loan request. When applying to a bank for a loan, be prepared to address the following points:

- *Character.* Bankers lend money to borrowers who appear honest and who have a good credit history. Before you apply for a loan, it makes sense to obtain a copy of your credit report and clean up any problems.
- *Capacity.* This is a prediction of the borrower's ability to repay the loan. For a new business, bankers look at the business plan. For an existing business, bankers consider financial statements and industry trends.
- *Collateral.* Bankers generally want a borrower to pledge an asset that can be sold to pay off the loan if the borrower lacks funds.
- *Capital.* Bankers scrutinise a borrower's net worth, the amount by which assets exceed debts.
- *Conditions.* Whether bankers give a loan can be influenced by the current economic climate as well as by the amount.

Types of bank funding

Overdraft

The principal form of short-term bank funding is an overdraft, secured by a charge over the assets of the business. A little over a quarter of all bank finance for small firms is in the form of an overdraft. The overdraft was originally designed to cover the timing differences of, say, having to acquire raw materials to manufacture finished goods that are later sold.

If you are starting out in a contract cleaning business, say, with a major contract, you need sufficient funds initially to buy the mop and bucket. Three months into the contract they will have been paid for, and so there is no point in getting a five-year bank loan to cover this, as within a year you will have cash in the bank and a loan with an early redemption penalty!

However, if your bank account does not get out of the red at any stage during the year, you will need to re-examine your financing. All too often companies utilise an overdraft to acquire long-term assets, and that overdraft never seems to disappear, eventually constraining the business.

The attraction of overdrafts is that they are very easy to arrange and take little time to set up. That is also their inherent weakness. The key words in the arrangement document are 'repayable on demand', which leaves the bank free to make and change the rules as it sees fit. (This term is under review, and some banks may remove it from the arrangement.) With other forms of borrowing, as long as you stick to the terms and conditions, the loan is yours for the duration. It is not so with overdrafts.

Term loans

If you are starting up a manufacturing business, you will be buying machinery to last probably five years, designing your logo and buying stationery, paying the deposit on leasehold premises, buying a vehicle, and investing funds in winning a long-term contract. As the profits on this will be expected to flow in over a number of years, they need to be financed over a similarly long period of time, either through a bank loan or by inviting someone to invest in shares in the company. In other words, you need a long-term commitment. Term loans, as these long-term borrowings are generally known, are funds provided by a bank for a number of years.

The interest can be either variable, changing with general interest rates, or fixed for a number of years ahead. The proportion of fixed-rate loans has increased from a third of all term loans to around one in two. In some cases it may be possible to move between having a fixed interest rate and a variable one at certain intervals. It may even be possible to have a moratorium on interest payments for a short period, to give the business some breathing space. Provided the conditions of the loan are met in such matters as repayment, interest and security cover, the money is available for the period of the loan. Unlike in the case of an overdraft, the bank cannot pull the rug from under you if circumstances (or the local manager) change.

Just over a third of all term loans are for periods greater than 10 years, and a quarter are for 3 years or less.

Loan guarantee schemes

These are operated by banks at the instigation of governments in the UK, and in Australia, the United States and elsewhere. These schemes guarantee loans from banks and other financial institutions for small businesses with viable business proposals that have tried and failed to obtain a conventional loan because of a lack of security. Loans are available for periods between two and 10 years on sums from £5,000 to £2500,000.

The government guarantees 70–90 per cent of the loan. In return for the guarantee, the borrower pays a premium of 1–2 per cent per year on the outstanding amount of the loan. The commercial aspects of the loan are matters between the borrower and the lender.

Different countries have different conditions, and these can change from year to year, but the basic concept of governments taking a hand to encourage banks to be a little bolder in their approach to new and small firm lending has been well entrenched for over two decades. In recent years in the UK, between 4,000 and 8,000 government-guaranteed loans have been granted each year, for total sums of between £200 million and £300 million.

Other types of bank lending

Banks are usually a good starting point for almost any type of debt financing. If you import raw materials, the bank provides you with letters of credit. If you have a number of overseas suppliers who prefer settlement in their own currency, for which you will need foreign currency checking facilities or buying forward, banks can make the necessary arrangements. They are also able to provide many of the other cash-flow and asset-backed financing products described below, although they are often not the only or the most appropriate provider.

Shopping around for a bank

It is important to remember that banks are in business too. As well as the main clearing banks, a number of the former building societies and smaller regional banks are competing hard for small firm lending.

Abbey National, for example, set out in 2002 to recruit around 600 staff across the United Kingdom as part of a push to snatch market share from its rivals in the business banking market, in a drive to challenge the 'big four' clearing banks in the business banking and finance markets. The move came hot on the heels of an aggressive push by rival HBOS (the merged Halifax and Bank of Scotland) into the small-business banking market. Both groups then announced plans to offer a current account for small businesses, paying interest of 2 per cent.

Usage among small firms of telephone and Internet banking has significantly increased over the past few years. In 1998, 16 per cent of small firms used telephone banking, rising to 35 per cent by 2004. For Internet banking the proportion has risen from 14 per cent to 30 per cent. Branch location seems less likely to be a significant factor to bank customers in the future, so you no longer have to confine your search for a bank to those with a branch nearby. All the major clearing banks offer telephone banking and Internet services to their small business customers, or are in the process of doing so.

Giving bank guarantees

Where the assets of a business are small, anyone lending it money may seek the added protection of requiring the owner to personally guarantee the loan. In the case of limited companies, this is in effect stripping away some of the protection that companies are supposed to afford the risk-taking owner-manager.

Keep these seven factors firmly in mind when your bank raises this issue, as at some stage it almost inevitably will.

1. Resist any suggestion that you should provide any guarantees at all. Make it absolutely clear that this is just not an option as far as you are concerned.
2. Your next line of defence should be to offer the new assets themselves as security. Whatever assets you plan to buy with the funds should be comfort enough. If the bank will not accept those assets at the generally accepted discount, then perhaps you are not making a prudent investment. (A generally accepted discount might be 30 per cent of the value of any stock in trade, 50 per cent of debtors and 80 per cent of freehold property.)
3. If pressed, make any guarantee given as specific as possible. For example, set a maximum value.

4.　Try to secure the guarantee against specific assets only. Perhaps you could persuade the bank to limit its claims against you to, say, one particular property, even though you actually want the funds to finance new stock in trade.

5.　Set clear conditions for the guarantee to come to an end, for example when your overdraft or borrowings return to the level they were at before your most recent request for additional funds. Otherwise the bank may try to retain the extra comfort of the security of a personal guarantee as part of your permanent banking arrangements. In effect, this will leave you exposed to the threat of having the guarantee enforced for ever. It will also take away a negotiating option for any further financing you may need. If the bank already has your personal guarantee, you have little else to offer it.

6.　Make sure the conditions of the additional financing are clear, as are any events that could allow the bank to exercise its rights. For example, it is likely that any funds advanced by a bank will come with some strings attached. These could include what and how much of that money can be spent on which particular assets. So, if the funds are an advance for stock and you use them to buy a new vehicle, however necessary for the business that may be, you will be technically in breach of your loan 'covenants', as these conditions are known.

7.　If you believe that giving a personal guarantee materially changes the nature of the bank's risk, then it may be worth trying for a lower interest rate on the loan. (Banks charge interest at a rate above the base rate. A more risky loan to a small firm may be charged out at 4 per cent over a base rate of 8 per cent. That is 12 per cent in all. But if your personal assets include a second home worth £150,000 on which there is no mortgage, and the total financing you are looking to secure is, say, £50,000, then any financing with that as security should be charged at the rate prevailing for a mortgage. That might be 2 per cent over base, and if it were, your new borrowing rate would be only 10 per cent.)

Remember, everything in business finance is negotiable, and your relationship with a bank is no exception. Banks are in competition too, so if yours is being unreasonably hard, it may be time to move on. Obviously, to be able to move on, you need to have some advance notice of when the additional funds are needed. Rushing into a bank asking for extra finance from next week is hardly likely to inspire much confidence in your abilities as a strategic thinker. That is where your business plan will come into its own.

Credit unions

If you don't like the terms on offer from the high street banks, as the major banks are often known, you could consider forming your own bank. This is not quite as crazy an idea as it sounds. Credit unions formed by groups of small businesspeople, both in business and aspiring to start up, have been around for decades in the United States, the UK and elsewhere. They have been an attractive option for people on low incomes, providing a cheap and convenient alternative to banks. Some self-employed people such as taxi drivers have also formed credit unions. They can then apply for loans to meet unexpected capital expenditure for repairs, refurbishments or technical upgrading.

The popularity of credit unions varies from country to country. In the UK, for example, fewer than one in 300 people belong to one, compared with more than one in three in Canada, Ireland and Australia. Certainly, few could argue about the attractiveness of an annual interest rate 30 per cent below that of the high-street lenders, which is what credit unions aim for. Members have to save regularly to qualify for a loan, although there is no minimum deposit, and after 10 weeks, members with a good track record can borrow up to five times their savings, although they must continue to save while repaying the loan. There is no set interest rate, but dividends are distributed to members from any surplus, usually about 5 per cent a year. This too compares favourably with bank interest on deposit accounts.

Local Exchange Trading Systems (LETS)

Almost 450 LETS schemes are currently in operation and whilst some have only a dozen members while the largest, in Manchester, has over 380. All in all, over 40,000 people are involved in this method of trading. Anyone who joins a scheme offers skills or services, such as plumbing, gardening or the use of a photocopier, to other members. A price is agreed in whatever notional currency has been adopted, but no money changes hands. The system is more ambitious than straight barter. The provider receives a credit on his or her account kept by a local organiser, and a debit is marked up against the user. The person in credit can then set this against other services.

The trades that have used LETS successfully include restaurateurs, plumbers, carpenters, lawyers, retailers of all descriptions, cycle shops, freelance writers, piano teachers, translation agencies, cleaners, typists, gardeners, tree surgeons, security guards, bookkeepers and child-minders. No interest is paid on LETS, but all the usual tax and Value Added Tax rules apply to businesses trading in this way.

The benefits of using LETS are that you can start trading and grow with virtually no start-up capital. All you need are time and saleable skills – once you have 'sold' your wares, payment is immediate by way of a LETS credit. Also, using LETS means that the wealth is kept in the local community, which means customers in your area may be able to spend more with you. For example, one shop that used to accept 25 per cent of the value of its goods in LETS was surprised at how sharply its turnover increased when it increased the proportion to 50 per cent.

One of the keys to success in using LETS is to have an enterprising organiser who can produce, maintain and circulate a wide-ranging directory of LETS services and outlets.

Borrowing from family and friends

Those close to you might be willing to lend you money or invest in your business. This helps you avoid the problem of pleading your case to outsiders and enduring extra paperwork and bureaucratic delays. Help from friends, relatives and business associates can be especially valuable if you have been through bankruptcy or had other credit problems that would make borrowing from a commercial lender difficult or impossible.

Their involvement brings a range of extra potential benefits, costs and risks that are not a feature of most other types of finance. You need to decide which of these are acceptable.

Some advantages of borrowing money from people you know well are that you may be charged a lower interest rate, may be able to delay paying back money until you are more established, and may be given more flexibility if you get into a jam. But once the loan terms are agreed to, you have the same legal obligations as you would with a bank or any other source of finance.

In addition, borrowing money from relatives and friends can have a major disadvantage. If your business does poorly and those close to you end up losing money, you may well damage a good personal relationship. So, in dealing with friends, relatives and business associates, be extra careful not only to establish clearly the terms of the deal and put it in writing, but also to make an extra effort to explain the risks. In short, it is your job to make sure your helpful friend or relative will not suffer true hardship if you are unable to meet your financial commitments.

Many types of businesses have loyal and devoted followers, people who care as much about the business as the owners do. A health food restaurant, a specialist bookstore or an art gallery, for example, may attract people who are enthusiastic about lending money to or investing in the business because it fits in with their lifestyle or philosophy.

Their decision to participate is driven to some extent by their feelings, and is not strictly a business proposition. The rules for borrowing from friends and relatives apply here as well. Put repayment terms in writing, and do not accept money from people who cannot afford to risk it.

Financing cash flow

Customers often take time to pay up. In the meantime you have to pay those who work for you and your less patient suppliers. So, the more you grow, the more funds you need. It is often possible to 'factor' your creditworthy customers' bills to a financial institution, receiving some of the funds as your goods leave the door, hence speeding up cash flow.

Factoring is generally only available to a business that invoices other business customers, either in its home market or internationally, for its services. Factoring can be made available to new businesses, although its services are usually of most value during the early stages of growth. It is an arrangement that allows you to receive up to 80 per cent of the cash due from your customers more quickly than they would normally pay. The factoring company in effect buys your trade debts, and can also provide a debtor accounting and administration service. In other words, it takes over the day-to-day work of invoicing and sending out reminders and statements. This can be a particularly helpful service to a small, expanding business. It allows the management to concentrate on expanding the business, with the factoring company providing expert guidance on credit control, 100 per cent protection against bad debts, and improved cash flow.

You will, of course, have to pay for factoring services. Having the cash before your customers pay will cost you a little more than normal overdraft rates. The factoring service will cost between 0.5 and 3.5 per cent of the turnover, depending on volume of work, the number of debtors, average invoice amount and other related factors. You can get up to 80 per cent of the value of your invoice in advance, with the remainder paid when your customer settles up, less the various charges just mentioned.

If you sell direct to the public, sell complex and expensive capital equipment, or expect progress payments on long-term projects, then factoring is not for you. If you are expanding more rapidly than other sources of finance will allow, this may be a useful service that is worth exploring.

Invoice discounting is a variation on the same theme. However, the majority of small firms continue to prefer factoring to invoice discounting because it enables them to outsource their financial management controls. Factors collect in money owed by a firm's customers, whereas invoice discounters leave it to the firm itself, which could be an advantage for firms that fear the factoring method might reduce their contact with clients. Invoice discounting is in any case typically available only to businesses with a turnover in excess of £1 million.

Cash-flow financing accounts for £8 billion of business financing, up from £2 billion in 1990.

The most commonly used formula to value a business is the price/earnings (P/E) ratio. This indicates the number of times annual profits at which a business is valued. If you look up any listed company's performance in the financial press, you will see a P/E ratio, calculated as the share price divided by the earnings per share. So, if the share price of the business in question is £10 and the earnings per share are 80p, the P/E ratio is 12.5. This is another way of saying the company is worth 12½ years' profits. This is a reasonably typical figure, but a company in the Internet sector, for example, might have a quite different multiple in force. Two hundred and thirty-five years times earnings is an all-time record in this sector. For less glamorous sectors with much lower growth prospects, the P/E ratio might be in single figures. While it may seem a pretty rarefied idea to someone starting out in business, the stock market is where the framework for values is set.

So, if your business is in the food sector, and a typical P/E ratio in that sector is 12, that is where outsiders will start when they think about valuing your business. Then a few things get added and taken away. The first seriously negative event is the discount that will be applied because your business is not on the stock market. Private businesses are generally viewed as being worth at least a third less than a publicly quoted firm listed on a stock exchange. That is because shares in a public company are much more liquid. There are more shares and more buyers and sellers for a quoted than for an unquoted business's shares. Valuations are also affected by the numbers and skills of the founding team. A business run by one person is generally valued at around half the value of a comparable private company run by a team of three or more experienced managers. The reasoning here is that customers are probably loyal to the owner manager and may not come over to any new owner. That in turn means that the future value of the business will be lower, in the absence of extra sales effort.

One last factor that affects private business valuations is the economic cycle. At the bottom of the cycle (a downturn), on average small private firms sell on multiples of between 6 and 8. At the top of the cycle (a boom), the same firm may sell for between 10 and 12.

All these figures are illustrative only. Every business sale and every circumstance has unique elements to it that can greatly affect the final outcome.

How much equity should you sell?

The answer is as little as you can to raise the money you need now. If you are successful in business you will need to raise more money in the future. Also, as you grow and become profitable, your shares will be worth more. The more your shares are worth, the fewer you have to sell to raise a given amount of finance.

As a benchmark you should remember that retaining less than 76 per cent of the business will mean that you do not have absolute control. If outsiders have over 25 per cent of your shares they can challenge your decisions and slow you down, in much the same way as the House of Lords can hold back the Commons. If you end up with less than 50 per cent, then you have lost effective control. However, these figures represent the legal position, and may have little impact on the real position on the ground. If you are doing a great job and all is going to plan, it is unlikely that you will face any serious challenge to your decisions.

No outside investor in an early-stage venture will want to take so many shares away from you that it acts as a disincentive. Investors know they have to keep you motivated and feeling like the owner, rather than simply being their manager. So, plan on selling no more than a third, and ideally less than 15 per cent, of your shares on any initial round of financing.

SOURCES OF RISK CAPITAL

There are only a handful of types of organisation a new or young business can go to raise equity or risk capital. A description of these different sources is given below, and contact details are provided in Appendix 2.

Business angels

One likely first source of equity or risk capital will be a private individual with his or her own funds, and perhaps some knowledge of your type of business. In return for a share in the business, such investors will put in money at their own risk. They have been christened 'business angels', a term first coined to describe private wealthy individuals who back theatrical productions, usually a play on Broadway or in London's West End. By their very nature, such investments are highly speculative, as shows tend to either soar or bomb. The angel typically has a personal interest in the production, the arts in general, or perhaps in a member of the cast. He or she might also want to play some role in the production, or in negotiating an aspect of the business relationship between the players and the theatre or some other outside party. In any event, most angels are determined upon some involvement beyond merely signing a cheque.

There is no rational way to calculate either risk or reward in such ventures. A great writer and a great cast are not guarantors of success. In the same way, total unknowns can also triumph. The chances of losing money are high.

Business angels are a similar breed. They are informal suppliers of risk capital to new and growing businesses, often taking a hand at the stage when no one else will take the chance. They form a sort of investor of last resort, but while they often lose their shirts, they sometimes make serious money. One angel who backed Sage with £10,000 in its first round of £250,000 financing saw his stake rise to £40 million.

These angels often have their own agenda, and frequently operate through managed networks. Angel networks operate throughout the world, and in some cases these networks operate on the Internet. In the UK and the United States there are hundreds of networks, with tens of thousands of business angels prepared to put up several billion pounds each year into new or small business.

Research has unravelled these sketchy facts about business angels as a breed. Knowing them may help you find the right one for your business.

- Business angels are generally self-made, high-net-worth individuals, with entrepreneurial backgrounds. Most are in the 45 to 65 age group. Nineteen per cent are millionaires. Only 1 per cent of business angels are women.
- Fifty per cent of angels conduct minimal or no sector research. They meet their entrepreneur an average of 5.4 times before investing (compared with venture capitalists, who meet them on average 9.5 times), and 54 per cent of angels neglect to take up independent personal references compared with only 6 per cent of venture capitalists.
- Typically, business angels are investing 5–15 per cent of their investment portfolio in this way, and their motivation is, first and foremost, financial gain through capital appreciation, with the fun and enjoyment of being involved with an entrepreneurial business an important secondary motive. A minority are motivated in part by altruistic considerations, such as helping the next generation of entrepreneurs to get started, and supporting their country or state.
- Business angels invest in only a very small proportion of investments that they see: typically at least seven out of eight opportunities are rejected. More than 90 per cent of investment opportunities are rejected at the initial screening stage.
- Around 30 per cent of investments by business angels are in technology-based businesses. Most will tell you that they vigorously avoid investing in industries they know nothing about.
- The majority of business angels invest in businesses located in close proximity to where they live – two-thirds of investments are made in businesses located within 100 miles of their home or office. They are, however, prepared to look further afield if they have specific sector-related investment preferences or if they are technology investors.
- Ninety-two per cent of angels have worked in a small firm, compared, for example, with only 52 per cent of venture capitalists who have similar experience.

■ On average, business angels sell their shareholding in the most successful investments after four years (and 75 per cent sell within seven years). Conversely, half of the investments in which business angels lost money had failed within two years of the investment being made.

■ Angels fundamentally back people rather than propositions.

■ Business angels are up to five times more likely to invest in start-ups and early-stage investments than venture capital providers in general.

One estimate is that the UK has approximately 18,000 business angels, and that they annually invest in the region of £500 million.

Venture capital

Venture capital (VC) providers are investing other people's money, often from pension funds. They have a different agenda from that of business angels, and are more likely to be interested in investing more money for a larger stake.

VC is a means of financing the start-up, development, expansion or purchase of a company. The venture capitalist acquires an agreed proportion of the share capital (equity) of the company in return for providing the requisite funding. VC firms often work in conjunction with other providers of finance in putting together a total funding package for a business. VC has its origins in the late 18th century, when entrepreneurs found wealthy individuals to back their projects. Worldwide, several hundred VC firms invest.

VC is a medium to long-term investment of not just money, but time and effort. The VC firm's aim is to enable growth companies to develop into the major businesses of tomorrow.

VCs go through a process known as 'due diligence' before investing. This process involves a thorough examination of both the business and its owners. Past financial performance, the directors' track record and the business plan are all subjected to detailed scrutiny, usually by accountants and lawyers. Directors are then required to 'warrant' that they have provided *all* relevant information, under pain of financial penalties. The cost of this process will have to be borne by the firm raising the money, but it will be paid out of the money raised, if that is any consolation.

In general, VCs expect their investment to have paid off within seven years, but they are hardened realists. Two in every 10 investments they make are total write-offs, and six perform averagely well at best. So, the one star in every 10 investments they make has to cover a lot of duds. VCs have a target rate of return of 30 per cent plus, to cover this poor hit rate.

Raising venture capital is not a cheap option. The arrangement costs will almost always run to six figures. The deals are not quick to arrange either. Six months is not unusual, and over a year has been known. Every VC has a deal done in six weeks in its portfolio, but that truly is the exception.

VC providers will want to exit from their investment at some stage. Their preferred route is via a public offering (see below), but a trade sale is more usual.

While VC is big business, the value of funds invested in early-stage UK companies has remained modest, at just a few per cent of all the funds invested. While this is mainly attributable to the risk–reward relationship, the due diligence and transaction costs involved in investing in small companies are similar to those associated with investments in large companies, and so they are far higher per unit of funds invested. But don't despair. New venture capital funds are coming on stream all the time, and they too are looking for a gap in the market.

Going public

Taking your business to a stock market and raising risk capital from the general public is also a possibility. Not many do it, but at the peak a few hundred firms a year were funded in this way. There are two possible types of stock markets on which to gain a public listing. A full listing on the London Stock Exchange, the New York Stock Exchange or any other major country's exchange calls for a track record of making substantial profits, with decent seven-figure sums being made in the year you plan to float, as this process is known. A full listing also calls for a large proportion of the company's shares to be put up for sale at the outset. (In the UK this would be at least 25 per cent of the company's shares.)

In addition, you would be expected to have 100 shareholders now and be able to demonstrate that 100 more will come on board as a result of the listing. This is rarely an appealing idea to entrepreneurs, who expect to see their share price rise in later years and are loath to sell off so much of the business at what they believe to be a bargain basement price. There is also the threat of a takeover with so many of the shares in so many other people's hands. However, if going public appeals to you, the US market may be the best place to float. The value placed on new companies on its stock markets is between three and five times that in UK and European markets.

Junior markets such as London's Alternative Investment Market (AIM) are a much more attractive proposition for entrepreneurs seeking equity capital. Formed in the mid to late 1990s specifically to provide risk capital for new rather than established ventures, these markets have an altogether more relaxed atmosphere.

The AIM is the largest junior market in Europe. Over 350 firms are listed, and some £3 billion of new equity capital has been raised. AIM is particularly attractive to any dynamic company of any size, age or business sector that has rapid growth in mind. The smallest firm on AIM entered at under £1 million capitalisation, and the largest at over £330 million. The formalities are minimal, but the costs of entry are high and you must have a nominated adviser, such as a major accountancy firm, stockbroker or banker.

Going public also puts a stamp of respectability on you and your company. It will enhance the status and credibility of your business, and it will enable you to borrow more against the security provided by your new shareholders, should you so wish. Your shares will also provide an attractive way to retain and motivate key staff. If they are given, or rather are allowed to earn, share options at discounted prices, they too can participate in the capital gains you are making.

With a public share listing you can now join in the takeover and asset-stripping game. When your share price is high and things are going well, you can look out for weaker firms to gobble up – and all you have to do is to offer them more of your shares in return for theirs. You do not even have to find real money.

WORKSHEET FOR ASSIGNMENT 16: FINANCING REQUIREMENTS

Based on your financial projections, state how much cash you need to raise to set up your business, and how and when you propose to repay it.

Use the questions below as the format for your worksheet.

1. Based on the maximum figure in your cash-flow forecast, how much money do you need and what do you need it for?
2. How does this compare with the sum that you and your partners or shareholders are putting in (ie level of gearing)?

$$\text{Gearing} = \frac{\text{Total funds required for business}}{\text{Money put in by you} + \text{shareholders}}$$

For example, if you already have £1,000 of assets and are looking for a loan of £5,000, the funds required are £6,000. If you have already invested £500 and plan to put in a further £2,500, then your gearing is:

$$\frac{6{,}000}{500 + 2{,}500} = \frac{6{,}000}{3{,}000} = 2{:}1$$

3. Where do you expect to raise the funds you need to finance your business?
4. Prepare a schedule showing when you need these funds.
5. How and when will any borrowing be repaid?

Source of repayment   *Amount £*   *Date*

_____

_____

_____

Total £

6. If you plan to issue shares, how will you value the business?
7. What deal do you propose to offer to a potential investor? (Include some idea of how much equity you are prepared to sell.)
8. What exit route(s) could be open to potential investors?
9. What security, if any, is available as collateral for any loan?

Security   *Value £*

_____

_____

_____

Total £

10. Will you be receiving any grants or loans to help to finance your business (other than from the organisation to which you are now applying)?

Source   *Date*   *Funds provided*   *Amount £*

_____

_____

_____

Total £

11. What further private cash, if any, is available to invest in the business?

Source   *Date*   *Funds provided*   *Amount £*

_____

_____

_____

Total £

12. What are the key risks that could adversely affect your projections?
     (These could include technical, financial and marketing risks.)

     Risk area   *Financial impact on*
                                                    Sales   *Profits*
     _____

     _____

     _____

13. What contingency plans do you have either to manage or to minimise
     the consequences of these risks?

     Risk area   *Plan*   *Effect*
     _____

     _____

SUGGESTED FURTHER READING

Barrow, Colin (2000) *How to Survive the Business Downturn*, 'Part 4', Wiley, Chichester

Barrow, Colin (2004) *Business Accounting for Dummies*, John Wiley, New York

Phase 6

Business controls

Introduction

No one is likely to take any business proposition seriously unless the founder(s) can demonstrate at the outset that they can monitor and control the venture.

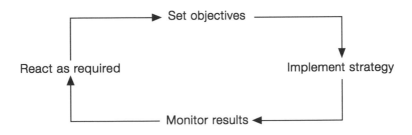

Figure 6.1 The control cycle

Just as your business plan should include a statement of objectives and strategy, it must also contain a brief description of how you will monitor results.

Every business needs to monitor financial, sales and market performance. Manufacturing businesses or those involved in research, development and fashion may have to observe results on a much wider scale.

In these assignments you should address the issues of importance to your type of business. If you do not have first-hand experience of working in a similar business, either find someone who has or find a professional adviser, such as an auditor, with that experience.

As a minimum, potential financiers will want to see that you have made arrangements to keep the books.

17

Financial controls

To survive and prosper in business, you need to know how much cash you have and what your profit or loss on sales is. For a business to survive, let alone grow, these facts are needed on a monthly, weekly or occasionally even a daily basis depending on the nature of the business.

While bad luck plays a part in some business failures, a lack of reliable financial information plays a part in most. However, all the information needed to manage well is close at hand. The bills to be paid, invoices raised, petty-cash slips and bank statements between them are enough to give a true picture of performance. All that needs to be done is for the information on them to be recorded and organised so that the financial picture becomes clear. The way financial information is recorded is known as 'bookkeeping'.

But it is not just the owner of a company who needs these financial facts. Bankers, shareholders and tax inspectors will be unsympathetic audiences to anyone without well-documented facts to back them up. If, for example, a tax authority presents a business with a tax demand, the onus then lies with the businessperson, using his or her records, to either agree with or dispute the sum claimed. If you are unable to adequately explain a bank deposit, the tax authority may treat it as taxable income. A bank manager faced with a request for an increased overdraft facility to help a small business grow needs financial facts to work with. Without them, the bank will generally have to say no, as it has a responsibility to the owners of the money it would be using.

Keeping even the simplest of records – perhaps as little as writing down the source of a deposit on a slip or in your cheque book – and recording the event in a book or ledger will make your relations with tax inspectors and bankers go much more smoothly.

If you just pile your bills, receipts and cheque stubs into an old shoebox and take it to an accountant at the end of the year (or when you run out of cash), it will cost a lot more to get your accounts done than if you had kept good records in the first place. In addition, you will have had a stressful period of being unsure of how well or badly you are doing.

Starting simple

If you are doing books by hand and don't have a lot of transactions, the single-entry method is the easiest acceptable way to go. This involves writing down each transaction in your records once, preferably on a ledger sheet. You record the flow of income and expenses through your business by making a running total of money taken in ('gross receipts') and money paid out ('payments' or, as they are sometimes called, 'disbursements'). Receipts and payments should be kept and summarised daily, weekly or monthly, in accordance with the needs of the business. At the end of the year, the 12 monthly summaries are totalled up – you are ready for tax time.

This simple record system is known as a 'cash book' – an example is given in Table 6.1.

In the left-hand four columns, the month's expenses are entered as they occur, together with some basic details and the amount. At the head of the first column is the amount of cash brought forward from the preceding month.

On the right, expenses are listed in the same way. The total of receipts for the month is £1,480.15 and that for expenses is £672.01. The difference between these two figures is the amount of cash now in the business. As the business shown in Table 6.1 has brought in more cash than it has spent, the figure is higher than the amount brought forward at the beginning of the month. The figure of £808.14 is the amount that is 'brought down' to be 'brought forward' to the next month. The total of the month's payments and the amount 'carried down' are equal to the sum of all the receipts in the left-hand columns.

If there are a reasonably large number of transactions, it would be sensible to extend this simple cash book to include a basic analysis of the figures – this variation is called an 'analysed cash book'. An example of the payments side of an analysed cash book is shown in Table 6.2 (the receipts side is similar, but with different categories). You can see at a glance the receipts and payments, both in total and by main category. This breakdown lets you see, for example, how much is being spent on each major area of your business, or who your most important customers are. The payments are the same as in Table 6.1, but now we can see how much we have spent on stock, vehicles and telephone expenses. The sums total both down the amount columns and across the analysis section to arrive at the same amount: £672.01. This is both a useful bit of management information and essential for your tax return.

If you are taking *or* giving credit, you will need to keep more information than the cash book – whether it is analysed or not.
You will need to keep copies of paid and unpaid sales invoices and the same for purchases, as well as your bank statements. The bank statements should

Table 6.1 A simple cash-book system

Receipts				Payments			
Date	Name	Details	Amount £	Date	Name	Details	Amount £
1 June	Balance	Brought forward	450.55	4 June	Gibbs	Stock purchase	310.00
4 June	Anderson	Sales	175.00	8 June	Gibbs	Stock purchase	130.00
6 June	Brown	Sales	45.00	12 June	ABC Telecoms	Telephone charges	55.23
14 June	Smith & Co	Refund on returned stock	137.34	18 June	Colt Rentals	Vehicle hire	87.26
17 June	Jenkins	Sales	190.25	22 June	VV Mobiles	Mobile phone	53.24
20 June	Hollis	Sales	425.12	27 June	Gibbs	Stock purchase	36.28
23 June	Jenkins	Sales	56.89				
							672.01
				30 June	Balance	Carried down	808.14
			1,480.15				1,480.15
1 July	Balance	Brought down	808.14				

then be 'reconciled' to your cash book to tie everything together. For example, the bank statement for the example given in Table 6.1 should show £808.14 in the account at the end of June. Figure 6.1 outlines how this works.

Building a system

If you operate a partnership, trade as a company or plan to get big, then you will need a double-entry bookkeeping system. This calls for a series of day books, ledgers, a journal, a petty-cash book and a wages book, as well as a number of files for copies of invoices and receipts.

The double-entry system requires two entries for each transaction – this provides built-in checks and balances to ensure accuracy. Each transaction requires an entry as a debit and as a credit. This may sound a little complicated, but you only need to get a general idea.

A double-entry system is more complicated and time-consuming if done by hand, since everything is recorded twice. If done manually, the method

Table 6.2   Example of an analysed cash book

Payments				Analysis			
Date	Name	Details	Amount £	Stocks	Vehicles	Telephone	Other
4 June	Gibbs	Stock purchase	310	310			
8 June	Gibbs	Stock purchase	130	130			
12 June	ABC Telecoms	Telephone charges	55.23			55.23	
18 June	Colt Rentals	Vehicle hire	87.26		87.26		
22 June	VV Mobiles	Mobile phone	53.24			53.24	
27 June	Gibbs	Stock purchase	36.28	36.28			
Totals			**672.01**	**476.28**	**87.26**	**108.47**	

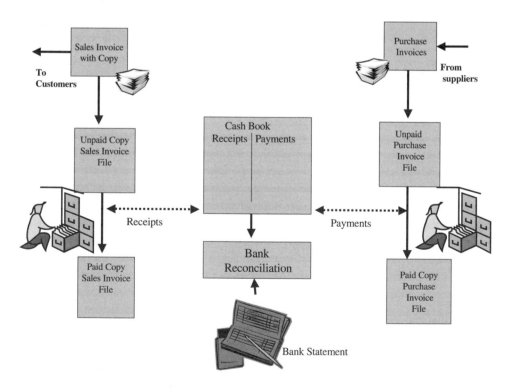

Figure 6.1   A simple system of business records

requires a formal set of books – journals and ledgers. All transactions would be first entered into a journal and then 'posted' (written) on a ledger sheet – the same amount would be written down in two different places. Typical ledger accounts include those for titled income, expenses, assets and liabilities (debts).

To give an example, a payment of rent in a double-entry system might result in two separate journal entries – a debit for an expense of, say, £250 and a corresponding credit of £250 – a double entry (see Table 6.3). The debits in a double-entry system must always equal the credits. If they don't, you know there is an error somewhere. So, double entry allows you to balance your books, which you can't do with the single-entry method.

Table 6.3 An example of a double-entry ledger

General Journal of Andrew's Bookshop			
Date	**Description of entry**	**Debit**	**Credit**
10th July	Rent expense Cash	£250	 £250

The records to be kept include :

- *Day books.* Sometimes called 'journals' or 'books of original entry', these are where each transaction is initially recorded in date order. Each day book is used to cater for one kind of transaction, so if there are enough transactions of a particular kind, you open a day book for it. For example, there may always be enough cash transactions to warrant a cash day book. If a firm sells on credit, then there will be a sales day book. Cash day books are described below.
- *Cash books.* Many small businesses trade in both cash (notes and coins) and cheques. For bookkeeping purposes these are all called cash, although initially a separate record is kept of each. The petty-cash book is used to record transactions in notes and coins. Money in is on the left-hand page and money out is on the right. The money out could include such items as stamps or office coffee. Always keep receipts, as one day you may have to verify these records. Once a week (or daily if the sums involved justify it), total the money in and out to get a cash balance. Check that it agrees with actual cash from the till or cash box.

The cash book records all receipts and payments made by cheque. Once again, money in is on the left-hand page and money out is on the right. Every week, add up both pages to arrive at the balance of the cash in your bank. This should be checked against your bank statement at least once a month to ensure that the basic information you are working with is correct.

- *Sales ledger and purchase ledger.* If your business gives credit to customers or takes credit from suppliers, you will need a sales and a purchase ledger. Each ledger should ideally have a separate page for every business that you deal with.

  On the right-hand side of the purchase ledger are listed the date, description, amount and cost of each item bought on credit. On the left-hand side a record is kept of all payments made to the supplier, along with the items for which the payments were made. Each month, by deducting the left-hand total from the right, you can see how much each supplier is owed. Suppliers ought to send you a statement and you can use that to check your own view of the situation.

  The sales ledger deals with customers in much the same way. One important difference is that credit sales are shown on the left-hand side of the ledger, while customers' payments appear on the right. This is simply an accounting convention to deal with credits and debits. It would also be very useful to keep a note of customers' (and suppliers') addresses, telephone numbers and contacts' names with each entry in the ledgers. This will ensure you have all the relevant information when chasing up payments or dealing with queries.

- *Capital or asset register.* Limited companies have to keep a capital register. This records capital items they own, such as land, buildings, equipment or vehicles, showing the cost at date of purchase. It also records the disposal of any of these items and the cumulative depreciation.

- *Nominal or private ledger.* This is usually kept by your accountant or bookkeeper. It brings together all the information from the 'primary ledgers' (the other basic records). Expenses from the cash books and purchase ledger are posted to the left-hand side of the nominal ledger. Income from sales (and any other income) is posted to the right. Normally, each type of expense or income has a separate page, which makes subsequent analysis an easier task.

- *The trial balance.* Every month, each page in the nominal ledger is totalled and used to prepare a trial balance. The sum of all the left-hand totals should end up equalling the sum of all the right-hand totals. This is the basis of double-entry bookkeeping, and is what gives you confidence that the figures are correctly recorded.

Using a computer

With the cost of a basic computerised accounting system starting at barely £50, and a reasonable package costing between £200 and £500, it makes good sense to plan to use such a system from the outset. Some advantages of using a computerised system are:

- No more arithmetical errors. As long as the information is entered correctly, it will be added up correctly. With a computer, a £250 rent expenditure, for example, is input as an expense (a debit) – the computer then automatically posts it to the rent account as a credit. In effect, the computer eliminates the extra step of the double-entry system and the need to master the difference between debit and credit.
- Using a computer, routine tasks such as filling in the tax return (as well as VAT in Europe and sales tax in the United States) take minutes rather than days. The system can ensure your returns are accurate and fully reconciled. With a computerised system, invoices will always be accurate. You can see at a glance which customers are regularly taking too long to pay. In addition, reminder statements can be automatically prepared.
- If your business is concerned with stock-holding, a computerised system can help you to match stock levels to demand. It could even provide profit-margin information quickly by product so you are able to see which products are worth promoting and which are less attractive.
- Your year-end accounts preparation and, where appropriate, audit will be greatly streamlined. This will save time and money, and allow you to monitor profits and cash flow accurately.

If your business has relatively few transactions each month, say no more than 20 or 30 items to record, a half-way house towards computerisation would be to use a spreadsheet. This will not give you the advantages of a double-entry accounting system, but with the number of items you need to record, the chances are you will not need one. Using a spreadsheet will reduce the chances of arithmetical errors, save time in adding and subtracting columns and make the calculations in an analysed cash book much easier to do. If you already have a spreadsheet, the only additional cost will be the time taken writing the relevant equations to apply to the various 'cells' in the spreadsheet.

There are also a number of Internet solutions available for small- and medium-sized businesses.

Cranfield MBAs Humphrey Drummond and Ali Hakeem established Ascot Drummond (www.ascotdrummond.co.uk) to provide a service for the self-employed and small businesses that do not want to spend their Friday evenings 'doing the books'. Daily and weekly records are sent to Humphrey Drummond at his London office, where they are scanned in; they are then downloaded in Pakistan, where Ali's team of accountants maintain and complete the books at minimal costs.

Two suppliers with a good range of products are:

The Sage Group PLC
Sage House
Benton Park Road
Newcastle upon Tyne NE7 7LZ

Quick Books
Intuit Service Centre
Freepost SCE127
Swindon
Wilts SN5 8ZZ

Tel: 0191 255 3000
Fax: 0191 255 0308
Web site: www.uk.sage.com

Tel: 0800 585058
Fax: 0845 6011571
Web site: www.intuit.co.uk

Starting up my business consumed all the cash we had. So, to save money I planned to do my own accounts. Unfortunately, we were so successful I never had time to do the books. Sure, we sent out invoices. And when the bank complained we were over our overdraft limit, I would call in a few favours and get some customers to pay up. I paid our bills when I had the money – or if we needed more supplies from someone we owed money to.

It just seemed that if we were so busy we must be making money. At the end of the year I realised I would never get the accounts done, so I took my shoeboxes full of bills to an accountant. As well as incurring an unexpected four-figure bill for all the work involved in sorting out the mess, the accountant revealed that we had lost money, not made it. To make matters worse, we had passed the threshold for VAT registration, and failed to register. I was now in trouble with the VAT man.

All in all, a very busy but totally unproductive year. With a good accounting system I would have seen where we were going wrong within three months.

(Name withheld to save embarrassment)

WORKSHEET FOR ASSIGNMENT 17: FINANCIAL CONTROLS

1. What bookkeeping and accounting system have you chosen and why?
2. What control information does it produce and with what frequency?
3. Who will keep the books and produce the accounts?
4. Who will your auditors be?

SUGGESTED FURTHER READING

Bannister, Tony (2004) *Straightforward Guide to Bookkeeping and Accounts*, Straight Forward Publishing, Brighton

Barrow, Colin (2001) *Financial Management for the Small Business*, 5th edn, Kogan Page, London

Kirkland, Keith and Howard, Stuart (1998) *Simple and Practical Book-keeping*, Kogan Page, London

Muggeridge, Les (1994) *A Guide to Accountancy Software*, 2nd edn, Kogan Page in association with the Institute of Chartered Accountants of Scotland, London

18

Sales and marketing controls

In the early weeks and months of any new venture, large amounts of both effort and money will be expended without any visible signs of sales revenue, let alone profits. Even once the business has been trading for some time, the most reliable predictor of likely future results will be the sales and marketing efforts for the immediate past. Your business plan should explain how you intend to monitor and control this activity.

Gordon Smith set up his business, the Supreme Garden Furniture Company, shortly after being made redundant. Using 800 square feet on the ground floor of an old Lancashire textile mill, he planned to produce a range of one- to four-seat garden benches in an authentic Victorian design, together with matching tables. Each item in the range was manufactured to a very high standard using top-quality materials, such as kiln-dried African Iroko hardwood.

With professional advice he drew up a business plan incorporating cash and profit forecasts, an assessment of the market and his likely competitors, the plant and machinery required and the start-up capital he would need.

His main customers would be garden centres and he planned to spend a couple of days a week out on the road selling, initially in Lancashire, Yorkshire and Cheshire. He also produced a leaflet and price-list which he intended to send to potential customers further afield. These he would follow up later.

Smith could incorporate the sales and marketing controls shown in Figure 6.1 (page 286) in his initial business plan to monitor his performance.

Once Smith had gained a number of customers, he found that future sales to *existing customers* were much easier than constantly seeking new customers. So, he kept records of existing customers, to monitor their purchases and plan follow-up visits.

From an analysis of his customer records Smith was subsequently able to discover that garden centres in the South-East placed average orders of £2,000 a time, while in his home area a £500 order was exceptional. In his business plan for his second year's trading he would be able to incorporate this information and alter his selling strategy accordingly.

Controlling your promotional costs and judging their cost-effectiveness is also an early, vital marketing control task.

Table 6.4 Example of how to monitor promotional costs

Week	No of enquiries received	No of leaflets sent	No of quotations given	No of customers seen	Estimate of sales worth of week's activity

Autoglass depots had a questionnaire placed next to the till, requiring the receptionist to ask each paying customer how they had heard of the Autoglass service. The questionnaire listed the communication channels used by the company, including local press adverts, *Yellow Pages*, leaflets to garages, and insurance company recommendations. Each month a summary list of items ticked was compared with depot promotional expenditure, enabling savings to be made in expensive but unproductive avenues (eg local press) and increasing expenditure on useful media (eg *Yellow Pages*). Later, the monitoring information required was obtained by incorporating the questions on to the customer invoice form itself. This ensured that information on work completed off-depot site was also collected.

Equally, advertising costs per sales lead generated and converted should be recorded, while tear-off coupons, discounts on production or special offer leaflets all help to measure the cost-effectiveness of your promotions.

WORKSHEET FOR ASSIGNMENT 18: SALES AND MARKETING CONTROLS

1. Describe your records for monitoring sales activities.
2. Draw up a customer record card for your business, or show your existing one.
3. What other marketing records do you plan to keep, eg for advertising costs and results?

A customer record card for the Supreme Garden Furniture Company

Customer's name, address, phone number, key contacts and best time to phone and visit

_____

_____

_____

_____

Buying record

Date	Products bought	Value	Comments (if any)
		£	
		£	
		£	
		£	

Visit/Phone record

Date	Purpose of call	Results	Action

Special requirements

_____

_____

Figure 6.2   Example customer record card

SUGGESTED FURTHER FEADING

Stewart, Grant (1999) *Successful Sales Management*, Financial Times/Prentice-Hall, London

Waterhouse, Steve (2003) *The Team Selling Solution: Creating and managing teams that win the complex sale*, McGraw-Hill Education, New York

19

Other business controls

Depending on the nature of your venture, your business plan will have to show how you plan to control other aspects of the firm's performance. These could include:

- manufacturing and production;
- personnel records/accident reports;
- quality and complaints;
- new product development/design.

Stock cards for the different stages of your production process (raw materials, work-in-progress, finished goods) are particularly important to help you identify fast- and slow-moving items and to help you identify correct safety stock levels. Equally, to permit customers to complain (better than them voting with their feet, without telling you) you will need to provide customer suggestion boxes or explanations as to how to contact key managers, eg by giving a name and contact address on a restaurant menu.

WORKSHEET FOR ASSIGNMENT 19: OTHER BUSINESS CONTROLS

1. What other business controls do you plan to introduce into your business at the outset?
2. Why do you consider them important?

SUGGESTED FURTHER READING

Barrow, Colin (1988) *Business Controls*, Open University, Milton Keynes
Gupta, Praveen (2003) *Six Sigma Business Scorecard: Creating a comprehensive corporate measurement system*, McGraw-Hill, New York

BUILD YOUR BUSINESS — NOT YOUR OVERHEADS

If you can tick ANY of the boxes below you should be talking to us.

- ☐ Cash flow under pressure?
- ☐ Keeping up to date with ledgers a problem?
- ☐ Chasing outstanding debt a hassle?
- ☐ The cost of maintaining an accounts department a big overhead on time and money?
- ☐ Paying more tax than you wish you had to?
- ☐ Tax audit fee too big?

Give us your headaches and you can get on with building your business and income.

Backroom
Business Solutions

www.backroomsolutions.com
Telephone: **020 8905 2526**

Changing the way you run your business could save you a fortune...

What are the most thankless and time consuming tasks of any business today? You will probably agree that managing the day to day finances and keeping track of the paperwork is everyone's bugbear. Finding and keeping staff to do these tasks or being forced to do them yourself is also a headache and in the end can be costly and stressful. Time is money and handing over essential but laborious day-to-day activities may be the answer to your problems.

Think about how much easier life would be without having to deal with delivery notes, invoices and credit notes. Then there is the chore of paying bills, banking payments and chasing people for money. If that isn't enough there is VAT, payroll, sickness, maternity leave and holiday cover.

Who has time to make money? What goes on behind the scenes is just as important as the product or service that you offer to your customers. In reality many businesses just struggle along, hoping that the paperwork will not get on top of them and that the accountants will sort out all the problems at the end of the month or at the end of the tax year!

How would you feel if all the really laborious parts of the business were collected up and dealt with on a daily basis so that everything could run smoothly and cashflow management was no longer a problem? Well, now you can, by handing over these tasks to Backroom Business Solutions (BBS), who will manage everything from paying bills to chasing people for money, for a fraction of the price of employing staff within your own company.

Trusting someone else with the inner workings of your business sounds risky and breaching confidentiality, but the essence of Backroom Business Solutions is that they become a wing of your own company and everything remains confidential as links are set up which are dedicated to your company and are controlled to keep them safe and secure.

So how would you benefit from having this service operating within your company? Simply by having a dedicated professional team keeping track of all the day to day finances you will be free to run the company and increase your business profits. BBS literally becomes your accounts department, Monday to Friday, throughout the year and handles all external telephone queries. They take care of the complete process from beginning to end; managing weekly cash flow, paying suppliers, chasing debt, making credit searches and much more. They can also produce tax accounts if necessary. BBS clients have access to information when they need it, Monday to Friday, 9 to 5. Management accounts and practical business analysis is provided so that they understand what is going on in their business.

Typical of the feedback from their clients are the comments from Dave Regan, who tells us that this service has had a hugely beneficial effect on his business. "It's allowed us to get on with growing our business whilst keeping on top of the finances and also, when we needed cash flow support, the Bank had confidence in supporting us because we have all the up to date financial information..."

The Management of BBS, which includes a qualified accountant, have in excess of 60 years practical business experience behind them working with Plc's and small companies across a wide spectrum of industries including the services sector, manufacturing, retail and medical. Their clients include software companies, distribution, legal, medical, mail order, travel, property, hotels, pharmaceuticals, and web designers. The costs and services are tailored to meet the needs of clients and are based on an interview and subsequent assessment of requirements.

Clients of Backroom Business Solutions have achieved significant benefits that would normally be financially prohibitive and the result is a real boost to income, profitability and peace of mind.

If you would like to talk to someone at BBS, for free advice, they are contactable by email on **enquiries@backroomsolutions.com** or by telephoning **020 8905 2526**.

The website is **www.backroomsolutions.com**

Phase 7

Writing up and presenting your business plan

20

Writing up and presenting your business plan

Up to now, the workbook assignments have focused on gathering data needed to validate a business idea, to confirm the business team's capability to implement their chosen strategy and to quantify the resources needed in terms of 'men, machinery, money and management'.

Now this information has to be assembled, collated and orchestrated into a coherent and complete written business plan aimed at a specific audience.

In this assignment we will examine the five activities that can make this happen:

1. packaging;
2. layout and content;
3. writing and editing;
4. who to send it to;
5. the oral presentation.

PACKAGING

Every product is enhanced by appropriate packaging, and a business plan is no exception. The panellists at Cranfield's enterprise programmes prefer a simple spiral binding with a plastic cover on the front and back. This makes it easy for the reader to move from section to section, and it ensures the plan will survive frequent handling. Stapled copies and leather-bound tomes are viewed as undesirable extremes.

A near-letter-quality (NLQ) printer will produce a satisfactory type finish, which, together with wide margins and double spacing, will result in a pleasing and easy-to-read document.

LAYOUT AND CONTENT

There is no such thing as a 'universal' business plan format. That being said, experience at Cranfield has taught us that certain layouts and contents have gone down better than others. These are our guidelines to producing an attractive business plan, from the investor's point of view. Not every sub-heading will be relevant to every type of business, but the general format should be followed, with emphasis laid as appropriate.

First, the cover should show the name of the company, its address and phone number and the date on which this version of the plan was prepared. It should confirm that this is the company's latest view on its position and financing needs. Remember that your business plan should be targeted at specific sources of finance. It's highly likely, therefore, that you will need to assemble slightly different business plans, highlighting areas of concern to lenders as opposed to investors, for example.

Second, the title page, immediately behind the front cover, should repeat the above information and also give the founder's name, address and phone number. He or she is likely to be the first point of contact and anyone reading the business plan may want to talk over some aspects of the proposal before arranging a meeting.

The executive summary

Ideally one but certainly no longer than two pages, this should follow immediately behind the title page.

Writing up the executive summary is not easy but it is the most important single part of the business plan; it will probably do more to influence whether or not the plan is reviewed in its entirety than anything else you do. It can also make the reader favourably disposed towards a venture at the outset – which is no bad thing.

These two pages must explain:

1. the current state of the company with respect to product/service readiness for market, trading position and past successes if already running, and key staff on board;
2. the products or services to be sold and to whom they will be sold, including details on competitive advantage;
3. the reasons customers need this product or service, together with some indication of market size and growth;
4. the company's aims and objectives in both the short and the longer term, and an indication of the strategies to be employed in getting there;
5. a summary of forecasts, sales, profits and cash flow;

6. how much money is needed, and how and when the investor or lender will benefit from providing the funds.

Obviously, the executive summary can only be written after the business plan itself has been completed.

The summary below, for instance, accompanied a 40-page plan:

PNU-CLEEN will assemble and market an already prototyped design for a vacuum cleaner. The design work was carried out by myself and my co-director when we were at Loughborough University taking a BSc course in design and manufacture. The prototype was made during my postgraduate course in industrial design engineering at the Royal College of Art in London.

The vacuum cleaner is somewhat special. Its design, powered by compressed air, is aimed at the industrial market and fulfils a need overlooked by cleaning equipment manufacturers.

The vacuum cleaner offers to the customer an 'at-hand' machine that can be used by its employees to keep their workplace or machine clean and tidy during production. This produces a healthier and more productive environment in which to work.

It is cheaper than electrical vacuum cleaners and more versatile. It is also far less prone to blockage, which is especially important considering the types of material found in manufacturing industry.

The vacuum cleaner can be produced at low unit cost. This, together with the market price it can command for what it has to offer, will mean that only a small turnover is needed for the company to break even. However, with the prospect of a sizeable market both in this country and abroad, the company has the chance of making substantial profits.

The company will concentrate on this product for the first five years to ensure that it reaches all of its potential market and this will make a sound base from which we can either expand into other products or incorporate the manufacturing side of the product into our own capabilities.

The financial forecasts indicate that break-even will be achieved in the second year of operations, and in year 3 return on investment should be about 40 per cent. By then sales turnover will be a little over £1 million, gross profits about £400,000, and profit before tax but after financing charges around £200,000.

Our P/E ratio from year 3 will be 10 to 1, which should leave an attractive margin for any investor to exit, with comparable stock being quoted at 19 to 1.

We will need an investment of £300,000 to implement our strategy, with roughly half going into tangibles such as premises and stock, and the balance into marketing and development expenses. We are able and willing to put up £100,000. The balance we would like to fund from the sale of a share of the business, the exact proportion to be discussed at a later stage.

The table of contents

After the executive summary follows a table of contents. This is the map that will guide the new reader through your business proposal and on to the 'inevitable' conclusion that they should put up the funds. If a map is obscure, muddled or even missing, then the chances are you will end up with lost or irritated readers unable to find their way around your proposal.

Each of the main sections of the business plan should be listed and the pages within that section indicated. There are two valid schools of thought on page numbering. One favours a straightforward sequential numbering of each page, 1, 2, 3 . . . 9, 10 for example. This seems to us to be perfectly adequate for short, simple plans, dealing with uncomplicated issues and seeking modest levels of finance.

Most proposals should be numbered by section. In the example that follows, the section headed 'The Business and Its Management' is Section 1, and the pages that follow are listed from 1.1 to 1.7 in the table of contents, so identifying each page as belonging within that specific section. This numbering method also allows you to insert new material without upsetting the entire pagination during preparation. Tables and figures should also be similarly numbered.

Individual paragraph numbering, much in favour with government and civil service departments, is considered something of an overkill in a business plan and is to be discouraged, except perhaps if you are looking for a large amount of government grant.

The table of contents below shows both the layout and the content that in our experience are most in favour with financial institutions. Unsurprisingly, the terminology is similar to that used throughout the workbook. For a comprehensive explanation of what should be included under each heading, look back to the appropriate assignments, set out in Table 7.1.

Table 7.1   Using the workbook assignment data

Section in business plan	Relevant assignments
1	Assignments 1 and 2
2	Assignment 3
3	Assignments 4, 5 and 6
4	Assignments 7, 8 and 9
5	Assignment 10
6	Assignment 10
7	Assignments 11–15
8	Assignment 16
9	Assignments 17–19

Table 7.2 Sample table of contents

Section	Page
Executive Summary	i, ii
1. The Business and Its Management	
History and Position to Date	1.1
Current or New Mission	1.2
Objectives, Near Term	1.3
Objectives, Long Term	1.4
The Management Team	1.5
Legal Structure	1.6
Professional Advisers	1.7
2. The Products or Services	
Descriptions	2.1
Readiness for Market	2.2
Applications	2.3
Proprietary Position	2.4
Comparison with Competition, Performance and Economics	2.5
Guarantees and Warranties	2.6
Future Potential/Product Development	2.7
Sources of Supply (if not a manufacturing/ assembling business)	2.8
3. Market and Competitors	
Description of Customers	3.1
Customer Needs and Benefits	3.2
Market Segments	3.3
Customer Decision Criteria	3.4
Market and Segment Size and Growth	3.5
Market Projections	3.6
Competition	3.7
4. Competitive Business Strategy	
Pricing Policy	4.1
Promotional Plans	4.2
Choice of Location and Premises	4.3
Distribution Channels	4.4
Anticipated Mark-up	4.5
Competitor Response	4.6

9. Business Controls

Financial	9.1
Sales and Marketing	9.2
Manufacturing	9.3
Other Controls	9.4

Appendices could include:

- management team biographies;
- names and details of professional advisers;
- technical data and drawings;
- details of patents, copyright, designs;
- audited accounts;
- consultants' reports or other published data on products, markets, etc;
- orders on hand and enquiry status;
- detailed market research methods and findings;
- organisation charts.

WRITING AND EDITING

You and your colleagues should write the first draft of the business plan yourselves. The niceties of grammar and style can be resolved later. Different people in your team will have been responsible for carrying out the various assignments in the workbook, and writing up the appropriate section(s) of the business plan. This information should be circulated to ensure that:

1. everyone is still heading in the same direction;
2. nothing important has been missed out.

A 'prospectus', such as a business plan seeking finance from investors, can have a legal status, turning any claims you may make for sales and profits (for example) into a 'contract'. Your accountant and legal adviser will be able to help you with the appropriate language that can convey your projections without giving them contractual status.

This would also be a good time to talk over the proposal with a 'friendly' banker or venture capital provider. They can give an insider's view as to the strengths and weaknesses of your proposal.

When your first draft has been revised, then comes the task of editing. Here the grammar, spelling and language must be carefully checked to ensure that your business plan is crisp, correct, clear and complete – and not too long. If writing is not your trade, then once again this is an area in which to seek help. Your local college or librarian will know of someone who can produce 'attention-capturing' prose, if you yourself don't.

However much help you get with writing up your business plan, it is still just that – your plan. So, the responsibility for the final proof-reading before it goes out must rest with you. Spelling mistakes and typing errors can have a disproportionate influence on the way your business plan is received.

The other purpose of editing is to reduce the business plan to between 20 and 40 pages. However complex or sizeable the venture, outsiders won't have time to read it if it is longer – and insiders will only succeed in displaying their muddled thinking to full effect. If your plan includes volumes of data, tables, graphs, etc, then refer to them in the text, but confine them to an appendix.

WHO TO SEND IT TO

Now you are ready to send out your business plan to a few carefully selected financial institutions that you know are interested in proposals such as yours.

This will involve some research into the particular interests, foibles and idiosyncrasies of the institutions themselves. If you are only interested in raising debt capital, the field is narrowed to the clearing banks for the main part. If you are looking for someone to share the risk with you, then you must review the much wider field of venture capital. Here, some institutions will only look at proposals over a certain capital sum, such as £250,000, or will only invest in certain technologies. Appendix 2 lists and describes the principal sources of finance for new business proposals in the UK.

It is a good idea to carry out this research before the final editing of your business plan, as you should incorporate something of this knowledge into the way your business plan is presented. You may find that slightly different versions of Section 8.5, 'The Deal on Offer', have to be made for each different source of finance to which you send your business plan.

Don't be disheartened if the first batch of financiers you contact don't sign you up. One Cranfield enterprise programme participant had to approach 26 lending institutions, 10 of them different branches of the same organisation, before getting the funds she wanted. One important piece of information she brought back from every interview was the reason for the refusal. This eventually led to a refined proposal that won through.

It is as well to remember that financial institutions are far from infallible, so you may have to widen your audience to other contacts.

Anita Roddick, the Body Shop founder, was turned down flat by the banks when she was starting up and had to raise £4,000 from a local Sussex garage owner. This, together with £4,000 of her own funds, allowed the first shop to open in Brighton. Today, there are hundreds of Body Shop outlets throughout the world. The company has a full listing on the Stock Exchange and Ms Roddick is a millionaire many times over. Anita's personal wealth is £30 million and she controls 1,800 shops – and one Sussex bank manager must be feeling a little silly!

Finally, how long will it all take? This also depends on whether you are raising debt or equity, the institution you approach and the complexity of the deal on offer. A secured bank loan, for example, can take from a few days to a few weeks to arrange.

Investment from a venture capital house will rarely take less than three months to arrange, and will more usually take six or even up to nine months. Although the deal itself may be struck early on, the lawyers will pore over the detail for weeks. Every exchange of letters can add a fortnight to the wait. The 'due diligence' process in which every detail of your business plan is checked out will also take time – so this will have to be allowed for in your projections.

THE ORAL PRESENTATION

If getting someone interested in your business plan is half the battle in raising funds, the other half is the oral presentation. Any organisation financing a venture will insist on seeing the team involved presenting and defending their plans – in person. They know that they are backing people every bit as much as the idea. You can be sure that any financier you are presenting to will be well prepared. Remember that they see hundreds of proposals every year, and either have or know of investments in many different sectors of the economy. If this is not your first business venture, they may even have taken the trouble to find out something of your past financial history.

Keep these points in mind when preparing for the presentation of your business plan:

- Find out how much time you have, then rehearse your presentation beforehand. Allow at least as much time for questions as for your talk.
- Use visual aids and if possible bring and demonstrate your product or service. A video or computer-generated model is better than nothing.
- Explain your strategy in a businesslike manner, demonstrating your grasp of the competitive market forces at work. Listen to comments and criticisms carefully, avoiding a defensive attitude when you respond.
- Make your replies to questions brief and to the point. If members of the audience want more information, they can ask. This approach allows time

for the many different questions that must be asked, either now or later, before an investment can proceed.

▪ Your goal is to create empathy between yourself and your listeners. While you may not be able to change your personality, you could take a few tips on presentation skills. Eye contact, tone of speech, enthusiasm and body language all have a part to play in making a presentation successful.

▪ Wearing a suit is never likely to upset anyone. Shorts and sandals could just set the wrong tone! Serious money calls for serious people.

▪ *Be prepared.* You need to have every aspect of your business plan in your head and know your way around the plan forwards, backwards and sideways! You never know when the chance to present may occur. It's as well to have a 5-, 10- and 20-minute presentation ready to run at a moment's notice.

WORKSHEET FOR ASSIGNMENT 20: WRITING UP AND PRESENTING YOUR BUSINESS PLAN

1. Who do you propose to send your business plan to first, and why have you chosen them?
2. Write a first draft of your business plan along the lines recommended.
3. Who can help you to edit and rewrite the final version of your plan?
4. Prepare and rehearse a presentation of your business plan.

SUGGESTED FURTHER READING

Cary, Lucius (1998) *The Venture Capital Report: Guide to venture capital in the UK*, FT/Prentice Hall, London

Gladstone, David and Gladstone, Laura (2002) *Venture Capital Handbook: An entrepreneur's guide to raising venture capital*, FT/Prentice Hall, New Jersey

Appendix 1

Market research information sources

DESK RESEARCH

The number of directories and data-gathering services is enormous. A small selection of the most important of these is set out below under the headings UK and Overseas.

Most of these organisations are international in nature, and operate wherever profitable business is to be done. Whatever your sector or interest, the chances are that there is a directory or information service.

Most of these services are fee-paying, and sometimes they are expensive. However, access to a large proportion of the data can be gained on a pay-as-you-use basis. Often the data are available through an intermediary such as a library (see under that heading). In this case, many data may well be free to visitors, and specialist services will be available either at a modest cost, or perhaps even also free if you are a library member. Some libraries may make some of the data available online.

DATA SOURCES

UK Market Data
Bank of England
Threadneedle Street
London EC2R 8AH
Tel: 020 7601 4444
Fax: 020 7601 5460
E-mail: enquiries@bankofengland.co.uk
Web site: http://www.bankofengland.co.uk/

The Bank of England publishes information on all aspects of its work in many formats, much of it available on this site. You can use the search page to find either the complete document (presented in one of two ways, as either a Web page or a PDF file readable with the latest Adobe Acrobat Reader – available free from Adobe's Web site) or a summary of the contents and/or details of how to obtain the publication from the Bank.

Hard copies of all publications (including those not available on this site) can be obtained by contacting the Bank's Public Enquiries Group.

Aside from a vast array of data on how the economy is working, the following small business reports are regularly produced, and make interesting and informative reading:

- *Quarterly Report on Small Business Statistics* (start-ups and failures, all by sector and geographic area;
- *The Financing of Technology-based Small Firms* reports;
- *Finance for Small Firms*;
- *Smaller Exporters: A special report*;
- *The Financing of Ethnic Minority Firms in the UK*;
- *Finance for Small Businesses in Deprived Communities*.

Benns Media Directory
Miller Freeman UK Ltd
Riverbank House, Angel Lane
Tonbridge, Kent TN9 1SE
Tel: 01732 362666
Fax: 01732 367301
Web site: http://www.millerfreeman.co.uk/

Directory covering the media industry across all of its sectors within the UK. Guide to newspapers, periodicals, broadcasting, reference publications and electronic media. There are also Europe and World editions. Priced at £152 per volume. Not yet on the Internet.

Accredited by the DTI, this UK business information site has a particular focus on providing information for the small and medium-sized (SME) business community in the UK and Ireland. It offers quick and easy access to detailed information on business areas SMEs need to know about, in a format that is straightforward and easy to use.

It provide links to company information, business briefings, business skills, business opportunities, direct marketing lists, company formation, company credit checks, venture capital, legal advice, business consultants, business health check and domain names. It also offers a facility to download essential Key Note Market Information straight to your desktop from as little as £10. Exclusive to bird-online are the new Snapshot and Digest Reports aimed particularly at SMEs, enabling the busy owner-manager to receive a concise and authoritative overview of a particular market. It also offers a 'pay as you go' facility for company reports, from £2 a report.

BRAD (British Rate and Data)
BRAD Group, EMAP Media
33–39 Bowling Green Lane
London EC1R 0DA
Tel: 020 7505 8000
Web site: www.brad.co.uk

BRAD is a monthly classified directory of media in the UK and the Republic of Ireland that carry advertising. Media are broken down into national and regional newspapers, consumer press, business press, new and electronic media (mostly Internet sites), television, video, cinema, radio, and posters and outdoor. This information is also available via subscription through BRADnet and BRADbase. The BRAD group also publishes Genesis, Alf and mailing list service Target Direct.

British Companies
Web site: http://www.britishcompanies.co.uk/

An annotated listing of links to British companies and organisations that deal in consumer products, organised into several dozen categories.

British Services
Web site: http://www.britishservices.co.uk/

An annotated listing of British companies and organisations that provide services, organised by category.

Companies House
Tel: 0870 3333636
Fax: 029 20 380517
Web site: http://www.companieshouse.co.uk/

By visiting any of the Companies House offices you can get the following information instantly from in-house computer screens:

- company number;
- company type;
- date of incorporation;
- a list of all documents filed in the last five years;

- details of serving directors and secretaries and of those who have resigned since 1991;
- a list of disqualified directors;
- images of accounts online to view or print (Cardiff and London);
- document packages;
- a choice of three company reports;
- mortgage information (Cardiff and London);
- insolvency details.

You can order prints of the information shown on the screen, and you may use the online ordering system to order a full search on microfiche, available within two hours at Cardiff, London and Edinburgh, or on the following day at the other offices.

Prices range from 10p per page of information copied on site, to £6.50 for a microfiche of a company's accounts. A special delivery of data can cost £25.

Company Plus
Centaur Communications
50 Poland Street
London W1F 7AX
Tel: 020 7970 4619
E-mail: companyplus@thelawyer.com
Web site: http://companyplus.thelawyer.com/

Company Plus provides access to two separate groups of reports: analysed reports by ICC (profile report, overview report, financial report, company directors report and individual directors report) and the original documents as filed at Companies House.

Directory of Directories
E-mail: info@alephsearch.co.uk
Web site: http://www.albedo.co.uk/sites/aleph/

AlephSearch is maintained by Albedo Systems, and contains links to selected Web-based directories, both unspecialised and specialised, from Accommodation to Zoology. The directories cover the world, but fairly thinly!

Directory of UK Associations
A S K Hollis, Hollis Directories Ltd
Harlequin House, 7 High Street,
Teddington, Middlesex YW11 8EL
Tel: 020 8977 7711
Fax: 020 8977 1133
Web site: http://www.hollis-pr.com/publications/ask.htm

Over 5,000 associations, pressure groups, unions, institutes, societies and more are profiled, representing every interest area from abrasives through to zoos, from industrial, professional and business sectors to government, charities and the consumer. Price £150.

Dun & Bradstreet
European and UK Headquarters
Holmers Farm Way
High Wycombe, Bucks HP12 4UL
Tel: 01494 422000
Fax: 01494 422260
E-mail: customerhelp@dnb.com
Web site: http://www.dnb.com/1

D&B, as it is generally known, has been one of the world's leading providers of business information for 160 years. It claims to have the largest company database available, with information on 66 million businesses and branches worldwide.

Experian
Talbot House, Talbot Street
Nottingham NG1 5HF
Tel: 0115 941 0888
Fax: 0115 934 4905
Web site: http://www.uk.experian.com/

Experian's data can help with decisions spanning everything from where to locate a business through to identifying a customer base, from whether to grant credit to an individual through to the financial reputation of a prospective business partner.

ICC Information Limited
Field House, 72 Oldfield Road
Hampton, Middlesex TW12 2HQ
Tel: 020 8481 8847
Fax: 020 8941 6014
E-mail: ipdatasupport@icc.co.uk
Web site: www.icc.co.uk/

ICC produces and maintains a database of all 1.6 million live, and 3.8 million dissolved, limited liability companies in the UK. To ensure up-to-date information, ICC has at least one share in approximately 95 per cent of British quoted companies, and also sources reports from Companies Registration Office in the UK.

Kelly's
Web site: http://www.kellys.co.uk/

Kelly's Directories are published by Reed Publications. They cover a wide range of business activities in the UK. Kellysearch.com is the latest version of the long-established *Industrial Directory*. The Web site contains all of the product and service listings that users of the hard-copy directories are used to, plus many more.

Because the Web site is a live source of information, it can keep you up to date with the latest in company details, news and special features. The Web site is completely free to use and allows you to search the extensive database of over 140,000 UK companies and over 100,000 product and service headings.

Key Note Ltd
Field House, 72 Oldfield Road
Hampton, Middlesex TW12 2HQ
Tel: 020 8481 8750
Fax: 020 8783 0049
E-mail: info@keynote.co.uk
Web site: http://www.keynote.co.uk

Key Note has built a reputation as an expert provider of market information, producing highly respected off-the-shelf publications that cover a comprehensive range of market sectors, from commercial and industrial to service and consumer titles.

Its report gallery has a listing of literally hundreds of reports covering everything from *Activity Holidays* to *Women's Magazines*. The executive summary, a generous 1,000 words plus a full index, is available free on every report, which should make it clear if the report is worth buying, or worth a trip to a major reference library that may well have a copy to view.

Reports are priced from around £300 upwards, with most in the £500 to £700 range.

Kompass United Kingdom
Reed Business Information
Windsor Court, East Grinstead House
East Grinstead, West Sussex RH19 1XA
Tel: 0800 0185 882
E-mail: jmason@reedinfo.co.uk
Web site: http://www.kompass.com/

Kompass claims to have details of 1.6 million UK companies, 23 million key product and service references, 3.2 million executive names, 744,000 trade and brand names and 50,000 Kompass classification codes in its UK directory. It also creates directory information in over 70 countries. Its Web site has a free access area that users may access without registration. It provides access to the following:

- limited search criteria: products/services, company/trade names, and geographical (worldwide, regions or countries);
- limited company lists;
- limited number of full company profiles (partial profiles contain only the contact details).

Media Pocket Book
NTC Publications Ltd
Farm Road, Henley-on-Thames
Oxfordshire RG9 1EJ
Tel: 01491 411000
Fax: 01491 571188
A statistical profile of British commercial media. Contains data on audiences, ad rates and ad spend for all media, plus key data on economics, demographics, digital TV and radio, ambient media and the Internet. Price £26.00.

Media UK Internet Directory
Media UK
2 King's Court, Skelmanthorpe
Huddersfield HD8 9DY
Tel: 0701 0701 218
Fax: 0701 0701 219
Web site: http://directory.mediauk.com/

Complete listing of all online media in the UK. Includes radio, television, magazines and newspapers with industry resources. A useful touch for publicity-conscious entrepreneurs is a tutorial on writing a press release.

Mintel International Group Ltd
18–19 Long Lane
London EC1A 9PL
Tel: 020 7606 4533
E-mail: info@mintel.com
Web site: www.mintel.com

A privately owned independent company, established and respected for over 27 years, Mintel publishes over 400 reports every year examining every conceivable consumer market. Reports cost several hundred pounds, but you can view the introduction and main headings. Most are available free in business libraries. Mintel also offers a number of reports on the US and European markets.

National Statistics
Web site: http://www.statistics.gov.uk/

The National Statistics Web site contains a vast range of official UK statistics and information about statistics, which can be accessed and downloaded free. There are 13 separate themes. Each one deals with a distinct and easily recognisable area of national life. So, whether you are looking to access the very latest statistics on the UK's economy, or research and survey information released by the government, or want to study popular trends and facts, click on one of these themes and explore!

The range of data is mind-boggling. For example, within the Economy Section it is possible to drill down to Household Final Consumption Expenditure, which includes personal expenditure on goods, both durable and non-durable, on second-hand goods, and on services. This shows trends in usage of almost everything you can think of.

Research Index
Research Index Ltd, 94 West Parade
Lincoln LN1 1JZ
Tel: 01522 524212
Fax: 01522 514257
E-mail: info@researchindex.co.uk
Web site: http://www.researchindex.co.uk/

Research Index, part of the Creditfax Group, is a database that indexes the headlines of news, views and comments on industries and companies worldwide, as reported in the UK national press and a range of quality business magazines. Every significant daily and Sunday newspaper, business magazine and periodical is indexed. It's a free way to find out what the press has to say about your competitors or suppliers.

Sources of Unofficial UK Statistics
Gower Publishing Ltd
Gower House, Croft Road
Aldershot, Hampshire GU11 3HR
Tel: 01252 331551
Fax: 0252 355505
E-mail: orders@bookpoint.co.uk
Web site: www.gowerpub.com

Sources of Unofficial UK Statistics gives details of almost 900 publications and services (including electronic publications) produced by trade associations, professional bodies, banks, consultants, employers' federations, forecasting organisations and others, together with statistics appearing in trade journals and periodicals. Titles and services are listed alphabetically by publisher, and each entry contains information, where available, on subject, content and source of statistics, together with frequency, availability and cost, and address, telephone and fax details for further information. This edition also includes details of Internet sites and information on whether statistics are available on those sites. The book concludes with a title index and a subject index to the entries. It is 368 pages long and costs £65.00.

Youth Research Group (YoRG)
4 Pinetrees, Portsmouth Road
Esher, Surrey KT10 9LF
Tel: 01372 468 554
Fax: 01372 469 788
Web site: http://www.yorg.com

These surveys are completed in school classes by 6- to 16-year-olds playing on multimedia workstations as they respond intuitively to their software. YoRG does not bore them with books of multiple-choice answers that are worse than homework. Its research programme involves them completely by using technology they love and understand. The survey sample consists of three waves of 7,000 respondents, conducted once each school term. Of this sample, 2,000 respondents complete all three waves, to allow for brand and attitude tracking annually. The remainder of the sample are new respondents each wave. This authoritative sample is applied to investigate information nodules, which are also complemented by new 'hot topics' throughout the year. Results are obtained within three weeks from commissioning. There are free profiles of various age groups and sexes on the Web site.

INTERNATIONAL MARKET DATA

Many of the providers listed in the UK section above also provide data on the international market.

For example, Benn's has Europe and World editions; Dun & Bradstreet has extensive coverage of the United States, Europe and Asia; Kelly, Keynote and Kompass all have international coverage, as do Mintel and Willing's Press Guide. Who Owns Whom has guides covering Australia and the Far East, mainland Europe and a North American edition.

Only providers that offer some sort of online service are listed, so only the Web address has been given here. Those that produce their information in hard copy and book form will in all probability be available in or through major reference or university libraries. (See under the heading 'Libraries'.) Where the source name is not the same as the title on the top line, it is given at the bottom of each entry.

AME Info
http://www.ameinfo.com/
A business directory providing access to 200,000 companies from 14 Middle Eastern countries. Also includes company news and news from selected industries, exhibitions and events, travel guide, country facts and much more.
Provided by: AME – Arabian Modern Equipment Establishment (klaus@ame info.com).

AskAlix
http://www.askalix.com/
A European business directory (using Dun & Bradstreet's data) that searches for businesses by the keyword entries they themselves submit. Currently lists businesses in the UK, Ireland, Germany, France, the Netherlands, Luxembourg and Sweden. Search by name, product or service and by location.
Provided by: Miami International Limited (info@askalix.com).

Big Book
http://www.bigbook.com/
Listings for businesses in the United States. You can search by business name, location and/or category. Listings include address, phone number and a street map showing the business location.
Provided by: BigBook (bigbook@northnet.com.au).

Cap Gemini Ernst & Young
http://www.capgemini.co.uk
This is an IT services and management consultancy with offices throughout Europe. It publishes strategic reports on IT and Internet issues, extracts of which can be found on its Web site.

Computer Technology Research Corporation
http://www.ctrcorp.com
An internationally recognised and respected research and publishing company. Its reports cover major technologies, trends, products, companies and markets concerning the computer industry. Some report data are free, the rest are catalogued and priced on the Web site.

Corporate Information
http://www.corporateinformation.com/
Business information site covering the main world economies. The site can be searched in four ways:

- Research a company: type in the name of a company and get a list of sites that cover the company. Over 350,000 profiles are indexed in the search engine.
- Research a country's industry: select one of 30 industries and 65 countries and get a list of companies in that particular industry, a list of relevant links and a short write-up about the industry.
- Research by country: there is a link library with thousands of links. Select from one of the over 100 countries and you can research companies, industries and economic information.
- Research reports: you can read research reports about over 15,000 companies. Each research report analyses sales, dividends, earnings, profit ratios, research and development, inventory and so on.

dNet
http://www.d-net.com/
Database of business directories. Directories are not online, but this site helps locate a type of directory, indicates whether it comes in print, CD ROM or otherwise, and gives contact information on how to purchase it. Also a database of mailing lists and labels.
Provided by: dNet Online Services, Inc.

dot com directory
http://www.dotcomdirectory.com/
One of the most comprehensive resources available to locate business information about companies on the Web. Gives links to companies' Web sites, company overviews, subsidiaries/divisions, and financial information. Use the site's search engine or browse by category.
Provided by: Network Solutions, Inc.

Euromonitor
http://www.euromonitor.com
Euromonitor International is a leading global information provider with 28 years of research expertise. It provides instant access to in-depth strategic analysis and up-to-date market statistics for dozens of global industries. You can download data direct, have reports despatched by e-mail or order a hard-copy version.

Reports cover sectors ranging from alcohol to tourism, and are not free. But you can see what's available and get an idea of its content before you buy, or try to track a report down in a library or elsewhere on the Internet.

Europages – European Business Directory
http://www.europages.com/
Europages provides 500,000 company addresses from over 30 European countries, hundreds of company brochures, access to key business information and links to yellow pages throughout Europe. This site has information that is searchable, company catalogues, phone numbers, products information, e-mail capability, and economic information. The site can be viewed in English, German, Spanish, French, Italian and Dutch.

Forrester Research
http://www.forrester.com
A US company that, following its purchase of UK-based Fletcher Research, has a strong presence in Europe. Its great strength lies in the Internet and e-commerce in general. Hundreds of IPOs relied on its data to support the sales forecasts in their business plans. A large population of its published data can be accessed on its Web site on a 90-day free trial basis.

FT.com
www.ft.com
Has global, UK and US sites, as well as full coverage of Asia, the Middle East, South America and Africa. The site is free; all you have to do is register. Once registered, you also get daily industry-specific news bulletins sent to you by e-mail, and a portfolio that tracks share prices, market news and broker recommendations.

The new Business.com Directory enables you to access 25,000 business categories and subcategories as well as hundreds of thousands of business-oriented Web sites. In addition, it incorporates over 10,000 company profiles and 58 Business.com industry profiles. The main site contains 10 million news articles sourced from 2,000 leading publications worldwide. Updated every 10 minutes.

The *Financial Times* itself publishes approximately 240 surveys annually, which appear with copies of the newspaper most days of the week. Topics include financial markets, global industries, business management, and developed and emerging countries. FT.com publishes these surveys as soon as they are available, as well as providing an index of previous surveys. Provided by: Pearson PLC.

Government statistics

Most countries have their own government sites for national statistics data. Below are listed some of the main sites, which in turn have links to other sources of general statistical data.

http://stats.bls.gov/
US site of the Bureau of Labor Statistics, this contains lots of statistical material on the US economy and labour force.

http://www.insee.fr/va/keyfigur/index.htm
French National Statistics Organisation.

http://www.statistik-bund.de/e_home.htm
German National Statistics Organisation.

http://petra.istat.it/
Italian National Statistics Organisation.

http://europa.eu.int/en/comm/eurostat/serven/part6/6theme.htm
Site of Eurostat, which is the statistical organisation of the European Communities

gopher://gopher.undp.org:70/11/ungophers/popin/wdtrends
United Nations world population figures.

Lexis-Nexis
http://www.lexis-nexis.com/
This organisation has literally dozens of databases covering every sector you can think of, but most useful for entrepreneurs researching competitors is Company Analyzer, which creates comprehensive company reports drawn from 36 separate sources, with up to 250 documents per source. So, when you get tired of scouring different databases to find out all there is to know about a competitor, customer or supplier, you could consider using Company Analyzer to access legal, business, financial and public records sources with a single search.

Company Analyzer provides access to accurate information about parent and subsidiary companies and their directors, to highlight potential conflicts of interest.

News Directory.com
http://www.newsd.com/
NewsDirectory is a guide to all online English-language media. This free directory of newspapers, magazines, television stations, colleges, visitor bureaux, governmental agencies and more can help you get to where you want to go, or find sites you didn't know about. It is a simple and fast site that can be used to access all the news and information that you can handle. You can link to:

- over 3,600 newspapers;
- over 4,800 magazines;
- hundreds of television stations;

- plus colleges, visitor bureaus, governmental agencies and travel links;
- more than 14,500 links in all.

Standard & Poor's
http://www.standardandpoors.com/
Standard & Poor's was established in 1860 to provide independent insight, analysis and information to those in the financial community to help them determine value in the marketplace. It is a pre-eminent global provider of independent financial analysis and information on companies, their shareholders and their directors.

Telebase
http://www.telebase.com/
Telebase designs, manages and markets online information services that help people find the information they need from some 500 databases from the world's leading electronic information services, including Dun & Bradstreet, LexisNexis, Experian, Thomson & Thomson, Standard & Poor's and the like. Available directly and under private label from more than 25 distributors via the Internet, these products provide quick and simple, single-point access to a wealth of detailed business and research information. You can search a wide variety of general interest, specialised or technical publications along with over 100 international and US national and regional news sources, and can gather detailed company information from premier business sources.

Thomas's Register
http://www.thomasregister.com/
ThomasRegister.com is one of the world's leading resources for information on industrial products and services. It provides details on more than 170,000 US and Canadian manufacturers, with extensive company and product information. The site also provides secure online ordering and links to thousands of manufacturer and online catalogues. You can search by product, company or brand name. You need to register for a free membership to use the site, and hard copies of the various registers are about £129.00 + VAT.

CARRYING OUT DESK RESEARCH

There are three main ways to do desk research: via the Internet; visiting a library to read physical or online directories; or commissioning someone else, perhaps a market research agency or a business studies student carrying out a supervised project.

Using the Internet

The Internet can be a powerful source of desk research. It has some particular strengths and weaknesses that you need to keep in mind when using it.

Weaknesses of the Internet

- Strong US bias.
- Patchy coverage.
- Often there is lack of authority.

Strengths of the Internet

- Access is cheap and information can be free.
- Good for background information.
- Information can be obtained quickly.
- Wide geographic scope.
- More organisations now have their own Web pages.

It would be a brave or foolhardy entrepreneur who started up in business or set out to launch new products or services without at least spending a day or two surfing the Internet.

There are two main ways to gather market research information on the Internet. The first is by using search engines. This can be seen as a passive action, simply gathering in data that is already out there. Some of the libraries listed later also provide routes to market research data on the Internet. These have the advantage over pure search engines of having had their content vetted by an information specialist.

The second and more active way to use the Internet for market research is to use one of the 11,000 bulletin or message boards, newsgroups and chat rooms to elicit the data you require. These cover almost every subject, organised loosely by topic. There is a good chance that a question posted within an appropriate user group by an entrepreneur will get a response from one of the millions of Internet users.

Libraries and library information sources

There are thousands of libraries in the UK and tens of thousands elsewhere in the world, which between them contain more desk research data than any entrepreneur could ever require. As well as the fairly conventional lending services in the area of business books, these libraries also contain all the reference and research databases listed in this section and many hundreds more besides. Libraries, in particular the reference libraries in larger towns and cities, also have Internet access to their data in various forms, and many offer fee-paying research services for business users at fairly modest rates.

Apart from public libraries, there are hundreds of university libraries, specialist science and technology libraries and government collections of data, which can be accessed with little difficulty.

Librarians are trained, among other things, to archive and retrieve information and data from their own libraries and increasingly from Internet data sources. Thus they represent an invaluable resource that entrepreneurs should tap into early in the research process. If personnel resources are limited, you may need to write or call ahead and schedule an appointment. It will help if you take the time to familiarise yourself with some standard types of business reference materials.

123 World.com
http://www.123world.com/libraries/
This site claims to be the ultimate source of authentic and reliable information about the library resources of the world on the Net. Using 123world.com you can find out about all the libraries in your vicinity or anywhere else in the world. Its list of libraries includes public libraries, research libraries, state libraries, national archives, libraries of different educational institutions, agricultural and technical libraries, business libraries, science libraries and many other specialist libraries. The listing also provides helpful information about various libraries.

The links in this directory will guide you to the official sites of the libraries that you are looking for, in alphabetical order.

The British Library Business Information Service (BIS)
96 Euston Road
London NW1 2DB
Tel: 020 7412 7454
Fax: 020 7412 7453
E-mail: business-information@bl.uk
Web site: http://www.bl.uk/services/information/business.html

BIS holds one of the most comprehensive collections of business information in the UK. Business information sources published in the UK are collected as comprehensively as possible; sources published elsewhere are taken selectively. It aims to cover the manufacturing, wholesale trading, retailing and distribution aspects of major industries and the following service sectors: financial services, energy, environment, transport, and food and drink.

City Business Library
1 Brewers' Hall Garden
London EC2V 5BX
Tel: 020 7332 1812
Fax: 020 7332 1847
Web site: http://www.cityoflondon.gov.uk/ (follow link Services – Libraries)
Opening hours: Monday to Friday 9.30 am to 5.00 pm
(There are no membership requirements.)

The City Business Library is one of the leading business information sources in the country, situated in the heart of the City of London. The collection is used by the City and the wider community of London, the UK and overseas. The experienced staff are on hand to help you find the business information you require. If they do not hold the information you need, they will try to advise you of a more appropriate source. The library has a collection of directories, market reports, books, periodicals and newspapers, plus CD ROMs and Internet sources. It has specialist collections covering the City, companies, countries, directories, the European Union, markets, periodicals and newspapers.

Consortium of University Research Libraries (CURL)
http://www.curl.ac.uk/
This is a searchable database of some of the elite UK university research libraries. Many of these universities offer market data-gathering services, such as that on offer from the City Business Library or Birmingham Library.

eLibrary.com
http://ask.elibrary.com
'Research without the legwork' is its slogan. eLibrary is a comprehensive general reference service that contains premium content from a wide variety of sources. eLibrary can be compared to a real-world library of that houses a wide collection of periodicals and books, but with eLibrary the doors are never locked.

This is, of course, an entirely paid-for service, but it is not that expensive. In any event you get seven days free to try it out, so it's no great risk. For less than the price of a typical newspaper subscription, you will get unlimited use of eLibrary and you can select either a monthly subscription plan for $14.95 or an annual subscription plan for $79.95.

The Internet Public Library
http://www.ipl.org/
The Internet Public Library (IPL) is a public service organisation run by the University of Michigan School of Information. Its goal is to provide library

services to Internet users. Activities include finding, evaluating, selecting, organising, describing and creating information resources. There are lots of useful links on the site, to sources of directories and databases.

lib-web-cats
http://lib11.library.vanderbilt.edu/ltg/lwc-search.pl
Maintained by Marshall Breeding, the Library Technology Officer for the Jean and Alexander Heard Library at Vanderbilt University, this site profiles, describes and maintains a directory of over 5,000 libraries worldwide.

Library Spot
StartSpot Mediaworks, Inc. attn: LibrarySpot.com Team
1840 Oak Avenue
Evanston, IL 60201, USA
E-mail: info@startspot.com
Web site: http://www.libraryspot.com/

LibrarySpot.com is a free virtual library resource centre for just about anyone exploring the Web for valuable research information. Forbes.com selected LibrarySpot.com as the Best Reference Site on the Web for 2001 and 2000, *USA Today* described it as 'an awesome online library' and the *Chicago Tribune* calls it 'the most useful single reference site on the Web. . . superb and then some'. The site is run by StartSpot Mediaworks, Inc. in the Northwestern University/ Evanston Research Park in Evanston, Illinois.

M25 Consortium of Higher Education Libraries
http://www.m25lib.ac.uk/
InforM25 enables simultaneous access to over 120 college and university library catalogues in the London area. It provides users with simultaneous searching of member libraries' catalogues using standardised protocols (http://www.M25lib.ac.uk/M25link/).

Mitchell Library
North Street
Glasgow G3 7DN
Tel: 0141 287 2905 (Business Information)
E-mail: business_information@cls.glasgow.gov.uk
Web site: http://www.mitchelllibrary.org/

The Mitchell Library provides an extensive service for the business community and other library users. Many of the services are free; however, there are subscription services on offer to business and corporate users.

The library carries out bespoke market research at a charge-out rate of £30 an hour for those within the Glasgow City Council administrative area and £50 an hour for those outside that area, provided they pay a £200 initial deposit. Casual users not paying a deposit are charged a 50 per cent premium.

Public Libraries of Europe
http://dspace.dial.pipex.com/town/square/ac940/eurolib.html
Started in 1996, this site gives a listing of European public libraries on the World Wide Web. It covers the whole of Europe, 42 countries so far, and the intention is to provide a complete country-by-country listing. For some countries a full listing already exists, in which case the site just provides a pointer to it.

UK Higher Education & Research Libraries
http://www.ex.ac.uk/library/uklibs.html
This is perhaps the most comprehensive listing of UK higher education libraries. Currently there are over 150 libraries and information services listed, including those of universities, university colleges, and institutes and colleges of higher education. While these libraries are intended for use by students, if you attend a business course at one of the colleges you will have free use of their resources. Otherwise, usually for a modest fee, you can make use of their business information service.

UK Libraries Plus
http://www.roehampton.ac.uk/uklibrariesplus/index.html
UK Libraries Plus is a cooperative venture between higher education libraries. It enables part-time, distance and placement students to borrow material from other libraries. In addition, there is a provision for full-time students and staff to use other libraries on a reference-only basis. Membership is open to any higher education institution in the UK, and over half are now members. A full list for participating institutions is given, with direct links to their Web sites.

The WWW Virtual Library (VL)
http://vlib.org/
The VL is the oldest catalogue of the Web, started by Tim Berners-Lee, the creator of html and the Web itself. Unlike commercial catalogues, it is run by a loose confederation of volunteers, who compile pages of key links for particular areas in which they are expert. Even though it is not the biggest index of the Web, the VL pages are widely recognised as being among the highest-quality guides to particular sections of the Web. The central affairs of the VL are coordinated by an elected council.

While the VL covers almost every field of human endeavour, it has a large section on business, with a subheading for marketing, among other business headings. Marketing itself has a further dozen headings. Much of the information, including tutorials and 'lessons', is absolutely free.

MARKET RESEARCH AGENCIES

If the market research information you need cannot easily be found either by yourself or by the information service of a library, you may well have to call on a professional market researcher. This will almost certainly be a more expensive way to gather market data, but you will undoubtedly save time and may well get more relevant and timely data.

The organisations listed below should between them provide links to a market researcher or market research firm anywhere in the world. But before you go the expensive route, do contact your local college and see if any of its business studies students can do the work for you.

Cobweb Information Ltd
Hawthorn House, Forth Banks
Newcastle upon Tyne NE1 3SG
Tel: 0191 2612853
Fax: 0191 2611910
E-mail: sales@cobwebinfo.com.
Web site: http://www.cobwebinfo.com/

Cobweb is a specialist provider of information services for businesses, their advisers and other professional intermediaries. Its content is of particular benefit to new-start and small/medium enterprises. The production team continually researches, creates, updates and publishes a practical and authoritative range of business titles, subjects and products.

The knowledge base provides a blend of when, how, where and why content subjects covering thousands of business topics and types, market sectors, regulations, sources of business funding, advice, expertise, contacts and much more. Published services are available in hard copy, on CD ROM and via the Internet. As well as off-the-shelf information packages, Cobweb can customise any individual service to a particular client's requirements, to give it its brand, add its own content, or produce customised content from scratch.

ESOMAR
Vondelstraat 172
1054 GV Amsterdam
Netherlands
Tel: (+31) 20 664 21 41
Fax: (+31) 20 664 29 22
E-mail: email@esomar.nl
Web site: http://www.esomar.nl/mr_associations.html

ESOMAR's mission is to promote the use of opinion and marketing research for improving decision making in business and society, worldwide. Founded in 1948, ESOMAR currently unites 4,000 members in 100 countries, both users and providers of opinion and marketing research. All ESOMAR members and the management of companies with a full entry in the Directory have entered into a written undertaking to act in full conformance with the ICC/ESOMAR International Code of Marketing and Social Research Practice in all their research dealings. Non-political in its policies, ESOMAR is open to all persons who are actively involved in or concerned with marketing and opinion research.

The membership listing, which includes the UK's Market Research Society, is on the Web site.

European Information Researcher's Network
c/o Instant Library Ltd, Charnwood Wing
GRTC, Ashby Road
Loughborough, Leicestershire LE11 3BJ
Tel: 01509 268 292
Fax: 01509 232 748
E-mail: eirene@instant-library.com
Web site: http://www.eirene.com/

EIRENE is a professional association representing over 65 information brokers from the EU, EFTA and East European countries. Members have adopted and are adhering to the European Code of Practice, which is subject to arbitration. Its online directory lists and describes the services of all its members, including details of their specialisations and their fee structure.

Market Research Society
15 Northburgh Street
London EC1V 0JR
Tel: 020 7490 4911
Fax: 020 7490 0608
General e-mail: info@mrs.org.uk
Web site: www.mrs.org.uk

The Market Research Society is the world's largest professional body for individuals employed in market research or with an interest in it. Founded in 1946, it is the largest body of its kind, with over 8,000 members working in most organisations currently undertaking market research in the UK and overseas.

The Research Buyer's Guide, produced annually, is perhaps its most useful service for entrepreneurs. This directory provides research buyers with crucial information on over 750 companies and consultants offering market research and related services throughout the UK and Republic of Ireland. It includes details of research markets, services and locations, contacts and an overview of each organisation's activities.

The online version of the Research Buyer's Guide is available at http:// www.rbg.org.uk/. As well as searchable up-to-date listings, this Web site also offers a bulletin board to display potential research projects.

The hard copy of the *Guide* costs £40, but the online guide is free, more useful and more up to date. There you can browse listings of organisations and freelancers, or use the QuoteMail facility to e-mail selected suppliers.

FIELD RESEARCH

In some cases, the answers to your questions won't exist in published form since no one else will have been interested enough to have researched and published the data – for example, how many young people pass a particular shopfront each day. There you will need to undertake some original market research.

Who can help?

There are a large number of specialist market research companies and you can obtain a list from the Market Research Society, 15 Northburgh Street, London EC1V 0JR; tel: 020 7490 4911; fax: 020 7490 0608; Web site: www.mrs. org.uk. They will advise you how best to conduct your research, devise tests and questionnaires, and analyse the results.

Professional market research is a sophisticated operation and it isn't cheap: conducting interviews with 100 shoppers, for instance, could cost you £1,000. There are ways to get less expensive help, though. Students on business study courses have to carry out projects as part of their course work. Very often this includes a market research task and tutors are keen to ensure that this project resembles real life as closely as possible, so you may be able to get them to undertake some of your market research for a modest fee. Contact the marketing department of a local college or polytechnic. One college has set up a full-time business in this field and its services are professionally recognised, at about one-third of the market price. Contact: Scanmark, Buckinghamshire Chiltern University College, High Wycombe, Bucks HP11 2JZ; tel: 01494 522 141; fax: 01494 603194; www.bcuc.co.uk.

Sharing the costs

Designing a questionnaire and interviewing a balanced sample of respondents is an expensive and time-consuming business. One way round the problem is to use an 'omnibus' survey, which asks questions on behalf of a number of different clients, so cutting the costs. Several market research firms carry out market research on a regular basis, so all you have to do is tell them the questions you want to ask. Most surveys are conducted face to face, but some are done by telephone. There are general surveys covering a national representative sample, and specialist surveys for those interested in only a particular market sector, for example, young people, motorists, mothers with 0- to 2-year-olds, etc.

General Omnibus Operators are run by firms whose names will already be familiar to you – Gallup, MORI and NOP, for instance. Their charges include an entry fee, usually payable once only, and a charge per question. These sums are between £100 and £200, and £150 and £400 respectively, depending on the sample size.

Specialist surveys are carried out less frequently than general surveys – monthly, quarterly or less often.

If you're interested in things medical or pharmaceutical you can choose between Taylor Nelson Sofres and Healthcare's Omnimed at about £200 a question.

Travel and Tourism Research offers a *Travel Agents Omnibus Survey* (200 agents, minimum fee £2,000). Produce Studies' *AgriQuest* is a panel of 800 farmers (minimum fee from £780), and *Omnicar* from Sample Surveys investigates the attitudes and behaviour of 1,000 motorists (no entry fee, £550 per pre-coded question, open ended £760). Infratest Burke Surveys look at the alcohol-drinking habits of 1,830 adults each month (around £400 per question).

Firms with products or services tailored to particular age groups might like to contact Taylor Nelson Sofres, which does monthly surveys of children and teenagers, mothers with different-aged children and, occasionally, grandmothers as well (£190 entry fee, around £145–£380 per question depending on the sample size). Taylor Nelson Sofres conducts several consumer omnibuses (1,500 adults (16+), no entry fee, £425–£1,000 per question) and Research Surveys of Great Britain, a *Baby Omnibus* (not a sample of highly articulate infants but of 700 mothers with 0- to 2-year-olds, entry fee £150, £260 per question).

If you're operating from Scotland or Ulster, or wish to test-market in these areas, System Three offers a monthly omnibus of 1,000 Scots (£225 entry fee, £270 per question) and Ulster Marketing Services, a Northern Irish survey (1,100 adults, no entry fee and from £460 per question, which buys you a full report with commentary).

Business to Business. Those wanting to question other businesses can use *Business Line* from Taylor Nelson, a quarterly survey of 2,000 small businesses employing between 1 and 49 employees (no entry fee, £1,520 per single question).

ADDRESSES

Audience Selection
66 Wilson Street
London EC2A 2JX
Tel: 020 7608 3618
Fax: 020 7868 6666
Web site: www.tnsofres.com

British Market Research Bureau Ltd
Hadley House
79–81 Uxbridge Road
Ealing
London W5 5SU
Tel: 020 8566 5000
Fax: 020 8579 9208
Web site: www.bmrb.co.uk

Business and Market Research Plc
Buxton Road
High Lane
Stockport
Cheshire SK6 8DX
Tel: 01663 765115
Fax: 01663 762362
Web site: www.bandmr.co.uk

Infratest Burke
Wembley Park
Harrow Road
Wembley
Middx HA9 3DE
Tel: 020 8782 3112
Fax: 020 8900 1500
Web site: www.sample-surveys.com

Market & Opinion Research International
32 Old Queen Street
London SW1H 9HP
Tel: 020 7222 0232
Fax: 020 77222 1653
Web site: www.mori.com

NOP Research Group Ltd
245 Blackfriars Road
London SE1 9UL
Tel: 020 7890 9000
Fax: 020 7890 9001
Web site: www.nop.co.uk

Produce Studies Research
Northcroft House
West Street
Newbury
Berkshire RG14 1HD
Tel: 01635 46112
Fax: 01635 43945
Web site: www.promar-international.com

Public Attitude Surveys Ltd
Rye Park House
London Road
High Wycombe
Bucks HP11 1EF
Tel: 01494 532771
Fax: 01494 521404
Web site: www.infratestburke.com

Research International
17 Russells Crescent
Horley
Surrey RH6 7DJ
Tel: 01293 823513

Research Surveys of Great Britain Ltd
AGB House
West Gate
London W5 1UA
Tel: 020 8566 3010
Fax: 020 8967 4060
Web site: www.tnsofres.com

Sample Surveys Ltd
121 Kennington Park Road
London SE11 4JT
Tel: 0870 707010
Fax: 020 7840 7901
Web site: www.sample-surveys.com

System Three
19 Atholl Crescent
Edinburgh EH3 8HJ
Tel: 0131 221 9955
Fax: 0131 221 9944
Web site: www.nfo-europe.com

Taylor Nelson AGB plc
Brenchley House
Week Street
Maidstone
Kent ME14 1RF
Tel: 01622 778899
Fax: 01622 778880
Web site: www.tnsofres.com

Taylor Nelson Sofres
44–46 Upper High Street
Epsom
Surrey KT17 4QJ
Tel: 01372 801010
Fax: 01372 749547
Web site: www.tnsofres.com

Travel and Tourism Research Ltd
4 Cochrane House
Admirals Way
London E14 9UD
Tel: 020 7538 5300
Fax: 020 7538 3229
Web site: www.tnsofres.com

Ulster Marketing Surveys Ltd
115 University Street
Belfast BT7 1HP
Tel: 028 9023 1060
Fax: 028 9024 3887
E-mail: dpatterson@ums-research.com
Web site: www.ums-research.com

Appendix 2

Sources of finance and financial advice for new and small businesses

We strongly recommend you to take professional advice before entering into any financial commitment.

ORGANISATIONS THAT CAN HELP OR ADVISE ON LENDING MATTERS

Association of British Credit Unions
Holyoak House, Hanover Street
Manchester M60 0AS
Tel: 0161 832 3694
Fax: 0161 832 3706
E-mail: Infor@abcul.org

Banks

Abbey Business
http://www.anbusinessbank.co.uk/ (main business Web site)
http://www.anbusinessbank.co.uk/html/information/startup_intro.html
(briefing for small business start-ups)

ABN AMRO
http://www.abnamro.com/ (main business Web site)
http://www.abnamro.com/com/Productsandservices/commercial/commer
cial.asp (financing your business Web site)
Its share of the small business banking market in both the US Midwest and
the Netherlands is over 30 per cent and it is growing in Belgium, Italy, Thai-
land, India, Taiwan and Hong Kong. Some presence in the UK.

AIB (Allied Irish Bank)
http://www.aib.ie/gb/ (main UK business Web site)
http://www.aib.ie/gb/business/finance/financeyourbusiness.asp (small
business finance Web site)

Alliance and Leicester
http://www.mybusinessbank.co.uk (small business banking Web site)

Barclays
http://www.barclays.com/ (main Web site)
http://www.smallbusiness.barclays.co.uk/ (small business Web site)

Co-operative Bank
http://www.co-operativebank.co.uk/ (main Web site and information on
financing your business)

HBOS (Halifax Bank of Scotland)
http://www.hbosplc.com/ (Web site with links to all banking services)
http://www.bankofscotland.co.uk/ (business Web site, with link to services
for small business)

HSBC
http://www.hsbc.co.uk/ (main business banking Web site)
http://www.ukbusiness.hsbc.com/sab/sab00001.jsp (starting a business Web
site)

Lloyd's TSB
http://www.success4business.com/ (main business banking Web site)
http://www.smallbusiness.co.uk/ (helpful hints on finance, with a strong
Lloyd's TSB bias)

NatWest
http://www.natwest.co.uk/ (main Web site)

Royal Bank of Scotland
http://www.royalbankscot.co.uk/ (main business Web site)
http://www.royalbankscot.co.uk/small_business/ (small business Web site)

Yorkshire Bank
http://www.ybonline.co.uk/business/ (main business Web site)

Business Money Ltd
Strode House, 10 Leigh Road
Street, Somerset BA16 0HA
Tel: 01458 841112
Fax: 01458 841286
http://business-money.com/
The online version of *Business Money*, an independent review of finance and banking for business; offers articles from the current edition plus links to pages supplying current financial news.

ECGD
http://www.ecgd.gov.uk/
ECGD, the Export Credits Guarantee Department, is the UK's official export credit agency. It is a separate government department reporting to the Secretary of State for Trade and Industry. It has over 80 years' experience of working closely with exporters, project sponsors, banks and buyers to help UK exporters compete effectively in overseas markets where the private sector may be unable to help. It does this by arranging finance facilities and credit insurance for contracts ranging from around £20,000 up to hundreds of millions of pounds. There is special help for smaller exporters. It also provides overseas investment insurance for UK-based companies investing overseas.

Factors and Discounters Association
Administration Office, 2nd Floor Boston House
The Little Green
Richmond, Surrey TW9 1QE
Tel: 020 8332 9955
Fax: 020 8332 2585
http://www.factors.org.uk

Finance and Leasing Association
Imperial House, 15–19 Kingsway
London WC2B 6UN
Tel: 020 7836 6511
Fax: 020 7420 9600
http://www.fla.org.uk
E-mail: info@fla.org.uk

Funds4Growth
Blue Chip Publishing Ltd
51 Newhall Street
Birmingham B3 3QR
Tel: 0121 248 0375
E-mail: steveanstey@bluechippublishing.co.uk
Web site: http://www.funds4growth.com
Complete a brief registration form, select a funding category and Funds Finder will give you a shortlist of likely providers. Detailed information on each is available within the database. You can then e-mail requests to any or all via a secure link. Funds4Growth takes no fees for any transactions from either you or your chosen provider. You deal directly with the lender

LETSLINK UK (Local Exchange Trading Systems)
54 Campbell Rd
Southsea, Hants PO5 1RW
Tel: 01705 730 639
E-mail: lets@letslinkuk.org
Web site: http://www.trendmonitor.com/LETSLINKUK/

UK Banks Guide
http://www.ukbanksguide.co.uk/
UK Banks Guide is an easy way to locate high street banks and building societies. It provides a comprehensive directory of UK bank sites on the Internet, covering online banking, business banking, private banking, offshore banks and international banks.

ORGANISATIONS THAT CAN HELP OR ADVISE ON EQUITY MATTERS

UK Business Angels
Beer & Partners Ltd
The Bell House, West Street
Dorking, Surrey RH4 1BS
Tel: 01306 742104
Fax: 01306 884999
E-mail: beerprt@netcomuk.co.uk
Web site: www.beerprt.com

Business Angels Network West, North Yorkshire & The Humber
Parkview House, Woodvale Office Park
Woodvale Road
Brighouse, West Yorkshire HD6 4AB
Tel: 01484 406275/406106
Fax: 01484 710110
E-mail: ken.ormerod@cktec.co.uk
Web site: www.businessangelsnetwork.co.uk

Business Direct in association with the *Daily Telegraph*
40–42 Cannon Street
London EC4N 6JJ
Tel: 020 7329 2939
Fax: 020 7329 2626
E-mail: contact@business.direct.uk.com
Web site: www.business-direct.uk.com

Business Investment Network Ltd
c/o Business Link Milton Keynes & North Bucks
Tempus, 249 Midsummer Boulevard
Central Milton Keynes
Tel: 01908 259267
Fax: 01908 230130
E-mail: binl@mk-chamber.co.uk
Web site: www.binl.co.uk

Business Link West
16 Clifton Park
Bristol BS8 3BY
Tel: 0117 973 7373 or 0976 238166 (mobile)
Fax: 0117-923 8024
E-mail: peter.hepburn@blw.westc.co.uk

Capital Match
King Business Centre, Reeds Lane
Sayers Common, Hassocks
West Sussex BN6 9LS
Tel: 01273 833881
Fax: 01273 833277
E-mail: Cadmus@globalnet.co.uk

Capital Network Ltd
2nd Floor, Don Valley House
Savile Street East
Sheffield S4 7UQ
Tel: 0114 281 3831
Fax: 0114 281 2772
E-mail: capnet@blsheffield.co.uk

Cavendish Management Resources (CMR)
1 Harley Street
London W1N 1DA
Tel: 020 7636 1744
Fax: 020 7636 5639
E-mail: cmr@cmruk.com
Web site: www.cmruk.com

Dunstable Management Group
PO Box 18
Dereham, Norfolk NR20 4UL
Tel: 01362 637948
Fax: 01362 637581
E-mail: dunstable@altavista.net

East Midlands Business Angels Ltd
PO Box 333
Newark, Nottinghamshire NG23 6FQ
Tel: 01636 708717
Fax: 01636 708717
E-mail: emba.co.uk@virgin.net
Web site: www.embaltd.co.uk

The Enterprise Forum
45 The Close
Norwich NR1 4EG
Tel: 01603 628912
Fax: 01603 628912
E-mail: lalance@wxs.nl

Entrust
Portman House, Portland Road
Newcastle upon Tyne NE2 1AQ
Tel: 0191 244 4000
Fax: 0191 244 4001
E-mail: enquire@entrust.co.uk
Web site: www.entrust.co.uk

EquityLink (Head Office)
Business Link Hertfordshire
45 Grosvenor Road
St Albans, Hertfordshire AL1 3AW
Tel: 01727 813533
Fax: 01727 813443
E-mail: info@EquityLink.co.uk
Web site: www.equitylink.co.uk

Bedfordshire & Luton Chamber Business
Kimpton Road
Luton, Beds LU2 0LB
Tel: 07970 485 016
Fax: 01582 522450
E-mail: hugo.burnettgodfree@chamber-business.com

Business Link Berkshire & Wiltshire
Emlyn Square
Swindon SN1 5BP
Tel: 01793 428364
Fax: 01793 485186
E-mail: keith.farmer@blbw.co.uk

Business Link Oxfordshire & Buckinghamshire
Unit B, The Firs
Bierton, Bucks HP22 5DX
Tel: 0845 606 4466
Fax: 0870 161 5860
E-mail: gordon.huntly@businesslinksolutions.co.uk

Cambridge Business Services Ltd
Business Link
Centenary House, St Mary's Street
Huntingdon PE29 3PE
Tel: 01480 846414
Fax: 01480 846478
E-mail: john.cresswell@c-b-s.org.uk

Business Link for Essex
Alexandra House, 36a Church Street
Great Baddow, Chelmsford
Essex CM2 7HY
Tel: 01245 241536
Fax: 01245 393837
E-mail: nick.athorne@essex.businesslink.co.uk

Business Link Hertfordshire
45 Grosvenor Road
St Albans, Herts AL1 3AW
Tel: 01727 813533
Fax: 01727 813443
E-mail: stuart.mcroberts@herts.businesslink.co.uk

Business Link Kent
26 Kings Hill Avenue
Kings Hill, West Malling
Kent ME19 4AE
Tel: 01732 878051
Fax: 01732 874818I
E-mail: ian.netherton@businesslinkkent.com

Business Link for London
Centre Point, 103 New Oxford Street
London WC1A 1DP
Tel: 0845 6000 787
Fax: 020 7010 000
E-mail: hotline@bl4london.com
Web site: http://www.bl4london.com

Lovewell Blake Equity Introductions Ltd
102 Prince of Wales Road
Norwich NR1 1NY
Tel: 01603 663300
Fax: 01603 692254
E-mail: hrj@lovewell-blake.co.uk

Southern Enterprise Ltd
The Martlet Heights
The Martlets, Burgess Hill
West Sussex RH15 9NJ
Tel: 01444 254980
Fax: 01444 254255
E-mail: janet.poulter@abbacus.co.uk

First Stage Capital
15–16 Margaret Street
London W1W 8RW
Tel: 020 7637 9292
Fax: 020 7436 1312
E-mail: info@firststagecapital.com
Web site: www.firststagecapital.com

Gorilla Park
42–46 Princess Street
London E1 5LP
Tel: 020 7920 2500
Fax: 020 7920 2501
E-mail: info@gorillapark.com

Great Eastern Investment Forum
Richmond House
16–20 Regent Street
Cambridge CB2 1DB
Tel: 01223 357131
Fax: 01223 720258
E-mail: geif@nwbrown.co.uk
Web site: www.geif.co.uk

IDJ Limited
81 Piccadilly
London W1J 8HY
Tel: 020 7355 1200
Fax: 020 7495 1149
E-mail: csmontefiore@idj.co.uk
Web site: www.idj.co.uk

Investor Champions plc
24 Bennetts Hill
Birmingham B2 5QP
Tel: 0121 643 8898
Fax: 0121 643 3331
E-mail: info@investorchampions.com
Web site: www.investorchampions.com
Contact: Bob Barnsley

LEntA Ventures
London Business Incentive Scheme (LBIS) Ltd
28 Park Street
London SE1 9EQ
Tel: 020 7940 1548
Fax: 020 7403 1742
E-mail: lenta.ventures@gle.co.uk
Web site: www.businessangels-london.co.uk

LINC Scotland
Queens House, 19 St Vincent Place
Glasgow G1 2DT
Tel: 0141 221 3321
Fax: 0141 221 2909
E-mail: info@lincscot.co.uk
Web site: www.lincscot.co.uk

MBAngels
Association of MBAs
15 Duncan Terrace
London N1 8BZ
Tel: 020 7837 3375
Fax: 020 7278 3634
E-mail: MBAngels@Talk21.com

Mercantile 100
HLB Kidsons CA
Breckenridge House, 274 Sauchiehall Street
Glasgow G2 3EH
Tel: 0141 307 5000
Fax: 0141 307 5005
E-mail: egrant@kiglasg.kidsons.co.uk
Web site: www.hlbkidsons.co.uk

National Business Angels Network
40–42 Cannon Street
London EC4N 6JJ
Tel: 020 7329 2929 or for info pack: 020 7329 4141
Fax: 020 7329 2626
E-mail: info@nationalbusangels.co.uk
Web site: http://www.nationalbusangels.co.uk

One London Business Angels
c/o Greater London Enterprise, 28 Park Street
London SE1 9EQ
Tel: 020 7940 1547
Fax: 020 7403 0300
E-mail: businessangels@one-london.com

Oxfordshire Investment Opportunity Network
Oxford Centre for Innovation
Mill Street
Oxford OX2 0JX
Tel: 01865 811143
Fax: 01865 209044
E-mail: oion@oxfordinnovation.co.uk
Web site: http://www.oion.co.uk

Selling Solutions
The Maltings, East Tyndall Street
Cardiff CF1 5EA
Tel: 029 20 485668
Fax: 029 20 452789

Solent Business Angels
Deepsprings, Emsworth
Hampshire PO10 8RL
Tel: 01243 373 959
Fax: 01243 375 082
E-mail: solent.angels@dial.pipex.com

South West Investment Group
Trevint House, Strangeways Villas
Truro, Cornwall TR1 2PA
Tel: 01872 223883
Fax: 01872 242470
E-mail: swig@btinternet.com

TEChINVEST
North West Development Agency
Muirfield House, Kelvin Close
Birchwood, Warrington
Cheshire WA3 7PB
Tel: 01925 400301/400302/400100
Fax: 01925 400400 or 830456
E-mail: tecinvest@nwda.co.uk
Web site: www.techinvest.org

Triodos Match
Brunel House, 11 The Promenade
Clifton, Bristol BS8 3NN
Tel: 0117 980 9746
Fax: 0117 973 9303
E-mail: mail@triodosmatch.co.uk
Web site: www.triodosmatch.co.uk

VentureNet
Highfold Studios, Shophouse Lane
Albury, Surrey GU5 9DN
Tel: 01483 205008
Fax: 01483 205009
E-mail: vnet@enterprisesupport.com
Web site: www.enterprisesupport.com

The Venture Site
5 The Maltings
Walkern, Hertfordshire SG2 7NP
Tel: 01438 861930
Fax: 01438 861089
E-mail: info@venturesite.co.uk
Web site: www.venturesite.co.uk

Winsec Corporate Exchange Ltd
1 The Centre, Church Road
Tiptree, Colchester CO5 0HF
Tel: 01621 815047
Fax: 01621 817965
E-mail: corpex@winsec.co.uk
Web site: www.winsec.co.uk

Xenos – The Wales Business Angel Network
3rd Floor, Oakleigh House
Park Place, Cardiff CF10 3DQ
Tel: 029 2033 8144
Fax: 029 2033 8145
E-mail: Info@xenos.co.uk
Web site: www.xenos.co.uk

Xenva Ltd
79 George Street
Ryde, Isle of Wight, PO33 2JF
Tel: 01983 817017
Fax: 01983 817001
E-mail: info@xenva.com
Web site: www.xenva.com

Yorkshire Association of Business Angels
c/o UniVentures International Limited
Woodhouse Business Centre, Wakefield Road
Normanton, West Yorkshire WF6 1BB
Tel: 01924 891125
Fax: 01924 892207
E-mail: a.burton@luniventures.co.uk
Web site: www.yaba.org.uk

Online directories of UK business angels can be found at:
http://www.startups.co.uk/directories.asp
and for most other European countries at:
http://www.eban.org/

UK VENTURE CAPITAL PROVIDERS

Some of these firms are very focused, only serving a single industry or a small
geographic area of the UK. Others have a wider vision and see the world as
their market, and will consider almost any business sector. One VC even
suggests it would be prepared to consider a business in sufficient trouble to
require rescuing!

3K Digital
Level 4, 16 Old Bond Street
London W1X 3DB
Tel: 020 7355 3322
Fax: 020 7355 3407
E-mail: info@3kdigital.com
Web site: http://www.3kdigital.com

Aberdeen Murray Johnstone Private Equity
55 Spring Gardens
Manchester M2 2BY
Tel: 0161 236 2288
Fax: 0161 236 5539
E-mail: private.equity@aberdeen-asset.com
Web site: http://www.aberdeen-asset.com

Abingworth Management Ltd
Princes House, 38 Jermyn Street
London SW1Y 6DN
Tel: 020 7534 1500
Fax: 020 7287 0480
E-mail: info@abingworth.co.uk
Web site: http://www.abingworth.com

ABN AMRO Capital Limited
199 Bishopsgate, London EC2M 3XW
Tel: 020 7678 8000
Fax: 020 7678 2050
E-mail: ian.taylor@uk.abnamro.com
Web site: http://www.privateequities.com

Accelerator Media (UK) Ltd
30 St James's Square
London SW1Y 4AL
Tel: 020 7968 4288
Fax: 020 7968 4298
E-mail: proposals@acceleratormedia.com
Web site: http://www.acceleratormedia.com

Accenture Technology Ventures
60 Queen Victoria Street
London EC4N 4TW
Tel: 020 7844 3333
Fax: 020 7844 9512
E-mail: techventures@accenture.com
Web site: http://www.accenturetechventures.com

ACT Venture Capital Ltd
Windsor Business Centre, 58 Howard Street
Belfast BT1 6PJ
Tel: 04890 500 880
Fax: 04890 500 888
E-mail: info@actvc.ie
Web site: http://www.actventure.com

Advent International plc
123 Buckingham Palace Road
London SW1W 9SL
Tel: 020 7333 0800
Fax: 020 7333 0801
E-mail: tfranks@uk.adventinternational.com
Web site: http://www.adventinternational.com

Advent Venture Partners
25 Buckingham Gate
London SW1E 6LD
Tel: 020 7630 9811
Fax: 020 7828 1474
E-mail: info@adventventures.com
Web site: http://www.adventventures.com

Albany Venture Managers Ltd
Forth House, 28 Rutland Square
Edinburgh EH1 2BW
Tel: 0131 221 6517
Fax: 0131 221 6511
E-mail: info@albanyventures.co.uk
Web site: http://www.albanyventures.co.uk

Albemarle Private Equity Ltd
1 Albemarle Street
London W1S 4HA
Tel: 020 7491 9555
Fax: 020 7491 7245
E-mail: Albemarle@btinternet.com

Alchemy Partners
20 Bedfordbury
London WC2N 4BL
Tel: 020 7240 9596
Fax: 020 7240 9594
E-mail: jmoulton@alchemypartners.co.uk
Web site: http://www.alchemypartners.co.uk

Alta Berkeley Venture Partners
9–10 Savile Row
London W1S 3PF
Tel: 020 7440 0200
Fax: 020 7734 6711
E-mail: infol@alta-berkeley.com
Web site: http://www.alta-berkeley.com

Amadeus Capital Partners Ltd
5 Shaftsbury Road
Cambridge CB2 2BW
Tel: 01223 707000
Fax: 01223 707070
E-mail: info@amadeuscapital.com
Web site: http://www.amadeuscapital.com

Apax Partners Ltd
15 Portland Place
London W1B 1PT
Tel: 020 7872 6300
Fax: 020 7636 6475
Web site: http://www.apax.com

Atlas Venture Ltd
55 Grosvenor Street
London W1K 3BW
Tel: 020 7529 4444
Fax: 020 7529 4455
E-mail: london@atlasventure.co.uk
Web site: http://www.atlasventure.com

Avlar Bioventures
St John's Innovation Centre, Cowley Road
Cambridge CB4 0WS
Tel: 01223 422255
Fax: 01223 426888
Web site: http://www.avlar.com

Bamboo Investments plc
Manfield House, 1 Southampton Street
London WC2R 0LR
Tel: 020 7845 8500
Fax: 020 7240 8266
E-mail: Plans@bamboo-investments.com
Web site: http://www.bamboo-investments.com

BancBoston Capital
Bank of Boston House, 39 Victoria Street
London SW1H 0ED
Tel: 020 7932 9053
Fax: 020 7932 9117
Web site: http://www.bancboscap.com/www.bancbostoncapital.com

Bank of America Equity Partners
43 Grosvenor Street
London W1K 3HL
Tel: 020 7809 5985
Fax: 020 7809 5999
E-mail: firstname.lastname@bankofamerica.com
Web site: http://www.baepeurope.com

Barclays Private Equity Ltd
5 The North Colonnade, Canary Wharf
London E14 4BB
Tel: 020 7512 9900
Fax: 020 7773 4805
Web site: http://www.barcap.com

Barclays Ventures
Third Floor, 50 Pall Mall
London SW1Y 5AX
Tel: 020 7441 4213
Fax: 020 7441 4212
E-mail: barclays.ventures@barclays.co.uk
Web site: http://www.barclaysventures.com

Baring Private Equity Partners Ltd
33 Cavendish Square
London W1M 0BQ
Tel: 020 7290 5000
Fax: 020 7290 5020
E-mail: mail@bpep.com
Web site: http://www.bpep.com

BC Partners Ltd
43–45 Portman Square
London W1H 6DA
Tel: 020 7009 48
Fax: 020 7009 4899 00
E-mail: london@bcpartners.com
Web site: http://www.bcpartners.com

Birmingham Technology (Venture Capital) Ltd
Aston Science Park, Love Lane
Birmingham B7 4BJ
Tel: 0121 250 3500
Fax: 0121 359 0433
E-mail: derekh@astonsciencepark.co.uk
Web site: http://www.astonsciencepark.co.uk

Cabot Square Capital Advisors Ltd
Byron House, 7–9 St James's Street
London SW1A 1EE
Tel: 020 7579 9320
Fax: 020 7579 9330
E-mail: contact@cabotsquare.com
Web site: http://www.cabotsquare.com

Cambridge Research & Innovation Ltd
13 Station Road
Cambridge CB1 2JB
Tel: 01223 312856
Fax: 01223 365704
E-mail: enquiries@cril.co.uk
Web site: http://www.cril.co.uk

Catalyst Fund Management & Research Ltd
15 Whitcomb Street
London WC2H 7HA
Tel: 020 7747 8600
Fax: 020 7930 2688
E-mail: info@catfund.com
Web site: http://www.catfund.com

Cinven
Pinners Hall, 105–108 Old Broad Street
London EC2N 1EH
Tel: 020 7661 3333
Fax: 020 7661 3888
E-mail: info@cinven.com
Web site: http://www.cinven.com

Close Brothers Private Equity
12 Appold Street
London EC2A 2AW
Tel: 020 7426 4000
Fax: 020 7426 4004
E-mail: enquiries@cbpel.com
Web site: http://www.cbpel.com

Company Guides Ltd
13 Christopher Street
London EC2A 2BS
Tel: 020 7247 6300
Fax: 020 7247 6900
E-mail: enquiries@companyguides.com
Web site: http://www.companyguides.com

Compass Investment Management Ltd
33 Cork Street
London W1X 1HB
Tel: 020 7434 4484/3488
Fax: 020 7434 3155
E-mail: invest@compass.uk.com
Web site: http://www.compass.uk.com

CVC Capital Partners Limited
Hudson House, 8–10 Tavistock Street
London WC2E 7PP
Tel: 020 7420 4200
Fax: 020 7420 4231/4232/4233
E-mail: info@cvceurope.com
Web site: http://www.cvceurope.com

Derbyshire First Investments Ltd
95 Sheffield Road
Chesterfield, Derbyshire S41 7JH
Tel: 01246 207 390
Fax: 01246 221 080
E-mail: info@dfil.co.uk(general enquiries); ahay@dfil.co.uk(investment)
Web site: http://www.dfil.co.uk

Duke Street Capital
Dukes Court, 32 Duke's Street
St James's
London SW1Y 6DF
Tel: 020 7451 6600
Fax: 020 7451 6601
E-mail: mail@dukestreetcapital.com
Web site: http://www.dukestreetcapital.com

ECI Ventures Ltd
Brettenham House, Lancaster Place
London WC2E 7EN
Tel: 020 7606 1000
Fax: 020 7240 5050
E-mail: janet.brooks@eciv.co.uk
Web site: http://www.eciv.co.uk

Electra Partners Europe Ltd
65 Kingsway
London WC2B 6QT
Tel: 020 7831 6464
Fax: 020 7404 5388
E-mail: info@electraeurope.com
Web site: http://www.electraeurope.com

Enterprise Equity (NI) Ltd
78a Dublin Road, Belfast BT2 7HP
Tel: 028 9024 2500
Fax: 028 9024 2487
E-mail: info@eeni.com
Web site: http://www.eeni.com

Enterprise Ventures Ltd
Lancaster House, Centurion Way
Leyland, Lancashire PR26 6TX
Tel: 01772 819400
Fax: 01772 819046
E-mail: ventures@enterprise.plc.uk
Web site: http://www.enterprise.plc.uk

Equity Ventures Ltd
28 Grosvenor Street
London W1X 9FE
Tel: 020 7917 9611
Fax: 020 7917 6002
E-mail: mail@equityventures.co.uk
Web site: http://www.equityventures.co.uk

ETCapital Ltd
St John's Innovation Centre, Cowley Road
Cambridge CB4 0WS
Tel: 01223 422010
Fax: 01223 422011
E-mail: directory@etcapital.com
Web site: http://www.etcapital.com

GLE Development Capital
52/54 Southwark Street
London SE1 1UN
Tel: 020 7403 0300
Fax: 020 7089 2301
E-mail: tracy.m@gledc.co.uk
Web site: http://www.gledevelopmentcapital.co.uk

Granville Baird Capital Partners
5th Floor, Walsingham House
London EC3N 4AH
Tel: 020 7488 1212
Fax: 020 7667 8481
E-mail: private.equity@granvillebaird.com
Web site: http://www.gbcp.co.uk

Graphite Capital
Berkeley Square House, Berkeley Square
London W1X 5PA
Tel: 020 7825 5300
Fax: 020 7825 5399
E-mail: info@graphitecapital.com
Web site: http://www.graphitecapital.com

Gresham Trust plc
One South Place
London EC2M 2GT
Tel: 020 7309 5000
Fax: 020 7374 0707
E-mail: info@greshamtrust.co.uk
Web site: http://www.greshamtrust.co.uk

Henderson Private Capital Ltd
4 Broadgate
London EC2M 2DA
Tel: 020 7410 3173
Fax: 020 7858 2799
E-mail: kathryn.fisher@henderson.com
Web site: http://www.henderson.com

Hermes Private Equity Management Limited
Lloyds Chambers, 1 Portsoken Street
London E1 8HZ
Tel: 020 7680 2290
Fax: 020 7702 9452
E-mail: private.equity@hermes.co.uk
Web site: http://www.hermes.co.uk

HSBC Ventures (UK) Ltd
36 Poultry
London EC2R 8AJ
Tel: 020 7260 7935
Fax: 020 7260 6767
E-mail: Venturesuk@hsbc.com
Web site: http://www.hsbc.co.uk

Innvotec Ltd
1 Castle Lane
London SW1E 6DN
Tel: 020 7630 6990
Fax: 020 7828 8232
E-mail: cvk@innvotec.co.uk (see regional offices)
Web site: http://www.innvotec.uk.com

Interregnum plc
22–23 Old Burlington Street
London W1S 2JJ
Tel: 020 7494 3080
Fax: 020 7494 3090
E-mail: enquiries@interregnum.com
Web site: http://www.interregnum.com

Kleinwort Capital Ltd
PO Box 18075, Riverbank House, 2 Swan Lane
London EC4R 3UX
Tel: 020 7623 8000
Fax: 020 7626 8616
E-mail: info@kleinwortcapital.com
Web site: http://wwwkleinwortcapital.com

Legal & General Ventures Ltd
5th Floor, Bucklersbury House, 3 Queen Victoria Street
London EC4N 8NH
Tel: 020 7528 6456
Fax: 020 7528 6444
E-mail: enquiries@ventures.landg.com
Web site: http://www.legalandgeneralventures.com

London Ventures (Fund Managers) Ltd
4th Floor, 17 Golden Square
London W1F 9JH
Tel: 020 7434 2425
Fax: 020 7434 2426
E-mail: lvfm@compuserve.com
Web site: http://www.londonventures.co.uk

Matrix Private Equity
9–10 Savile Row
London W1S 3PF
Tel: 020 7439 6050
Fax: 020 7287 2312
E-mail: info@matrixpe.com
Web site: http://www.matrixpe.com

MMC adVentures Ltd
Braywick House, Gregory Place
London W8 4NG
Tel: 020 7938 2220
Fax: 020 7938 2259
E-mail: enquiries@mmcadventures.com
Web site: http://www.mmcadventures.com

NBGI Private Equity
Old Change House, 128 Queen Victoria Street
London EC4V 4HR
Tel: 020 7661 5678
Fax: 020 7661 5667
E-mail: info@nbgiprivateequity.co.uk
Web site: http://www.nbgiprivateequity.co.uk

Northern Enterprise Ltd
3 Earl's Court, 5th Avenue
Team Valley, Gateshead NE11 0HF
Tel: 0191 442 4300
Fax: 0191 442 4301
E-mail: enquiries@nel.co.uk
Web site: http://www.nel.co.uk

Northern Venture Managers Ltd
Northumberland House, Princess Square
Newcastle upon Tyne NE1 8ER
Tel: 0191 244 6000
Fax: 0191 244 6001
E-mail: new@nvm.co.uk
Web site: http://www.nvm.co.uk

Penta Capital Partners Ltd
150 St Vincent Street
Glasgow G2 5NE
Tel: 0141 572 7300
Fax: 0141 572 7310
E-mail: info@pentacapital.com
Web site: http://www.pentacapital.com

Phoenix Equity Partners
33 Glasshouse Street
London W1B 5DG
Tel: 020 7434 6999
Fax: 020 7434 6998
E-mail: enquiries@phoenix-equity.com
Web site: http://www.phoenix-equity.com

Prelude Technology Investments Ltd
Sycamore Studios, New Road
Over, Cambridge CB4 5PJ
Tel: 01954 288090
Fax: 01954 288099
E-mail: Prelude@prelude-technology.co.uk
Web site: http://www.prelude-technology.co.uk

ProVen Private Equity Ltd
42 Craven Street
London WC2N 5NG
Tel: 020 7451 6500
Fax: 020 7839 8349
E-mail: info@proven.co.uk
Web site: http://www.provenprivateequity.com

Royal Bank Ventures
Waterhouse Square, 138–142 Holborn
London EC1N 2TH
Tel: 020 7842 0136
Fax: 020 7427 9911
E-mail: info@rbventures.co.uk
Web site: http://www.rbventures.co.uk

Scottish Equity Partners
17 Blythswood Square
Glasgow G2 4AD
Tel: 0141 273 4000
Fax: 0141 273 4001
E-mail: enquiries@sepl.co.uk
Web site: http://www.sepl.co.uk

Seed Capital Ltd
Magdalen Centre, Oxford Science Park
Oxford OX4 4GA
Tel: 01865 784466
Fax: 01865 784430
E-mail: luciusc@seedcapital.demon.co.uk
matthew@seedcapital.demon.co.uk
Web site: http://www.oxfordtechnology.com

Sovereign Capital Ltd
25 Buckingham Gate
London SW1E 6LD
Tel: 020 7828 6944
Fax: 020 7828 9958
E-mail: enquiries@sovereigncapital.co.uk
Web site: http://www.sovereigncapital.co.uk

Thompson Clive & Partners Ltd
24 Old Bond Street
London W1S 4AW
Tel: 020 7491 4809
Fax: 020 7493 9172
E-mail: mail@tcvc.com
Web site: http://www.tcvc.com

UK Steel Enterprise Ltd (formerly British Steel (Industry) Ltd)
The Innovation Centre, 217 Portobello
Sheffield S1 4DP
Tel: 0114 273 1612
Fax: 0114 270 1390
E-mail: investment@uksteelenterprise.co.uk
Web site: http://www.uksteelenterprise.co.uk

Wales Fund Managers Ltd
Cedar House, Greenwood Close
Cardiff Gate Business Park
Cardiff CF23 8RD
Tel: 029 20 546250
Fax: 029 20 546251
E-mail: info@wfml.co.uk
Web site: http://www.wfml.co.uk

WM Enterprise
Wellington House, 31–34 Waterloo Street
Birmingham B2 5TJ
Tel: 0121 236 8855
Fax: 0121 233 3942
E-mail: mail@wm-enterprise.co.uk
Web site: http://www.wm-enterprise.co.uk

Yorkshire Fund Managers Ltd (part of the Yorkshire Enterprise Group)
Saint Martins House, 210–212 Chapeltown Road
Leeds LS7 4HZ
Tel: 0113 294 5050
Fax: 0113 294 5002
E-mail: YFM@yorkshire-enterprise.co.uk
Web site: http://www.yorkshire-enterprise.co.uk

Online directories of venture capital providers

British Venture Capital Association
Essex House, 12–13 Essex Street
London WC2R 3AA
Tel: 020 7240 3846
Fax: 020 7240 3849
E-mail: bvca@bvca.co.uk
Web site: http://www.bvca.co.uk/
Online directory of all its UK VC members, plus lots of helpful information
about raising VC money.

European Venture Capital Association
Minervastraat 4
B-1930 Zaventem (Brussels)
Belgium
Tel: (+32) 2 715 00 20
Fax: (+32) 2 725 07 04
E-mail: evca@evca.com
Web site: http://www.evca.com/
Over 850 members to be found on their online search engines. The directory
can be searched by country, amount of money you are looking for and in a
variety of other ways.

NVCA (National Venture Capital Association)
1655 North Fort Myer Drive, Suite 850
Arlington, Virginia 22209, USA
Tel: 703 524 2549
Fax: 703 524 3940
E-mail: www.nvca.org
Web site: http://www.nvca.org/
The Association has an online directory of its 250 mostly US VCs, and lots of
useful information about raising money, preparing business plans and finding
advisers.

Venture Capital: On the Net (1000)
http://advocacy-net.com/venturemks.htm
Just what it says. Links to 1000 VC Web sites around the world.

London Stock Exchange
Old Broad Street
London EC2N 1HP
Tel: 020 7797 4404
Fax: 020 7797 2001
Web site: http://www.londonstockexchange.com
The ones to talk to about going public.

GRANTS, AWARDS AND COMPETITIONS

Unlike debt, which has to be repaid, or equity, which has to earn a return for the investors, grants and awards are not refundable. So, although they are often hard to get, they can be particularly valuable.

Grants

Support for business comes in a very wide variety of forms. The most obvious is the direct (cash) grant but other forms of assistance are also numerous. The main types are as follows.

Direct grant

This is a cash item, which may be offered for activities such as training, employment, export development, recruitment or capital investment projects. It is rare to obtain 100 per cent grant funding. Most schemes require the recipient company to put up a proportion of the cost, with a figure of 50 per cent being typical.

Repayable grant

This is where cash funding is offered for a project with the intention that the sums are repaid out of future revenues. The grant is not repayable in the event the project fails.

Soft loan

This is a loan where the terms and conditions of repayment are more generous (or softer) than those that would prevail if the loan were made available under normal commercial terms. The interest rate may be less than the ongoing commercial rate for a similar loan and/or the repayment term may be longer. Sometimes the loan may be interest-free.

Equity finance

Here a capital sum is injected into the business where the provider does not expect interest or repayment of the loan itself. Rather, the provider of funds takes an equity share of the business, in the hope/expectation that the value of the stake will appreciate at some time in the future, enabling a sale of the stake to facilitate a return on the original investment.

Free or subsidised consultancy

Often it is a particular skill or skills that a company lacks. This is particularly so in the case of start-ups and new companies. Some schemes provide these skills at free or subsidised rates by paying, in whole or in part, the fees of accredited or approved consultants who possess the skills the organisation lacks.

Access to resources

A number of schemes provide access to valuable publicly owned facilities (such as research facilities operated by the Ministry of Defence).

Best practice transfer

There are now a number of well-established quality and best practice initiatives such as Investors in People and ISO 9000. The cost of transferring such 'best practice' procedures to small firms is often subsidised by government.

Shared cost contract

The costs of research and development programmes can be prohibitive for small firms acting alone. Sharing the costs of such programmes with others, whereby all participants share in the costs and the consequent resulting know-how, can be a solution. Such arrangements are often brokered, and sometimes part-financed, by public bodies or institutions.

Subsidies

Some awarding bodies, while not always advancing direct cash grants, will subsidise the costs of approved products or services used by firms.

Location

Many grants are location-specific. There are several schemes that operate across the whole of the UK, and are available to all businesses that satisfy the outline criteria, but in addition to these there are a myriad of schemes that are administered locally. Thus the location of your business will be absolutely crucial, and funding that might be available to you will be strongly dependent on the area into which you intend to grow or develop. Additionally, there may well be additional grants available to a business investing in or into an area of social deprivation, particularly if it involves sustainable job creation.

Industry type

In order to satisfy the local economic or political agenda, many funding schemes are allocated towards the development of particular industry sectors.

IMPROVING YOUR CHANCES OF GETTING A GRANT

The assistance provided for enterprise is limited, so you will be competing for grants against other applicants. You can enhance your chances of success by following these seven rules:

1. *Keep yourself informed about what grants are available.* Grants are constantly being introduced (and withdrawn) but there is no system that lets you know automatically what is on offer. You have to keep yourself informed.

2. *Do not start the project for which you want a grant before you make the application.* The awarding body will almost certainly take the view that if you can start the project without a grant, you must have had sufficient funds to complete it without assistance. Better still, show the project is dependent on the grant being made.

3. *Make sure your application is in respect of a project.* Usually, grants are given for specific projects, not for the normal organic growth of a business. If, for example, you need new equipment to launch a product, make sure your application emphasises the project, not the equipment. State the advantages of the project's success (for example, it will safeguard or create jobs) and explain that the purchase of the equipment is a prerequisite for that success.

4. *Try to get in first.* The chances of a successful application are always highest just after a scheme is launched. That is when there is the most money 'in the pot', and it is also the time when those administering the scheme are keenest to get applications in and grants awarded. Competition is likely to be less fierce.

5. *Make your application match the awarding body's objectives.* The benefits of your project should fit in with the objectives of the awarding body and the grant scheme itself. So, if the grant is intended to help the local community, or the country in the form of potential exports, for example, make sure these are included. Most grant applications require the submission of a business plan, so make sure you have an up-to-date one.

6. *Make sure you have matching funds available.* It is unusual for a grant to finance 100 per cent of the costs of any project. Typically nowadays a grant will contribute 15–50 per cent of the total finance required. Those making the decision about the grant are spending public money. They have a duty to ensure it is spent wisely, and they will need to be absolutely convinced that you have, or can raise from other sources, the balance required.

7. *Talk to the awarding body before you apply.* Make contact with an individual responsible for administering the scheme. You will be given advice on whether it is worth while your applying, before you start spending time and effort on making the application; you may get some help and advice on completing the application form; you may get an insight into how you should shape your application.

HELP WITH GRANTS

Business Link
http://www.businesslink.org/

Department of Trade and Industry
http://www.dti.gov.uk/

Funders online
51 rue de la Concorde
B-1050 Brussels, Belgium
Tel: (+32) 2 512 8938
Fax: (+32) 2 512 3265
E-mail: webmaster@fundersonline.org
Web site: http://www.fundersonline.org
The directory is designed to help you track down in a quick and efficient way specific types of information provided on a funder's Web site, such as its grants list programmes description or newsletter; to enable you to find funders according to their country of location and fields of activities.

Grants On-line
75 Hazelwood Drive,
Verwood, Dorset BH31 6YG
Tel: 01202 828674
E-mail: services@mycommunity.org.uk
Web site: http://www.co-financing.co.uk/
The site provides access to the latest information on grants from the European Union, UK government, National Lottery, Regional Development Agency (RDA) grants and UK grant-making trusts. It is designed to guide you through the external funding maze, save you valuable time in identifying relevant external funding opportunities and to ensure that you have the most up-to-date information available. There is a 14-day free trial offer, and the standard subscription is £150 per annum.

j4b
51 Water Lane
Wilmslow, Cheshire SK9 5BQ
E-mail: enquiries@j4b.co.uk
Web site: http://www.j4b.co.uk/
The mission of j4b is to help businesses everywhere to find out about any grants, financial assistance, subsidies and help in kind that may be available to them. j4b was set up in 2000 to find easier ways through the information jungle, which puts most businesses off trying to find out about their possible entitlement. The site is updated continuously. It is free to use. There are no upfront fees for applicants to pay and j4b does not receive a commission on successful applications. Registered users receive targeted alerts about grants that might apply to them.

UK Fundraising
http://www.fundraising.co.uk/grants.html
Has free links to grants and funding resources, listed by geographical region.

BUSINESS COMPETITIONS

If you enjoy publicity and like a challenge, you could look out for a business competition to enter. Like government grants, business competitions are ubiquitous, and like national lotteries they are something of a hit or miss affair.

But one thing is certain. If you don't enter you cannot win. There are more than 100 annual awards in the United Kingdom alone, aimed at new or small businesses. For the most part, these are sponsored by banks, the major accountancy bodies, chambers of commerce, and local or national newspapers, business magazines and the trade press. Government departments may also have their own competitions as a means of promoting their initiatives, for exporting, innovation, job creation and so forth.

The nature and the amount of the awards change from year to year, as do the sponsors. But looking out in the national and local press, or contacting one of the organisations mentioned above, should put you in touch with a competition organiser quickly, as will an Internet search. Money awards constitute 40 per cent of the main competition prizes. For the most part, these cash sums are less than £5,000. However, a few do exceed £10,000 and one UK award is for £50,000. Other awards are for equally valuable goods and services, such as consultancy or accountancy advice, training, and computer hardware and software.

Business Competitions Directory

Categories: three awards to Web sites that are exceptionally well constructed. Sites are judged based on ease of navigation, content, graphic quality, page layout and design by the Book-Look's award team.
Further details:
E-mail: support@book-look.co.uk
Web site: http://www.book-look.co.uk/awards/awards/htm

Biotechnology & Biological Sciences Research Council (BBSRC): UK Bioscience Business Plan Competition

Categories: the competition aims to increase awareness of the issues involved in developing a bioscience business and help the formation of new bioscience business ventures. The competition is set in two rounds. In round one, participants have access to training in key commercialisation issues, and in round two, 18 ideas are been selected for development into full business plans. The costs of participation in the competition are fully met by funds provided by sponsors. Those progressing to round two receive up to £4,000. The ultimate

winners receive a prize of £20,000 and two runners-up receive £10,000 to assist with further development of their business.
Further details:
BBSRC
Polaris House, North Star Avenue
Swindon, Wilts SN2 1UH
Tel: 01793 413200
Fax: 01793 413201
Web site: http://www.bbsrc.ac.uk/business/skills/plan/Welcome.html

Business in the Community Awards for Excellence

Categories: the awards are run in association with the *Financial Times*, sponsored by the Department of Trade and Industry and recommended by the British Quality Foundation. The criteria are to:

- celebrate and recognise achievement;
- identify and share best practice;
- inspire others to consider how they make an impact on society;
- encourage companies to continually improve the impact of their core business;
- raise awareness of the benefits of responsible business practice.

All finalists for the Awards for Excellence are entitled to use the Impact Endorsement Mark.
Further details:
Business in the Community
137 Shepherdess Walk
London N1 7RQ
Tel: 0870 600 2482
E-mail: rebecca.fowkes@bitc.org.uk
Web site: http://www.bitc.org.uk/awards.html

Business Weekly Awards

Categories:

- Innovation One to Watch, for companies and consultancies with innovative technology, starting up or developed, which appear to the judges as strong commercial potential.

- Growth and Expansion, for companies demonstrating strong growth in the last 12 months, in turnover, staff numbers, physical premises, new products or markets.
- Private Company of the Year, for the private business that in the opinion of the panel of judges has made the most commercial progress in the previous 12 months.
- Quoted Company of the Year, for the public business that the judges feel has made the most commercial progress in the previous 12 months.

The Awards are easy to enter: just e-mail.
E-mail: awards@businessweekly.co.uk
Web site: http://www.businessweekly.co.uk

Cambridge Evening News Business Excellence Awards

Launched in the early 1990s, these awards are now firmly established as the premier awards of their kind in the Cambridge region. The winners are invited to a glittering awards presentation.

Categories:

- Businesswoman of the Year;
- Businessman of the Year;
- Small Business of the Year;
- Business of the Year;
- Business Investment;
- Business Innovation;
- Business Training.

Further details:
Cambridge Newspapers Ltd
Winship Road
Milton, Cambridge CB4 6PP
Tel: 01223 434203
Fax: 01223 434211
E-mail: editorial@cambridge-news.co.uk
Web site: http://www.cambridge-news.co.uk/businessawards/

Centrica-New Statesman Upstarts Awards

These awards are divided: three winners each receive a cheque for £15,000 and a fourth receives a cheque for £5,000 towards R&D.
Criteria:

- All entrants must be aged 18 or over and live in the United Kingdom.
- All entrants must be nominated by a business or organisation operating within the local community.
- Entrants are required to supply contact details of two referees who will be able to vouch for them, such as a doctor, JP, MP, solicitor, local councillor, religious denomination leader, company, charity or community organisation director.
- Organiser application forms must be duly completed.
- Individuals may present more than one proposed project. They must provide information explaining the entry: a typed or written summary, a cashflow projection to show how the award will be spent, a description of how the project or business will be promoted, and brief details of any team members.

Further details:
Upstarts Awards
New Statesman
7th Floor, Victoria Station House
191 Victoria Street
London SW1E 5NE
E-mail: upstarts@newstatesman.co.uk
Web site: http://www.upstarts.org.uk

Dragon Awards

Categories:

- Local Regeneration Award, recognising organisations that have developed an ongoing programme that is seen to support the social and economic regeneration of their local area.
- The Heart of the City Award, recognising firms located in the City, Docklands or City limits that participate in community involvement activities.
- The Small Business Award, which recognises small businesses that have worked with their local community. Businesses with fewer than 100 staff and a turnover of less than £3 million can apply.

- Corporate Community Involvement Newcomer Award, recognising organisations that have implemented corporate community involvement activities with distinction within the last 18 months.
- The London Partnership Award, recognising a single community project that has actively engaged business partners from a number of organisations.
- The Lord Mayor's Award, rewarding organisations that use their purchasing power to support local businesses by buying goods from the local community.

Further details:
The Corporation of London's Economic Development Unit
Tel: 020 7332 3608
E-mail: dragonawards@corpoflondon.gov.uk

E-Business Innovation Awards

Categories:

- International eGovernment Awards;
- Awards for Small/Medium Businesses;
- Global ebusiness Innovations.

To enter, submit by e-mail a 600-word text in three paragraphs explaining:

- The Challenge;
- The Solution;
- The Achievement.

Further details and advice:
Tel: 01489 872 802
E-mail: awards@abfl.co.uk
Web site: http://www.ecommerce-awards.com

Ecommerce Awards

The Ecommerce Awards are organised by UK online for business and Inter-Forum. The awards are sponsored by Cisco Systems and the Royal Bank of Scotland Group. There are over £125,000 worth of prizes. There is no charge for entry.

Further details:
Stuart Hillston (Project Director)
Tel: 01296 641 856
Fax: 01296 641 857
E-mail: stuart@ecommerce-awards.co.uk or info@ecommerce-awards.co.uk
Web site: http://ecommerce-awards.co.uk

Entrepreneur of the Year

Criteria: a regional national and international annual award scheme identifying and recognising the achievements of outstanding entrepreneurs within successful growing dynamic businesses. The programme celebrates their successes and the spirit that entrepreneurs bring to the economy in terms of job creation and the UK's competitiveness. The awards are endorsed by the Department of Trade and Industry, the British Chambers of Commerce, the Design Council, the Community Action Network and the Institute of Directors.

The overall UK Entrepreneur of the Year goes forward to the Ernst & Young World Entrepreneur of the Year Awards the following year.
Further details:
Will White
Media Relations Manager, Ernst & Young
Becket House, 1 Lambeth Palace Road
London SE1 7EU
Tel: 020 7951 3264
E-mail: wwhite@uk.ey.com
Web site: http://www.ey.com/global/gcr.nsf/

Evening Press Business Awards

There are eight awards in the categories of this award for the York region:

- Small Business of the Year;
- Exporter of the Year;
- Growth Business of the Year;
- Best Environmental Company;
- Progress through People;
- Use of New Technology;
- New Business of the Year;
- Business Personality of the Year.

There is an online entry form for those wishing to submit via the Web. Alternatively, for further details contact:
Sky Ferrey, PA to the Editor
Evening Press, 76–86 Walmgate
York YO1 9YN
Web site: http://thisisyork.co.uk/york.businessawards

Growing Business Awards

There are eight categories:

- New Product of the Year;
- International Initiative of the Year;
- Most Promising Young Company;
- Innovative Company of the Year;
- Entrepreneur of the Year;
- Best Business Advisor;
- Company of the Year;
- E-Business of the Year.

Entries are judged by a panel of eminent and impartial adjudicators. Entering one or more category is allowed. Award winners may state in advertising/promotional activity and on their stationery that they are a winner, but this must include the category and year in which the award was won.
Further details:
Iona Reid Scott, The Growing Business Awards
Real Business, 23rd Floor Millbank Tower
Millbank, London SW1P 4QP
Tel: 020 7828 0999
Fax: 020 7630 0733
E-mail: awards@caspianpublishing.co.uk
Web site: http://www.growingbusinessawards.co.uk

The Internet Industry Awards

The Internet Services Providers' Association (ISPA) was established in 1995 as a trade association to represent Internet services providers in the UK. ISPA promotes competition, self-regulation and the development of the internet industry. It sponsors awards in the categories:

■ Consumer Awards;
■ Business Awards;
■ Industry Awards;
■ Internet Watch Foundation Award.

There are 15 awards split into separate categories, governed by different rules and procedures for each section. A summary is published on the ISPA Web site.
Further details:
ISPA UK
23 Palace Street
London SW1E 5HW
Tel: 020 7233 7234
Fax: 020 7233 7294
E-mail: secretariat@ispa.org.uk
Web site: http://www.ispaawards.org.uk

Mayor's Awards for Business Achievement

These were introduced in 1989 by the Mayor of the time in King's Lynn, Norfolk to publicly recognise the achievements of local businesses. The awards are launched in October of every year, visits to shortlisted companies take place mid-late January of the following year, and the process culminates at the Presentation Dinner at the Town Hall at the end of February/beginning of March. Awards are given for:

■ Businesses with over 100 employees;
■ Businesses with less than 100 employees;
■ Staff Development and Training;
■ Local Service Enterprise with 20 employees (or part-time equivalents).

Prizes range from money to advertising (in the *Lynn News* and on KL.FM), and from marketing assistance (from Business Link) to hand-made engraved shields.
Further details:
Borough Council of King's Lynn & West Norfolk
King's Court, Chapel Street
King's Lynn, West Norfolk PE30 1EX
Tel: 01553 616200
Web site: http://www.west-norfolk.gov.uk

Oxford University Business Plan Competition (Oxford Science Enterprise Centre)

Criteria for this award are that it:

- should be original, or a significant improvement on an existing business;
- can be a product, process or service;
- must make 'significant use of design or technology'.

Invitations are open to entrepreneurs, researchers, students and new companies. To enter, you first write a two-page summary of your idea. If this is accepted, you then enter a full business plan outlining how your business would work. Shortlisted business plans are showcased at Venturefest for judging. The winner receives a £10,000 prize and there is also a prize of £1,000 for the best new idea.

Further details:
Oxford Centre for Innovation
Mill Street, Oxford OX2 0JX
Tel: 01865 811145
Fax: 01865 204950
E-mail: info@venturefest.com
Web site: http://www.venturefest.com

Parcelforce Worldwide Small Business Awards

These awards are designed to recognise and reward the UK's leading small businesses. Entrants receive recognition for the efforts of their employees, good public relations (winners' stories are always in demand, which generates great coverage that is seen by competitors, customers and employees alike), prizes worth up to £130,000, and, for new businesses, the opportunity to meet and network with other SMEs. The criteria are:

- the company must be independently owned, UK based and have 30 or fewer employees;
- company turnover should be £50,000 plus per annum;
- the company should have been established at least two years before the entry deadline.

For further details and entry form:
Web site: http://www.parcelforce.com/awards/qualify.asp

The Queen's Awards for Enterprise

These are the UK's top award for business performance, and are awarded in three categories:

- International trade;
- Innovation;
- Sustainable development.

General information can be downloaded from the Web site.
For further details:
The Queen's Award Office
Tel: 020 7222 2277
E-mail: info@queensawards.org.uk
Web site: http://www.queensawards.org.uk

SDC Innovation Awards

Introduced to nurture and encourage innovation in every sector of the coloration industry, each category carries a prize of £2,500 to be spent on education and/or research in the field of colour. The awards are for:

- Colour in Design – for innovation in the use of colour in design as applied to any material in any format.
- Colour in Process – for the innovative application of colour in industry, with particular emphasis on productivity, styling, energy savings and environmental improvements.
- Colour in Research – for innovation in colour research into the development of colorants and the use, application and control of colour.

Further details:
Tel: 01274 725138 Extension 203
Fax: 01274 392888
E-mail: secretariat@sdc.org.uk
To download an application form:
Web site: http://www.sdc.org.uk/general/innovawards.htm

UK Green Chemistry Awards

There are three annual awards for green chemistry technology that offers significant improvements in chemical processes, products and services through research and commercial exploitation of novel chemistry, to achieve a more sustainable, cleaner and healthier environment. One is an Annual Academic

Award of £10,000 to a young academic (under 40) preferably working in collaboration with industry, and there are two Annual Awards to UK companies for technology, products or services, one of which goes to an SME.
Further details: Mike Lancaster, Green Chemistry Network Manager
Tel: 01904 434549; Fax: 01904 434550
E-mail: greennet@york.ac.uk
Web site: http://www.chemsoc.org.uk

Women into Business Conference and Awards

Criteria: the Women into Business awards are seeking to reward women whose achievements and genuine commitment through their influence have made a significant contribution to their business throughout the year.
Application forms and further details are available from:
The Small Business Bureau Ltd, Curzon House, Church Road, Windlesham, Surrey GU20 6BH
Tel: 01276 452010/452020; Fax: 01276 451602
E-mail: info@sbb.org.uk
Web site: http://www.smallbusinessbureau.org.uk

At Macnair Mason we look at our business through the eyes of our clients and help our clients look at their business through the eyes of their customers (or clients).

The business of business is simple. It is about three things:
- selling a product or service at a margin above cost
- selling enough to compensate for time, capital and risk
- generating a positive cash flow

The twin strategies of efficient cost management and product or service differentiation create these three things.

The quality of a business depends upon the quality of management decisions. The quality of decisions depends in turn upon the quality of information. What you can measure, you can manage. What gets measured gets done.

A business is a system consisting of the following elements:

INPUT ✈ PROCESS ✈ OUTPUT

If you want to change the output of the system your only options are to work on the inputs and/or the process.

A typical management information system measures the financial aspects of system input for accountability and the financial aspects of system output to determine profitability. Accounting systems, in other words, monitor before the event, and after the event, but practically give no attention to the activities involved in the process of converting input to output. The only management information concerning the activities comes from casual observation, "we must be doing okay because we're busy".

The mere act of measurement does not, in and of itself, change the object of measurement. If we want to pro-actively influence outcomes we must take action on the processes that determine the outcome.

For example, to increase profit we must:
- Increase revenue without causing expenses to increase at the same or higher rate.
- Decrease expenses without causing gross profit to decline at the same or higher rate.

Some people subscribe to the idea that you need to be leaner, meaner, tighter, tougher or die. For organisations that have become complacent and lazy this is the right prescription.

But for the vast majority of businesses focusing on expense reduction by being "meaner, tighter and tougher" with suppliers, team members and customers is wrong. The key is to find the value point.

We need to look for ways to increase gross profit at a faster rate than expenses increase. We can do that through pricing, changing sales mix or increasing sales volume. But that can only be achieved if we have a superior competitive strategy that is sensitive to the needs and wants of customers or clients.

Returning to the systems concept

INPUT ✈ PROCESS✈ OUTPUT

There are just four ways to grow a business:

1. Increase the number of customers or clients (of the type you want)

2. Increase the frequency of transactions with you

3. Increase the average value of each transaction

4. Increase the efficiency of the business process.

At Macnair Mason we will work as part of your management team to create business performance excellence by:

- determining the business strategy and communicating it to the team members
- determining what needs to be done to implement the strategy
- identifying the processes that are required to be performed
- prioritising the key processes and eliminating redundancy
- re-engineering key processes and developing key performance indicators (KPI's)
- monitoring business performance

HOW DO WE HELP YOU IMPROVE THE PROFITABILITY OF YOUR BUSINESS?

1. We start with a full day Planning Session with the owners and managers of the business to:
    - Identify what your core business strengths and weaknesses are
    - Identify the opportunities that are there to be exploited
    - Work on a Mission Statement for the business
    - Set up an agenda for the work to be done

2. We work with your customers to identify their key frustrations with your business

3. We help you and your team develop a customer service strategy

4. We help you review and redesign, if necessary, your operating procedures

5. We assist you to redesign your organisational structure so that it fits in with your new strategy

6. We work with you to define Key Performance Indicators for each part of the business

7. We work with you to develop a marketing plan

8. We assist you in pulling it all together with a Management Control Plan

If you would like more information about our Business Development Programme please contact us on 020 7767 3500.

The New Frontier of Management

Management is facing an exciting new frontier as scientists explore more deeply into Performance Psychology. This has brought into focus how we transfer knowledge. Do we do it through traditional training or through coaching and mentoring. Of course the answer is all of them and none of them, because all brains have their own unique way of learning, therefore, what suits one brain does not suit another so there cannot be one unified approach.

The new frontier approach is to allow the person who is being educated or trained to allow us to look at their learning system and then change the knowledge to suit. Then having embedded the knowledge into bite-size pieces we must allow the individual to go and practise the new skills in real life situations, for we now know the importance of changing and reframing their life experiences, every human must do this to learn, for that is what learning is – re-framing their real life experiences.

1. The problem is more complex when you introduce emotional intelligence in to the equations, for due to recent research, emotional intelligence is more relevant to human performance then IQ. For it is whole person which must be developed at the same time as particular skills for the workplace. This is based on the notion that as our emotional brain occupies 85%, our logical objective thinking brain occupies 15% of our whole brain. Also those involved with training must accept the fact that learning has nothing to with education, learning is what the brain does starting from birth and ending at the day of our death.

2. Our philosophy can be summed up in saying that we care and support individuals to release their unique potential and come to practical strategies to ensure that the most important fact on the balance sheet is the output of all the brains engaged by the organisation.

The Approach

1. Because each human being is unique each development programme is designed to meet the needs of the specific individuals which it has been designed to serve. Note the term development programme, the sooner we get rid of the concept of training and start to view people as individuals and develop them, the sooner we will be able to cope with the new frontiers which is continually expanding due the rate of change accelerating in our lives.

2. Without a specially designed feedback system lasting for a minimum of 12-months, development of the human mind cannot be achieved.

3. After every activity, it should be embedded to allow participants to apply them in real life, this is where the feedback system comes into play.

4. Each group activity within the programme is must be delivered in a brain compatible way so that each individual learning system can be utilised.

5. All activities are designed in a modular format to reduce work disruptions.

6. All modules are designed to meet the specific needs of the participants.

The Structure of the Development Programme

Each development module lasts for 3-hours and 2-modules can be run in any one day.

The modules allows for any structure to be designed to suit the needs of the participants as soon as the basic skeleton has been set out by Senior Management who will also set the measurable parameters. In addition in many of the modules, participants can have a significant input into the module design. To enable effective feedback each module contains a distance learning section which is designed to embed the skills within the structural part of the module.

The writer has had personal experience using this approach in the following programmes and it has worked dramatically.

1. Developmental thinking which includes creative and innovative thinking. This releases the awesome power of every brain within an organisation.

2. Learning skills which are the fundamental requirement of any technical training, currently data input into our brains is exploding at unparalleled levels due to the World Wide Web, yet little or nothing is done to train our brains to cope with the explosion. Traditional education certainly has not.

3. High Performance Management.

4. High Performance Sales.

5. Effective Leadership.

6. Self-Managed Teams.

Investing Angels

Somewhat understandably, when high-growth ambitious companies approach business angels – individual investors – for financial support, the eager entrepreneur can fall into the trap of assuming that the only investment required to close the deal is on the part of the angel parting with his pounds. However, without equally critical investment in terms of business planning on the part of the entrepreneur, this final, fiscal end game is unlikely to be achieved.

Business planning is critical to any early-stage company when approaching business angels, or indeed any other source of funding, for finance. But as with any type of communication, a thorough understanding of the audience that you are pitching to is critical if the message is to get through - a 70 page 'business plan' is often not appropriate.

So what is a business angel?

An angel investor, unlike a VC, is intimately involved in any investment decision he or she makes through the commitment of his or her own disposable cash. Angels may have made their cash in a number of different ways. Some will be entrepreneurs that have started and sold businesses successfully, some will be highly paid individuals, either still working or perhaps recently retired, and others may have inherited their wealth.

In common with VCs, some angels choose to become closely involved with their investments, particularly where they have either sector expertise, or functional expertise that is currently lacking or poorly serviced in the investee company, e.g. financial skills. More often than not, they will have a network of industry or investor contacts that can prove invaluable to a young company.

The common denominator shared by angels, regardless of their background or skills, is that they understand the risks involved in investing into early-stage, high-growth companies – only one in ten of the companies they invest into is likely to succeed and make significant financial returns.

To help reduce the investment risk, an angel is therefore looking for an investment opportunity demonstrating attributes that will help its drive towards success.

Appropriate for angel funding?

By no means exhaustive, the below list reviews some of the characteristics that angel-seeking companies must display:

Unique proposition – for a company to be attractive to an angel, its product, service, technology or concept must be unique.

Market driven – importantly, following careful research, there should either be a proven need for the product or service, or the company must be creating a need that they can then fulfil and exploit.

Ambitious growth – leading on from the market need, the size of the market (which must be a growing one) should be significant, the market accessible, the team ambitious, and the product or service scalable to the point of becoming a large business.

Protectible position – with technology companies, the IP position needs to have been seriously considered, i.e. with the help of experts. However, whether high, low or no tech, any company must be able to demonstrate its ability to sustain its competitive advantage and commercial viability within acceptable cost expectations.

Realistic financials – however, gone are the days of capturing '50% of a £3bn market by year 2, company valued at £10m even though pre-revenue'. Although many angels made serious amounts of money in years 1999 – 2001, high-growth companies can no longer make ludicrous claims as to their potential market share or value. Alternative models for delivery of revenue should have been reviewed.

Strong management – angels invest most importantly into the management of a company – a company with the best business opportunity but unconvincing or incomplete management will inevitably fail. No credible investor will invest into a business unless the team they are investing into has all the ambition and ability to make it work, although sometimes angels may themselves fill gaps in the early team.

Reaching angels

Making your business investment ready obviously requires considerable effort in terms of business planning and the communication of the offering. But one last aspect to consider is that of finding and pitching to business angels. Doing this on an ad hoc basis can be time consuming and ineffectual, and as a result many companies choose to find business angels via formal groupings – business angel networks – which exist across the UK.

The Great Eastern Investment Forum, part of the NW Brown Group, is one of the UK's leading business angel networks, existing to introduce high-quality, high-growth companies from across the UK to business angels seeking robust investment opportunities. For information on how to be considered as one of these companies, please call Andrea Blakesley on 01223 720213 or email andrea.blakesley@geif.co.uk.

Notes

Great Eastern Investment Forum - www.geif.co.uk

GEIF is a leading business angel network located in Cambridge, providing a matching service between high growth companies seeking funding and business angels seeking quality investment opportunities. Since its establishment in 1995, GEIF angels have provided invaluable management input and funding to over 80 early-stage UK-based companies. In 2003 alone, GEIF angels invested £1.2m into companies coming through the forum, £900K of which was matched by GEIF Ventures, its co-investment fund, making a total of over £2m. Membership of GEIF includes private investors, corporate investors, venture capitalists and corporate advisers with access to high net worth individuals.

For further information, please contact Andrea Blakesley on 01223 720213 or email andrea.blakesley@geif.co.uk.

GEIF Ventures - www.geifventures.co.uk

GEIF Ventures is a £5 million co-investment fund within the NW Brown Group established with the commitment by the DTI to co-invest with Great Eastern Investment Forum business angels into promising businesses. GEIFV is able to co-invest initially up to £100,000 and, if appropriate, follow up its investment by another £400,000 after 9 months. GEIFV is not a lead investor and can only invest when a company receives an investment from GEIF business angels.

NW Brown Group - www.nwbrown.co.uk

NW Brown Group was founded in Cambridge in 1974. It offers a comprehensive range of financial services to private clients (including Investment Management, Stockbroking, Personal Financial Planning, and Insurance) and corporate clients (Corporate Pensions, Employee Benefits, Commercial Insurance, Venture Capital (First Cambridge Gateway Fund), Corporate Finance and Seed and Early Stage Finance through GEIF and GEIF Ventures).

Index

INDEX OF ADVERTISERS